the pictorial encyclopedia of
TRANSPORT

the pictorial encyclopedia of
TRANSPORT

Ing. J. Tůma

Hamlyn
London · New York · Sydney · Toronto

Translated by Alena Einhornová
Designed and produced by Artia for
The Hamlyn Publishing Group Limited
Astronaut House, Feltham, Middlesex, England

ISBN 0 600 38762 3
Printed in Czechoslovakia
3/05/07/51—01

Contents

Foreword

This book covers the evolution of world transport and the revolutionary changes which have left a deeper imprint on the history of mankind than have any of the other fields of technology. The railroad has now celebrated its 150th anniversary and about one hundred years ago the internal combustion engine began its work of advancing the mechanisation of transport on the roads and in the air. Our ancestors watching the sky, envied the birds their freedom and speed of movement, which the human body alone could never imitate; and it is relatively only a short time since men, after tremendous efforts, succeeded in flying a distance of one mile, using a flying machine as light and fragile as a spider's web. But since then they have never stopped researching and improving, and in due course the jet engine became a practical reality, and with it present-day supersonic travel. At the beginning of the 16th century, a journey round the world took two years; at the beginning of this century, over a month. Today, in great comfort aboard the Concorde, this distance could be covered in one day, even with refuelling stops.

Despite the constant increases in speed, the comfort and safety of passengers has not been neglected, but have been constantly improved. Almost inevitably there have been accidents, but these spurred the scientists, designers and engineers to find out why they had happened and to discover the means of preventing them happening again. There is still a long way to go in this field, but accidents are not the only disadvantage to follow in the wake of the quest for speed. The massive development of the automobile industry and of other forms of transport have given great freedom of movement to all who wish it, but have brought with them air pollution, particularly in the big cities. And ecologists are alarmed by the pollution of the oceans of the world by oil from the giant super-tankers, and of the upper layers of the atmosphere by modern jet engines and by rocket propulsion.

As a result of public alarm there are more and more frequent appeals to authority to legislate for 'cleaner' engines and for an enforced reduction of their noise level. The engineers are doing what they can to co-operate, but it does seem that at the stage they have reached technically, the only solution is to ban or at least restrict mechanical transport in certain areas. Nevertheless, economists predict that the amount of transport of all kinds needed to move freight and goods alone will be tripled by the year 2 000. The astronomic estimated figures of ton/miles of cargo and passenger/miles for the year 2 000 exceeds by far the capacities of conventional present-day means of transport, as well as that of the routes they cover. Twenty-four lanes is the maximum that makes any sort of sense for a motorway, and 10,000 is the maximum number of aircraft which can simultaneously be operated over the world's air routes while at the same time maintaining acceptable standards of safety and efficiency.

These are problems which have to be tackled and solved, so technical research continues into both the conventional and the unconventional, using among other things the science of cybernetics for the development of automated transport. Completely new concepts of traction and suspension have been evolved. Vehicles hover on air cushions or on magnetic lines of force; their appearance changes radically; trains are losing their wheels; aircraft are getting rid of their wings, but wings added to ships help them to skim above the water rather than move through it. Engines have been developed without moving parts, which simply change energy directly into movement, and a welcome reduction in noise-level is one result. In order to achieve greater efficiency and higher speeds, ship propellers are replaced by water jets. Automated rail cars have been tested which may take over the function of the car, at least in towns.

These are few examples only of the way things are going, for the process of development is unceasing and, as far as can be predicted, will ever be so.

1 The Role of Transport in the Development of Civilisation

The development of civilisation is directly connected with the development of transport. Transport has made the world accessible for the inquisitive man and become an essential part of his everyday life. It determines the pulse and rhythm of the economy in any country and state. Without transport, furnaces of metallurgical works and power stations would be put out of operation, machines in factories would stop working, millions of people would die of starvation and life would return to the conditions of thousands of years ago.

'There are three things contributing to the greatness of mankind', wrote the enlightened English monk Roger Bacon in his epistle *De nullitate magiae*, two centuries before the discovery of America. 'Fertile soil, a hard-working nation and the possibility of an easy transport of persons and commodities from one place to another.' In this book, which was published in Hamburg four hundred years after Bacon's death, we find surprising prophecies of a man who in his time could have known only teams of oxen and ships that sailed in coastal waters. 'Then we will be able to build machines driving ships faster than a crew of oarsmen and necessitating only one man to set the direction. We will be able to drive vehicles with unusual speed and without the assistance of animals. And one day we will be able to construct machines with wings that fly like the birds ...'

Contrary to these dreams the universal genius Leonardo da Vinci proposed in his sketches how to design such machines. But his self-propelled vehicles and flying machines equipped with airscrews could not be set in motion, because they had no engine to replace the inadequate strength of human muscles.

When, however, in the middle of the eighteenth century, pioneers of technology started to put into practice the daring wishes of man striving for faster motion, they were looked upon as dreamy eccentrics. Terrified villagers used to chase engineers and surveyors measuring and surveying the future railroads, they attacked courageous aeronauts whose balloons were driven by wind on to their land. Steam-driven vehicles were regarded as works of the devil himself and stones were hurled at their creators. Even royal courts were alarmed. In England—which otherwise was a country favouring

1. Only seventy years ago a hero on a flying machine tried in vain to leave an automobile behind

2 a

technological advance—an Act was approved ordering the steamers to go dead slow and setting unrealisable conditions: the steam engine was to trap its own smoke; the shameful red signal flag regulation (see page 41), interfering with the development of transport, was abolished only in 1896.

In the second half of the nineteenth century, new and daring transport routes started being constructed the world over with feverish haste and zeal. In 1869, the legendary transcontinental Pacific Railroad line opened up the rich resources of the American prairies and the Pacific Coast. In the same year, the Suez Canal, designed and built by F. M. Lesseps, shortened the sea transport route to India and the Far East by several thousand miles. A canal through the Panama Isthmus connected the Atlantic and Pacific oceans. The ever-expanding European railway network made it necessary to run the longest tunnels of the world through the Alps. The railway conquered Siberia, cut through African deserts and Indian jungles, climbed in the Andes above the clouds.

The introduction of the combustion engine

For more than a century steam was the king of transport. It was only the internal combustion engine which put an end to its sovereignty. In an automobile it was lighter and cleaner and opened the way for individual transport. The combustion engine was at the beginning a mere attraction, later on it was a luxury of the well-to-do, and finally, thanks to Henry Ford, the automobile became available to the populace, penetrating the most remote corners of the world. At present it appears to be a kind of a voracious object which—together with engine locomotives, ships and planes— swallows 90 per cent of all liquid fuels. The automobile occupies up to 50 per cent of the surface area of large cities, suffocating them with its products of combustion. On average 600 persons a day meet their death under its

2a. The triphibian *Epouvante*, from Verne's novel, *The Lord of the World*, amazed the spectators by a speed of 110 mph, although its undercarriage does not look very reliable

2b. A sports car easily reaches the same speed

2 b

wheels. Though most condemn it, it still can give a feeling of the freedom of movement and of independence. The vicious circle of production and consumption can no longer be interrupted. In the USA, the country with the most highly developed automobile industry in the world, a new human being is born every nine seconds, but a new car leaves the production lines of the giant car factories every five seconds. Scientific congresses and municipalities have to deal ever more frequently with problems of environmental protection.

The combustion engine made it possible for man to take off from the ground. In the beginning man could fly for a very short distance only, but soon the English Channel and finally the Atlantic Ocean were conquered. Air travel was a new form of transport. Aircraft offered unprecedented speeds, although it took a long time before people stopped being afraid of these speeds. But in the end a proud feeling of victory over nature prevailed. The American saying 'time is money' was accepted in Europe as well and nowadays everyone flies ever more frequently. The cruising speed on long-distance flights has reached the supersonic area. Moreover the capacity of giant planes now equals that of express trains. Following this development, the magnificent and fast passenger ships, which had been competing for 50 years to become symbols of the fastest among the fast—competing for the Blue Riband—lost their passengers in the course of several years and today are ending their lives as floating hotels. The mobility of man in modern times has increased in an unparalleled way.

World transport today

Approximately 1 million miles of railway lines and about 15½ million miles of roads and motorways wind round our planet. Day and night, about 200,000 locomotives and engines roll over the railway lines with about 10 million carriages and wag-

3a

3a. The fictional *Epouvante* when flying looked like a butterfly and had flapping wings

3b. The supersonic *Concorde* seems to be at first sight more simple; it can, however, transport 100 passengers at a speed of 1,350 mph

3b

4

ons. Roads are saturated with nearly $^1/_2$ milliard passenger cars and trucks. About 60,000 ships — mainly cargo — under 150 different flags cruise the oceans of the world. Several thousand planes take off daily from about 500 main world airports covering in several hours the distance between the continents.

A timetable of all the regular railway, bus, sea and air routes and lines throughout the world would need about 500,000 densely printed pages, occupying the space of a small library. That is why information about communications, providing of services, sales and bookings of air and railway tickets has

4. Present-day parking lots at certain exhibitions and sport stadiums occupy areas larger than that of the event itself. Photograph shows aerial view of 5,000 cars — only one eigth of the total capacity at the Hannover Fair parking lot

to be taken over by computers connected by tele-communication networks.

The possibilities offered by present-day transport to passengers and cargoes are inexhaustible. Nearly all the fantastic sci-fi ideas of the French writer Jules Verne have been outdone by reality. The respectable Mr. Phileas Fogg from the novel *Around the World in 80 Days* would cover this distance in one day only enjoying the comfort of the supersonic Concorde. For a tour of the world he might choose also an atomic submarine, because some of them—imitating Verne's *Nautilus*—navigate during trials round the entire globe, moving on and under the surface of the oceans and even under the icebergs in the area of the two poles. At the same time they consume only a minimum amount of nuclear fuel.

It is an undeniable fact that the steam locomotive contributed more to the unification of the world than all the philosophers and politicians during the history of civilisation. Countries had to agree on uniform couplings and brakes. International institutions work out and check agreements about the design and operation of railways, ships and planes. By strict safety regulations they protect human lives from negligence and improvisation which might have fatal consequences.

5. Increase in average speed of different means of transport during the last 150 years

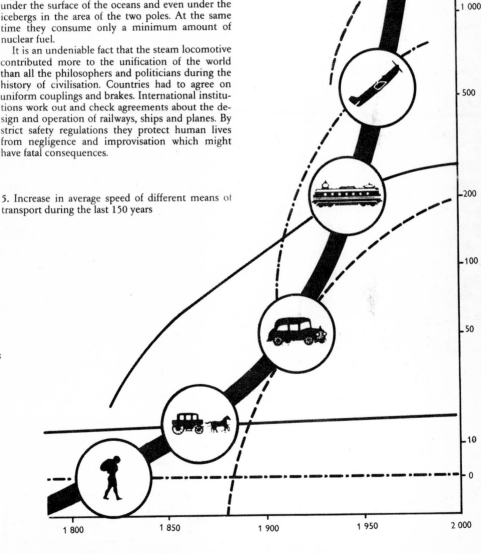

Trends of world transport

World transport harmoniously links speed, safety and economy, and in passenger transport comfort while travelling as well.

Speed: Spectacular news reports about various records are certainly incompatible with efforts to increase the speed of transport; this can be achieved only by looking for ways and means to increase the average cruising or commercial speed while still maintaining economic and safety requirements.

First speed records were accompanied by fatal tragedies involving the inventors and designers during dangerous trials and experiments. Nowadays, the struggle for speed takes place in wonderfully equipped research centres. Each means of transport faster than its predecessor is usually tested in wind tunnels, the computers and simulators ruling out any hazard risks during the trials.

Trains in service reach speeds up to 125 mph. In 1955, however, French engineers broke the world record with a modified electric engine reaching a speed of 331 kmh (205.5 mph). The trend towards higher speeds compels designers to look beyond the traditional wheels and rails and to consider in-stead cars hovering on an air or magnetic cushion.

Also, the speed of ships and boats can be increased above the 30 mph limit only with the help of wings or air cushions, if the transport is to remain economical.

Automobiles with turbine or jet engines have already broken world records by approaching speeds of former jet planes (over 600 mph).

Even in passenger transport jet planes have entered the supersonic age; during the process of further speed increases in the supersonic field, aircraft are going to lose their conventional wings.

Speed records of manned flight, however, belong to cosmonauts who attain speeds of about 12,000 mph when orbiting the Earth.

Safety: Increasing transport speeds accompanied by ever-higher traffic density of all lines and routes require the assistance of automation and cybernetics. Railway safety on main lines has already been ensured for years by automatic systems independent of the operator's perception. Ships and planes use radar to enable man to see many miles ahead in the night, in fog and bad weather conditions. Automated landing systems find an ever larger field of application; air transport can thus operate practical-

6

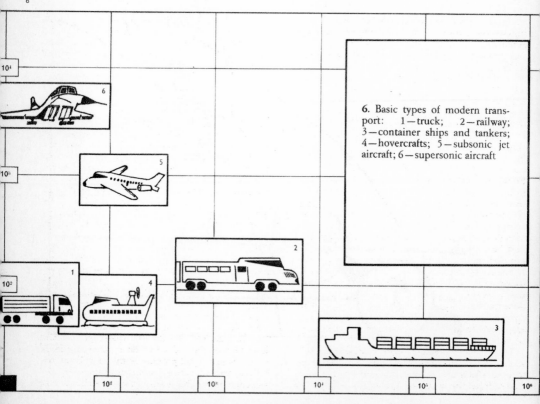

6. Basic types of modern transport: 1 — truck; 2 — railway; 3 — container ships and tankers; 4 — hovercrafts; 5 — subsonic jet aircraft; 6 — supersonic aircraft

7. Luxury comfort for passengers in the Grosse Mercedes, Type 600 *(Mercedes-Benz)*

ly under any weather conditions and 'blind' landings can be carried out. Only road transport resists automation. Regardless of improved active and passive car safety, over 200,000 people die on the roads of the world every year—more than during wars. All possibilities promising to improve this situation are tested—from 'safe' cars to anti-collision radar and electronically controlled motorways. It seems that the latter approach would be the most efficient one; in financial terms, however, it is not justifiable. But human society will certainly come to the conclusion that the value of life cannot be expressed by figures and that efforts to save lives are worth any expenditure.

Economy: This plays an important role especially in cargo transport. Experts are right when they say that 'the cheapest transport is no transport', since on the average products and raw materials become, because of transport, one quarter more expensive though their value does not increase. Huge transport investments are therefore under careful study. For each individual case the most convenient way of transport is selected, and individual means of transport are combined in the most advantageous way. Uneconomic railway lines are put out of operation; the same is true of old ports incapable of receiving large modern ships. Trans-shipped goods are concentrated in fully mechanised trans-shipment points.

The introduction of containers represented a substantial reduction of cargo transport costs. The containers, which are merely standardised boxes or crates, travel by modified ground, water and air transport literally 'from house to house', simplifying the former expensive goods handling.

The development of oil and natural gas consumption opened the way for a fully automated long-distance pipe-line transport which, in comparison with road tanker or wagon transportation costs, is three to five times less expensive. Gigantic oil and natural gas pipe lines cover in many countries distances of several hundred miles.

The economical use of transportation facilities which differ from country to country has been for years a matter of state control. By fixing taxes and transportation prices, states are trying to control transport in such a way as to reduce losses to the minimum. It is likely that in the future uniform transport systems will be established; individual means and ways of transport will be allotted the most advantageous areas and even the future big projects of transport constructions will be submitted to this division.

Comfortable travel: For many decades this has been—besides the 'floating hotels'—ensured by the passenger car. Trends of transport development indicate, however, that in the year 2000 there will be one car per inhabitant in the most developed countries, and the so-called 'fast variant' of the development allows for even two cars per inhabitant in the USA. But cities cannot be reconstructed from the very foundations and thus the passenger car will lose, first in the cities and later on even outside them, its privileged position as the most comfortable and therefore attractive means of transport. Designers of new public transport systems already take

8

this into consideration. Noiselessness, good lighting, automatically shaped seats, the possibility of listening to the radio and watching TV programmes are becoming a matter of course both in express trains and on board planes and lately even in long-distance motor-coaches. Part of the comfort is also a larger range of services offered during the travel. In some trains, aircraft, ships and road transport, the use of a telephone is available.

The following chapters should make the reader acquainted with the tremendous progress achieved in individual fields of transportation during the last 150 years. They illustrate in brief what obstacles had to be overcome before the modern integrated world transport network—to be accepted sooner or later by all the countries of the world— began to loom.

8. The giant *Tokyo Bay* tanker in the Miraflores Locks when passing through the Panama Canal in 1972—there was only 18-in clearance at each side and a little more at the bow and stern

2 The History of Transport

The assumption that man used to maintain and modify the paths leading to places with better nutrition sources and better hunting opportunities is very likely correct. Prehistoric man used to bridge swamps and brooks with branches. He dragged his hunting trophies on forked branches and this 'device' probably represented the origin of the sledge. Short circular trunks were used as rollers. When cut and shortened even more they turned into the first wheels.

We shall never have any documents about a really revolutionary event—when primitive man ventured to cross a river, lake or bay using a tree trunk.

Later he started making canoes; in fact they were just tree trunks hollowed out by a crude chisel or fire. According to archaeological findings the first canoe appeared about 5—6,000 years ago. He made primitive rafts by joining trunks or branches together and also used animal skins stuffed with grass or inflated by air.

Oared ships and primitive sailboats

The history of navigation began in the Mediterranean area which, because of favourable natural conditions, became the cradle of European civilisation. Scenes on ancient Egyptian vases, murals and reliefs indicate that the first sailboats appeared in Egypt about 3000 B.C. From joined reeds or

9. Some natives still make rafts in the same way as they did one thousand years ago

10. Naval expedition of the Egyptian Queen Hatshepsut from the region Punt in the first half of the fifteenth century B.C.

11

11. An ancient Greek vase with a scene from Odyssey shows the arrangement of a Greek single-sail, single-bank oared ship (1100—800 B.C.)

12. Chinese junk with bamboo mat sails. Its hull was sometimes divided into water-proof compartments

13. Large Greek trireme with rectangular sails supplementing the oarsmen. A copper-plated ram at the bow served to pierce the sides of enemy vessels

bundles of papyrus boats developed into larger coast vessels without keels or ribbing made of chiselled acacia, sycamore and cedar boards connected by wooden nails and reinforced in the transverse and longitudinal directions by ropes. In the years 5000—2000 B.C. ships were provided with paddles,

the paddlers facing the direction of the boat. Later on paddles were replaced by oars, the oarsmen facing in the opposite direction. Long oars at the stern helped to steer the boat. A large rectangular sail enabled navigation only in the direction of the wind. Ancient Egyptians did not yet know how to make full use of sails.

During the period of the New Egyptian Empire (1500 B.C.) oared ships up to 84 ft long and with a crew of more than a hundred men used to sail along the coast of Africa. Historical documents are available describing the expedition of Queen Hat-

12

shepsut's fleet across the Red Sea to the ancient country Punt (present-day Somalia). The ships returned with a cargo of goods and slaves.

The strongest element of the Egyptian rulers' fleet were Phoenician ships with a simple yard sail. Because of the high-quality cedar wood from the Lebanon they had a firm frame consisting of the keel and ribbing covered by wooden outer plating. Phoenician galleys dominated the Mediterranean Sea about the year 1000 B.C., introduced the practice of piracy, but moreover were able to import tin from as far away as England.

According to the Phoenician example, Greeks in the following millenium started constructing galleys which differed by their size and number of oarsmen sitting on banks one above the other. The most simple ones were the *moneres* with one row of oars; the double-row *biremes* were faster, and in the fifth century B.C. the fastest *triremes* with three banks of rowers one above the other were widely used. Warships up to 235 ft long had as many as five levels for the oarsmen. The longest oars had to be balanced by lead. The Greeks became world-famous navigators. They introduced the geographical latitude and longitude terms; in the port of Alexandria they erected a 460-ft high lighthouse with a wood-tar pitch fire showing the way in the night.

In the Red and Arab Seas and in the Persian Gulf Arab merchantmen *dhau* with three triangular sails appeared. The Indians sailed in *patamaras*, slim ships provided with up to three triangular sails.

In the rivers of China junks with a bulky hull and a blunt lifted stern were the most frequently used vessel for thousands of years. The earliest junks had bamboo mat sails, later on fabric sails were used. Oars played only an auxiliary role. They were steered by a lever rudder at the stern. The Chinese began using a compass as early as the third century B.C.

The largest warships and merchantmen of ancient times were those constructed by the Romans. Their 132-ft long *triremes* could carry up to 1,000 tons of cargo. A rectangular main sail was complemented by a smaller bowsprit sail. The main propulsion force, however, was still represented by oarsmen selected from the lowest classes of citizens and from slaves.

The history of navigation of the Nordic and West European nations began with the Vikings. They built ships 35—100 ft long made of oak and propelled by up to 25 pairs of oars. They were without a deck and capable of carrying up to 35 tons of cargo. In windy weather they used simple yard sails.

The Vikings sailed west in their ships to the British Isles, towards the south they reached Sicily, in the northern direction they got as far as Iceland, and it is not unlikely that in about the year A.D. 980 they reached the coast of North America. Following the rivers the Vikings penetrated to the Black Sea.

The origin of vehicles

According to archaeological findings the dawn of the wheeled vehicle took place about 5,000 years ago. From primitive all-wooden, double-wheel carts development led to old Egyptian racing and war chariots which even had an elastic body bottom

13

14. Double-wheeled chariot of the Indian Harappa civilisation from findings at Mohendjo-Daro (2000 B.C.)

15. Hunting chariot of the Assyrian king Assurbanipal on a relief from Ninive (668—628 B.C.)

16. Chariot of a Viking priestess (about 850 B.C.) found at Oseberg *(Oslo University)*

17. A Roman mail-coach station (500 B.C.). Foreground shows stone mounting blocks for the horseman, while a watering place is shown in background. The road is paved with hexagonal stone slabs

consisting of leather belts. The Assyrian king Assur-banipal 2,600 years ago had the wheels of his hunt-ing chariot fitted with metal pins on their circum-ference. In order to reduce the weight of the wheel, spokes were fitted between the hub and rim.

For thousands of years, peasants in Egypt, China and India made do with a simple double-wheel cart with a fixed shaft and a yoke for a team of oxen. Field work required that wheels with a large diame-ter were used. In the Bronze and Iron Ages votive carts were used for religious rites. Scandinavian vo-tive chariots had four wheels — an exceptionally pre-cious relic from the ninth century is the chariot of a Viking priestess with a swivelling shaft, metallic axles, with 12-spoke wheels and a magnificent orna-mental woodcut on the body.

The ancient Romans were equipped with a choice of about 30 types of carts — ranging from the clumsy agricultural *plaustrums;* sports chariots for a standing rider; four-wheeled *harmaxes* where the passenger could even rest lying down; to festive carts ostentatiously ornamented with gold and ivory.

16

17

21

The development of roads

Wide and solid roads were built by the Chinese in 4000 B.C., while the Egyptians and Babylonians paved theirs. Under the Emperor Darius the Persians built a 1,250-mile road from Susa to Sardis. But the most famous network of roads was built by the Romans. The total length of all the roads enabling the Romans to control their huge empire measured 65,000 miles. The saying 'via-vita'—the road is life—was generally accepted. Main roads were 35 ft wide, the renowned Via Appia even 65 ft wide. Roads consisted of several layers of stones and pebbles whose thickness varied, the layers being bonded by mortar. Roads were bordered by milestones and stone mounting blocks for the horse traveller. Every four miles mail-coach stations were ready with fresh horses. The traffic was controlled by strict regulations and the state administration organised the transport of news, passengers and goods. Sixteen out of 19 main road arteries led to Rome.

Sails over the oceans

The development of navigation in the thirteenth and fourteenth centuries was conditioned by the Crusades. Ships similar to those of the Roman period—this time however equipped with triangular lateen sails—sailed from ports such as Genoa, Barcelona and Venice. To enable the highest possible number of warriors, horses and supplies, to be carried on the expeditions, the ships were more rounded and larger than earlier vessels. The warriors were accommodated in overhung superstructures called castles. A high mast carried a crow's nest. Such a ship, often referred to as a *nef, nave* or *nao,* was sometimes over 100 ft long and had a deadweight capacity up to 560 tons.

During the course of the fourteenth and fifteenth centuries ships were provided with a stern rudder. A square sail was set on a high mast amidships, a new cross mast was located aft and set with a lateen sail, which improved the manoeuvring capacity of the ship. Equipped with a compass (from the twelfth century) and with an astrolabe (from the fifteenth century) such ships could finally undertake long-distance journeys.

In the second half of the fourteenth century the Union of Harbour Towns—Hansa—was founded. Originally this union of North German Towns was a free association protecting the interests of merchants. At the climax of its activity 90 large towns belonged to Hansa. Until the beginning of the sixteenth century Hansa controlled import and export of commodities, granted privileges of commercial navigation and controlled even fishing. Countries of the Iberian Peninsula profiting from navigation experiences of the Nordic and Mediterranean sailors sent out expeditions to find a sea route to the riches of India. The Portuguese Bartholomeu Diaz sailed in 1487 round Africa discovering the Cape of Good Hope. Christopher Columbus discovered America in 1492. In 1498 Vasco da Gama reached Calcutta. In the years 1519—21 Ferdinand Magellan undertook the longest voyage. He sailed round South America into the Pacific, discovering the Philippine Islands.

These explorers sailed in carracks and caravels. The original small and fast single-mast caravels had a deadweight of about 200 tons. During the sixteenth century, they were equipped with up to three masts and lateen sails, with a foremast with a square sail. The carracks were developed in England from the original Venetian type. They were larger, had yard sails on the main and foremasts and their high castles hung over the hull.

Pirates and corsairs represented a permanent threat to merchantmen and ships of pioneers. Only after the defeat of the Tunisian pirates and of the Turkish fleet at Lepanto in 1581 did conditions for safe navigation improve. By that time the caravels started being replaced by galleons. The forecastle of the galleon was directly connected with a triangular extended bow provided with a beak-head and usually decorated with a figure-head. The stern was rather flat forming the transom, while the aftercastle had galleries richly decorated by carvings. The three or four masts were set with new square sails.

In the years 1577—80 Francis Drake sailed round the world with five ships. During innumerable expeditions new settlements and colonies were founded. In 1588 the fleet of Elizabeth I, Queen of England, defeated the Spanish Armada. Henceforward the centre of navigation, commerce and colonial conquests moved from Spain to England. In 1620 the English Puritan Pilgrim Fathers, on board the small galleon *Mayflower* with a deadweight capacity of 180 tons, reached the coast of America.

In the seventeenth century the Netherlands began to develop their fleet, concentrating mainly on the build-up of the Dutch merchant navy which by the middle of the century had twice as many ships as England and France together. Its bulky *fluyts* could be met on all the oceans. The Dutch pilots were the first to use charts worked out in 1569 by G. Kraemer-Mercator.

In the seventeenth century France founded the first shipbuilders school, where the shape of ships was scientifically studied. Hulls of galleons were constructed slimmer, the ships were three-masted. Triangular sails were added to the square sails set on the foremast, the lateen sail on the mizzen mast was modified and changed into a trapezoidal gaff. The rudder was controlled by a wheel turning in the horizontal plane. Superstructures in the fore and aft were lower, thus forming a full-rigged ship.

During the eighteenth century further explorations were undertaken, this time on scientific bases. The knowledge of astronomy, the use of sextants, octants, of naval chronometers and logs measuring the ship's speed contributed to the achievements of

18. Crusader ships riding at anchor at Constantinople—1202—04 *(Miniature by Jean Froissart, 1400)*

19. The Portuguese sailor in Spanish service, Ferdinand Magellan, set sail in 1519 with his six ships trying to reach the coast of Brazil. It took him one year before he found a strait leading to the Pacific. He was killed in a fight with the natives. Out of the 265 member crew, only 18 returned home after three years

18

19

20

21

James Cook, discoverer of Australia, New Zealand and Polynesia, of Vitus Bering, of the Englishman Hudson, of the French navigator Cartier, and many others. Thanks to their work instruments charts could be made more accurate. In the middle of the nineteenth century the seas of the world belonged to the clippers. These were slim, fast ships with several masts, a sharp bow and square sails. The first to build clippers was the American John Griffith. With the improved shape of the hull, maximum sail surface and also with the excellent knowledge and experience of their captains, the clippers attained record speeds of about 20 knots (1 knot = 1 nautical mile per hour = 1·15 mph.) During the Californian Gold Rush of 1848 fast clippers were used to transport the fortune seekers from the east coast of America and Europe. Twenty years later the clippers became famous for their fast transport of tea and wool from India, China and Australia. Among the best-known clippers were the English sailing ships *Rainbow, Lightning* and *Cutty Sark.*

The improvement of the steam engine towards the end of the nineteenth century, however, brought about the end of sailing ships. During the early part of the twentieth century, only a few full-rigged ships and schooners were built, mainly as training ships for naval schools.

Now designers and shipbuilders are again returning to the idea of utilising sails. The so-called 'Dyna-Ships', to be used for economical cargo transport and for pleasure trips, would be provided with nylon sails or plastic shields on six swivelling masts. The swivelling movement of the sails to the most

20. A replica of Columbus' ship, the *Santa Maria,* in the port of Barcelona

21. A frigate in a storm (Picture by Willem van de Velde jr, 1633—1707)

22. Norwegian barquentine *Regina Maris* set sail in September 1970 for a voyage to Australia following the route taken by Captain Cook

advantageous position would be controlled by a computer on board the ship in communication with meteorological satellites; only under a dead calm sea would a diesel engine be used as auxiliary equipment.

From coaches to horse omnibuses

After the disintegration of the Roman road network during the Middle Ages, heavy wagons were used once again to withstand the shocks from the unkept roads. It looked as though nothing had changed during a thousand years.

Royal, imperial and aristocratic coaches appeared in the fourteenth century. They had rich gold ornaments and magnificent woodcuts and carvings. Coronation and wedding coaches of emperors from the sixteenth and seventeenth centuries were examples of superb artistry.

In this period a number of exceptional attempts were made to build vehicles moving with the appli-

23

cation of human power instead of horse power, by means of levers, cranks, treadwheels, etc. as the Nuremberg watchmaker Johann Hautsch proposed. More successful was the vehicle with sails, designed by the Dutch mathematician Simon Stevin.

In the sixteenth century some countries started to look after the roads, collecting fees and taxes for this purpose. People began travelling in coaches. But it was not until the seventeenth century that travelling became a little more comfortable: coaches

24

CVRRVS VELIFERI II A. MAVRITII NASSOVII

25

26

27

23. The English clippers *Teaping* and *Ariel* in 1866 covered a distance of 15,500 miles from Fu-Tschau-Fu to London with a cargo of tea in 99 days

24. This sail vehicle by Simon Stevin could travel along the Dutch shore with 30 passengers at a speed of 16 knots

25. Double-team Mail coaches could reach a speed of 10 mph *(Reproduction of a painting by G. Wright, 'Behind Time')*

26. Exclusive coach of Prince Dietrichstein *(Kunsthistorisches Museum, Vienna)*

27. The first London omnibus for 18 passengers introduced by G. Shillibeer in 1829 *(Science Museum, London)*

28. A Wells Fargo stage coach as used in the American West

29. A carriage of the first Continental horse-drawn railway linking České Budějovice and Linz in Austria (1828). It was hauled by three horses and carried up to twelve passengers

30. A cock, a duck and a sheep in the basket of a 'Montgolfier' became, on 19 September 1783, the first balloonists of the world

were equipped with leaf springs at the end of which the body was fixed by means of leather belts. The front wheels were connected with the shaft and could be swivelled.

The number of horses per coach, and its decoration and equipment, depended on the wealth of the owner. Aristocratic coaches bore the coat-of-arms of their owner on the side.

Larger carriages which could be hired appeared for the first time in Paris during the reign of Louis XIV (1643—1715). The owner of these carriages was Nicolas Savage, who had a house next to the church of St. Fiacrius. Accordingly they became known as fiacres. Four-wheeled closed carriages, known as Berlins, also gained widespread popularity. The glass partition between the front and rear seats was later used in the design of coupés with glass windows. Landaus, whose two-section tops could be lowered independently, had many admirers as well. Travelling in double-wheeled phaetons

29

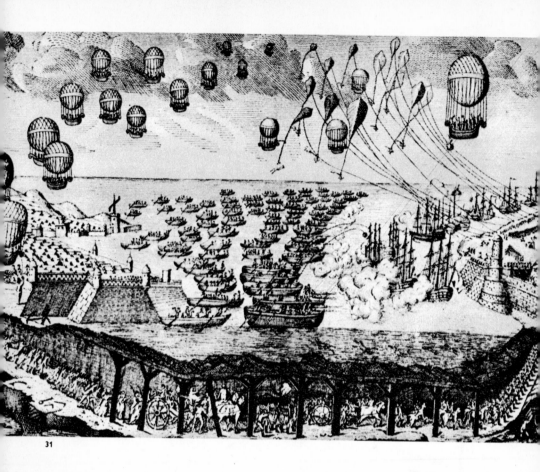

31

was especially agreeable on city roads, since the carriages were very light.

Further types of carriages developed from the two-wheeled phaeton were: gigs with big wheels and drawn by one horse; light open cabriolets; fashionable sulkies; and more simple low tilburies.

From the four-wheeled coupé the brougham with two seats and a forked shaft was born, and the landaulet, a smaller version of the landau, was very popular, as was the comfortable squalette. English gentry liked their mylords or breaks, while in Berlin and in Vienna the 'comfortable' with four seats won many passengers.

Up to the middle of the eighteenth century transport between towns had progressed from saddle or pack-horses to huge, lumbering stage wagons with a canvas top, to stage coaches. The first mail-carrying coach was introduced in 1784 by John Palmer, and was an immediate success; the mails had previously been carried by post boys on horseback. Mail coaches also carried up to eight passengers, four inside and four outside. Mail coaches provided a faster service compared with normal coaches, usually travelling throughout the night non-stop except for

changes of horses, until their destinations were reached. By 1830 mail coaches averaged 10 to 11 mph.

The most famous of all American vehicles was the Concord Coach, as used by the Wells Fargo Company for the overland routes in the West. By 1870, however, with the completion of the transcontinental railway, Concord coaches gave way to steam in the vast areas of the West.

In 1827, almost simultaneously in France and in England, rectangular carriages with a flat roof for 18 and sometimes even for 50 passengers appeared. They were called — very likely from the Latin word *omnis* (everybody) — omnibuses. They opened the age of mass public transport.

Horse-drawn railways

Already by the fifteenth century miners tried to make their work easier by letting their wagons run on rails made of timber poles. They used either to push the wagons themselves or put horses to them. Horses hauling four-wheeled wagons on rails could move cargoes four times heavier than they could

31. A plan for the invasion of Britain by balloons filled with soldiers, ships and a submarine tunnel. This proposal was submitted to Napoleon in 1804

32. Balloons filled with town gas were for decades an indispensable attraction of every major exhibition

32

cope with on the road. It was only in the mid-eighteenth century that mine wagons or cars were provided with flanged iron wheels to prevent derailment from the timber rails; as a protection during downhill travel they had block brakes. Flanged cast-iron rails, introduced by the English metallurgist Reynolds in 1768, were even safer. Ten years later his compatriot, 18-year-old John Curr, invented a rail with an elevated edge. He placed the rails not on longitudinal sleepers — as was the custom at that time — but on cross sleepers, using a gauge of 4 feet 8½ inches, which later became the standard size of gauge.

The Stockton and Darlington 'iron' railway was opened in 1825; it was 25 miles long. In sections with sharp gradients the horses were unharnessed and were replaced by a winch hauling the wagons with a rope. When the track was level again, the winch was disengaged and the horses once more took over.

A daring horse-drawn railway laid through hills and mountains between České Budějovice and Linz in Austria was built in 1828 by F. J. Gerstner. During its heyday up to a thousand cars ran daily in both directions; a single journey took 14 hours. At the Kerschbaum junction, the first railway station restaurant of the world was opened.

In the same year, a horse railroad from Baltimore to Ohio was being built in North America. It was opened as America's first common-carrier railway in May 1830.

The first German iron railway, leading from Fürth to Nuremburg, which was opened in 1835, and was designed for a 'mixed operation', since at that time the first steam locomotives appeared. After 1840 no more horse-drawn railways were built (except for use in cities), and the existing ones had to be reconstructed to take steam trains.

Ballooning

To be able to fly as a bird was the dream of mankind since time immemorial, but it was not until the invention of the hot-air balloon by the Montgolfier brothers towards the end of the eighteenth century that the really significant step towards this goal took place. The first balloon for public demonstration was made of pieces of cloth lined with

31

33

paper and fastened on a network of strings; it was filled with hot air from a specially-made fire and its capacity was about 22,000 cu ft. It was released from the French town of Annonay on 4 June 1783, where it rose to some 6,000 ft before the hot air cooled, and it returned to earth about 1·5 miles from the take-off point.

The Montgolfier brothers demonstrated their second and larger 'Aerostat' on 19 September 1783 before the king and queen of France at Versailles. On this flight, a cock, a duck and a sheep were put in the basket. After about 10 minutes aloft, the balloon descended about 1·25 miles distant, with the animals intact.

The first free flight of a manned 'montgolfier' balloon took place in Paris, on 21 November 1783, when Pilâtre de Rozier with the Marquis d'Arlandes as passenger, took 25 minutes on this historic flight, and they landed 5·5 miles away from the starting point.

During the same year, the French physicist J.A.C. Charles developed a balloon filled with hydrogen; its first flight on 27 August 1783 covered a distance of 15 miles. On 1 December 1783, in a larger hydrogen-filled balloon, Charles and a colleague Marie-Noel Robert made their first flight. After two hours and a 27-mile flight they landed successfully with their *charlière* in Paris. On 7 January 1785 the French aeronaut Jean Pierre Blanchard, accompanied by an American, Dr Jeffries, flew over the English Channel. Two hours after the take-off from Dover they landed near Calais. In June of the same year, De Rozier and his friend Romain were killed in what was probably the first recorded flying accident. This tragedy took place in a hybrid balloon—made from a hydrogen-filled envelope above a hot-air envelope—when the fire for the hot-air envelope ignited the hydrogen.

The importance of the balloon was not discounted by the military: a plan to attack England with a thousand balloons was even presented to Napoleon. But it was in the field of science that profited from balloons. For instance, in 1804, Gay-Lussac was able to study changes of pressure and temperature up to an altitude of 21,000 ft.

The death of two out of the three participants in an ill-advised attempt in 1875 to ascend in a balloon up to an altitude of nearly 32,000 ft showed the dangers of the thin atmosphere, and pressurised cabins were designed. In the years 1929 and 1930, Professor Auguste Piccard reached the stratosphere with such cabins — an altitude of about 53,000 ft. Balloons also became attractions at world exhibitions.

The main drawback of balloons was the impossibility to pilot them. The tragic fate of the expedition by Andrée, Strindberg and Fraenkel to the North Pole in 1897, as well as fatal flights of others, showed that the balloon could never become the longed-for airship of man's dreams.

Man with wings

Putting aside the legend about the flying Frenchman Besnier or the unsuccessful attempts of J. Degen in 1806, or those of other inventors trying to construct flying machines, it was concluded that flying with the help of wings could be put into reality only after a careful study of the flight of birds. Leonardo da Vinci was the first to undertake such studies. In the nineteenth century, naval captain J. M. Le Bris constructed a glider with wings like

those of an albatross. At the beginning he took off hauled by a rope drawn by horses. His idea has been taken up by present-day sportsmen with their man-flown kites hauled by motor cars or motor boats.

The German Otto Lilienthal became the pioneer of gliding flights. He undertook nearly 2,000 flying jumps, running downhill suspended beneath mono or bi-gliders. For that purpose he had an artificial hill made near Berlin. In 1896 the upper wing of his glider broke off and Lilienthal met his death — in the same way as his successor, P. S. Pilcher.

In the USA, the first to carry out gliding flights was O. Chanute, and the brothers Wilbur and Orville Wright from North Carolina were his faithful disciples. During 1902—03, they mastered to perfection gliding against the wind. All of them, however, came to the conclusion that flying with machines heavier than air would be possible only with the assistance of an engine.

33. After 33 years a film was found in a frozen camera which after developing showed an authentic picture of the *Ornen* balloon disaster. It was in 1897 that S.S. Andrée with two colleagues tried to reach the North Pole in this ill-fated balloon

34. Otto Lilienthal ready to jump with his mono-glider; this had flapping wings at the end of the main wings

The history of engines

The only energy man had as a reserve, capable of replacing beasts of draught, was the heat of the fire. The problem was how to convert it into useful mechanical work. An original proposal was presented by the Dutch physicist Christian Huygens in the seventeenth century. In a cylinder which was sealed

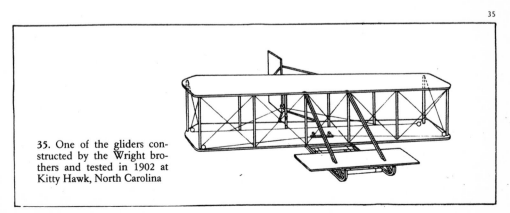

35. One of the gliders constructed by the Wright brothers and tested in 1902 at Kitty Hawk, North Carolina

at the top by a piston a certain quantity of gunpowder was burned. The combustion products were pushed out through the exhaust pipe and the atmospheric pressure forced the piston down to the bottom of the cylinder. At the same time it could lift a weight and thus carry out mechanical work. In these experiments, the principle of atmospheric machines was discovered. Gunpowder, however, was not a material to be trifled with, and the energy of the lifted weight could not really be used for transport. In 1687, the French physicist Denis Papin, living in England, replaced the explosion of gunpowder with the condensation of water vapours. The drawbacks and failures of his thermal engine were overcome by the English blacksmith Thomas Newcomen in 1705. Newcomen separated the steam boiler from the cylinder. He condensed the steam by injecting cold water under the piston. However, it was not until 1769 that James Watt constructed the first practical piston steam engine. Watt ignored the atmospheric principle and let the expanding steam affect alternately the two sides of the piston; he converted the to and fro movement of the piston into a rotating motion of a flywheel.

It took another 50 years of steam engine improvement before a steam locomotive or steamship was built, after which the steam engine dominated transport for nearly a hundred years. It was an irony of destiny that after it reached its highest development — for instance, the efficiency was raised from the original 0·1 per cent to about 16 per cent—it gave way to an engine with a higher efficiency of fuel combustion, which took place inside the cylinder.

The patent for the internal combustion engine was granted in 1859 to the Belgian Jean Lenoir. The patent application begins with the following words: 'The invention consists of the use of town gas together with air ignited electrically in order to acquire the driving force.' The German merchant Nikolaus A. Otto with the engineer Eugen Langen constructed soon afterwards an even more efficient engine burning an explosive mixture of liquid fuels and air created in a carburettor. But this engine functioned on the atmospheric principle and was therefore slow and too robust. In the course of time the idea of driving the pistons directly by the pressure of the combustion products prevailed. This was achieved in May 1876 by the German, Dr N. A. Otto who, with the assistance of Gottlieb Daimler, evolved a gas engine with a four-stroke cycle. By 1880, Karl Benz was making stationary two-stroke gas engines, and in 1885 Benz produced a two-seater tricycle and Daimler made a motorised bicycle—the age of the 'horseless carriage' had dawned. In 1897, Rudolf Diesel succeeded in adapting the internal combustion engine to run on cheaper grades of fuel oil by injecting the fuel directly into the cylinder and burning it by the heat of compressed air. Within the last 30 years, there has been much development of the diesel engine, especially in the marine field, where it has now supplanted the steam engine. Unlike the petrol engine, the diesel engine can be constructed for extremely high power outputs—some large, multi-cylinder slow-running (110 to 122 rpm) marine diesel engines are capable of producing over 2,300 hp per cylinder.

The pursuit of higher power outputs led to the design of rotary engines, or turbines. In ships, steam turbines found a wide field of application (until eclipsed by the diesel engine), while in aviation the turbine driven jet engine has supplanted the piston engine. Gas turbines are now penetrating into railway transport and even cars.

The beginning of steam navigation

In the sketch-books of Leonardo da Vinci, there are drawings of boats manually driven by small paddle-wheels and by screws. The age of mechanics in the sixteenth and seventeenth centuries added further ideas to these original designs, e.g. water or wind wheels fixed to boats. There existed, moreover, designs for rowing and paddling machines, of ships hauled by winches or pushed off the bottom by mechanical arms.

For the developing steam engine, the most convenient arrangement was represented by the slowly

36. An original sketch of Huygens' atmospheric piston machine

37. Diagrammatic representation of propulsion system used in road, water, rail and air transport from early days to the present

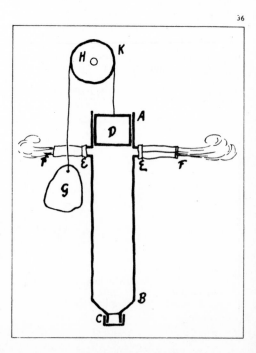

36

revolving paddle-wheel. The inventor of the atmospheric machine, Denis Papin, started experimenting with this configuration on the river Fulde, but he obtained no support and in the end the indignant boatman destroyed his boat. Even the patent of the Englishman Jonathan Hulls of 1737, concerning a barge with a paddle-wheel at the stern driven by Newcomen's atmospheric steam engine, remained only on paper. The American William

Henry tried a similar boat on the river Conestore, Pennsylvania, in 1763; the boat unfortunately sank during the trial. In Europe the French Marquis de Jouffroy was not successful either, although his paddle-wheel steamboat *Pyroscaphe* sailed for 15 minutes upstream on the River Saône in the presence of thousands of inhabitants of Lyons who were watching this spectacle in the year 1783.

In 1788 in Scotland, William Symington and

38. Sketch of Jonathan Hull's barge with a paddle-wheel at the stern. Patent taken out in 1737, but not built

39. Unsuccessful experiments of Symington and Miller with a two-paddle-wheel ship in 1788

40. During its famous voyage from the USA to Europe in 1819, the *Savannah* was mainly propelled by sails. In dead calm weather the paddle wheels driven by a steam engine propelled the ship at a speed of 4 knots

41. Symington's paddle-boat *Charlotte Dundas* in 1802. The single-cylinder steam engine was designed by James Watt

40

Patrick Miller built a twin-hull boat propelled by a small steam engine and by two paddle-wheels positioned in the middle of the boat. Unfortunately, the power output of the engine was very low, and the paddle-wheels being made of poor material either cracked or broke; Symington and Miller after falling out went their separate ways. Miller carried on developing paddle-wheel boats, this time propelled manually by means of a crank—in one of

these he reached Stockholm. Symington built the first paddle-wheel steamship *Charlotte Dundas* which was propelled by a single-cylinder steam engine designed by James Watt. In 1802 the ship hauled two 70-ton barges against a strong headwind over a distance of 19½ miles. But the waves caused by the paddle-wheels damaged the banks of the canal and the canal owners banned the building of a further eight steamers.

41

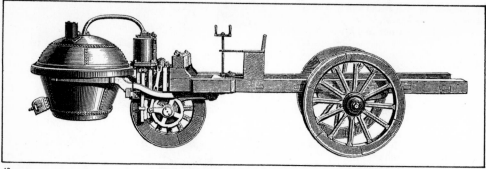

The American watchmaker John Fitch designed several types of steamboat which he tested on the river Delaware. One of them was propelled by paddle-wheels with a chain transmission moving alongside the ship like a tractor band. Another steamboat had a special rowing mechanism (Plate D). Still another was propelled by a screw. The most successful ship was the *Experiment* with a paddling mechanism at the stern. In 1787, Fitch started a regular transport service between Philadelphia and Trenton, the speed being 8 mph. It proved, however, to be a losing business and the impoverished inventor committed suicide.

A young American painter and engineer Robert Fulton (1765—1815) is generally considered the founder of steam navigation. First he constructed a small submarine and experimented with torpedoes. On the River Seine he carried out experiments with paddle-wheel steamboats, and tried to convince Napoleon that steamships could be used in the war against England. After his return to America he began, supported by Robert Livingston, patron of many American steamboat pioneers, to construct the *Clermont*, a 133-ft long paddle-wheel steamboat driven by an engine with a power output of about 20 hp. In spite of jeers, the *Clermont* began her voyage on 17 August 1807, sailing at an average speed of 4·7 mph up the Hudson river. Without any difficulties she covered the distance of 156 miles between New York and Albany. Thanks to another American inventor, John Stevens, and his son, large-scale building of steamboats was started in America. In 1823 more than 300 steamboats were ploughing through the waters of the rivers Mississippi, Ohio and St Laurence.

The first paddle steamer to run a regular service in Britain was Henry Bell's *Comet*. In 1812, with 20 passengers on board, the *Comet* left Glasgow and reached Greenock. In 1814 another paddle-steamer, the *Margery*, appeared on the Clyde. It was eventually sold to a French firm and in 1816 was the first steamboat to cross the Channel.

The first steam driven ship to cross the Atlantic was the wooden full-rigged sailing ship *Savannah*, with a gross tonnage of 320 tons and fitted with an auxiliary steam engine and paddles. On 24 May 1819, the ship left Georgia and after 30 days arrived in Liverpool. She crossed the ocean mainly under sail; in fact, the engines worked for only 80 hours, as they consumed all the fuel during the voyage.

Steam-driven vehicles

In Great Britain, at a time when the efforts of James Watt to improve the steam engine reached their zenith, several inventors were studying the possibility of driving vehicles with a steam engine. Watt himself did not wish to have imitators, and in 1784 he applied for a patent to protect his design of a steam-driven vehicle. As a result France was to become the cradle of the steam-driven vehicle. In 1769, Nicholas-Joseph Cugnot demonstrated his travelling steam carriage in the presence of military authorities in Paris. The Minister of Defence foresaw in the model a future vehicle for towing heavy guns, and he commissioned Cugnot to construct a larger steam carriage. The vehicle was finally manufactured towards the end of 1770. A double-cylinder steam engine directly drove the cranks of the single front wheel which served at the same time for steering the vehicle. Inevitably the vehicle was very clumsy. Also, Cugnot overlooked to install some kind of brake. The vehicle therefore could not travel faster than 2·5 mph and during the very first trial smashed against a wall. The historians quote this event as the first road accident. During the period of stormy and violent political changes France forgot Cugnot, who died at a time when the centre of the steam-driven vehicles development moved back to England.

In spite of the resistance of his employers, Watt and Boulton, a young engineer William Murdock started to build the first models of three-wheel steam carriages. He applied a higher pressure in the boiler, although this involved certain risks.

The first passengers to travel in a carriage drawn by a four-wheel steam-carriage appeared in the streets of Camborne on Christmas Eve, 1801. The designer was an English mining engineer, Richard Trevithick. It was also his idea to stimulate burning under the boiler by leading the exhaust vapours to a smoke-stack. In that way he increased the power output of the vehicle to such an extent that it could even climb hills. On the level it achieved a speed of 10 mph. In his second steam carriage, which he constructed together with his brother Vivian, Trevithick used huge rear wheels driven by gear wheels. By swivelling small front wheels the steam carriage could be steered. These experiments cost the inventor a lot of money. Trevithick came to the conclusion that the steam-driven vehicle could never work satisfactorily on bad roads, and consequently concentrated on steam locomotives.

Independently of the development of steam-driven vehicles in Britain, a steamer appeared in the USA in 1804. It was designed by a mechanic, Oliver Evans, and was, in fact, a four-wheel mobile and floating dredger or excavator called *Eructor amphibolus*. In the history of transport it holds the place of the first amphibious vehicle. In Britain, meanwhile, more practical steam-carriages were built. One of them was constructed in 1821 by Julius Griffith. Although by profession he was a correspondent, he enriched the technological design by an ingenious water-tube boiler. In order to reduce water consumption he introduced a multi-tube condenser. On the other hand, his fellow-countryman David Gordon—although by profession an engineer—led the development to an impasse. First he obtained a patent for a large rim-shaped carriage driven by a small locomotive which meshed its inner toothing in a way a squirrel turns a drum. In order to prevent wheel slippage he provided his second steam carriage with six iron arms, which were to push it off the ground using steam engine power. It was finally his son Alexander who contributed to the development of steam locomotion by founding, in 1832, the first specialised magazine in the world called *The Journal of Elemental Locomotion*. Through its pages he struggled for recognition of the usefulness of steam locomotion.

The increasing interest in the development of steam-driven vehicles resulted in a London surgeon, Goldsworthy Gurney, giving up his chosen profession. His first design was also based on vehicles pushed by mechanical arms. Later, profiting from the errors of his predecessors, Gurney built a steam-carriage with a double-cylinder steam engine inside the chassis. A safe tube boiler was located behind the body of the vehicle. In order to dissipate the fears of the passengers that the boiler might explode, he built the next coach as a carriage towed by a vehicle reminiscent of a locomotive. In 1831 he undertook a 220-mile journey. He met not only with difficulties concerning the water supply, but also with the indignant and alarmed population. People erected barricades on the roads and hurled stones at the carriage, so that finally he had to be protected by armed guards.

Another Englishman, Walter Hancock, provided steam-carriages with a new shape. He built seven steam omnibuses and opened a regular passenger transport service between London and Paddington. The most successful vehicles were the *Enterprise*, followed by *Autopsy* and *Era*. In subsequent omnibuses Hancock used a band brake and a steam feed pump.

Finally, in 1835, Dr William Church built a steam-carriage with a magnificent aspect. It was designed for up to 40 passengers and had a covered vertical boiler. In order to reduce shocks it was equipped with spring-cushioned wheels. Although it was characterised as 'a unity of perfect craftsman-

42. N.J. Cugnot produced this massive steam carriage of 1770 for moving artillery pieces

43. The bad state of roads compelled Trevithick to provide his second steam carriage built in 1802 with rear wheels larger than the front ones

44

ship, science and beauty', it had the reputation of not being very reliable.

The French designers were also unsuccessful in building fully reliable steam-carriages. A manufacturer of organs, Charles Dallery, returned to the heritage of Cugnot. In 1803 he built a vehicle *mobile* which could be used for travel both by land and by water. Another significant improvement in the design of steam-driven vehicles was introduced in 1828 by a watchmaker, Pecquer. To ensure smooth-

44. Oliver Evans approaching the Shuykill river in his amphibian steam dredger in 1804

45. Travelling from London to Bath in 1829, Gurney's steam-carriage achieved a speed of 12 mph

46. In May 1836 Walter Hancock ran a passenger transport service between London and Paddington using seven steam omnibuses

45

er trave round bends he provided them with a differential gear, increasing at the same time the draught under the boiler by means of a fan. In western Europe only road trains with two to three trailers and hauled by steam locomotives met with any enthusiasm. They were built by the Germans Dietz and his son.

In England, new technological improvements were introduced by Thomas Rickett. His three-wheel carriage, built for the Marquess of Statford, could change gears due to geared transmission and was equipped with block brakes. But only one historic steam-carriage, built in 1868 by the English colonel R.E.B. Crompton, was preserved. A number of his vehicles, looking like tractors and equipped with cushion tyres (invented in the USA by Charles Goodyear), hauled road freight trains in India, Java and Ceylon.

The promising development of steam-carriages was suddenly interrupted by the accident of Scott Russel's vehicle, whose boiler blew up during its journey from Glasgow killing several people. A campaign against steam-driven vehicles followed. Posters and topical pictures showed what a catastrophe the world may expect, if the 'fire' vehicles continued to be used ever more frequently (Plate ID.

Local communities raised their permission fees for steam locomotion, the railway was taking away passenger travel and freight, and the last nail in the steam-carriage's coffin was represented by the second 'Locomotive Act' of 5 July 1865—the well-

known Red Signal Flag Act. Each steam-carriage had to be attended by three persons, one of them being obliged to walk at least 60 yards ahead of the machine with a red signal flag to warn riders and coachmen approaching in the opposite direction. In villages and communities the speed was reduced to 2 mph, in free roads to 4 mph. 'Speeding' was punished with a £10 fine. This Act, abolished only in 1896, slowed down the development of automobiles by decades.

Triumph of the steam locomotive

The steam-carriage was placed on rails for the first time in 1803. In fact, it was the outcome of a £1,000 bet between Nicholas Humphrey, owner of the Pen-y-darran Ironworks in South Wales and a neighbouring ironmaster. To win his bet, Humphrey commissioned Richard Trevithick to build the first railway steam-carriage. The bet was: Could a cargo of 10 tons be moved from Pen-y-darran to the Glamorganshire Canal without the use of animal or manpower? On 21 February 1804, Trevithick's tramwagon (the term locomotive was introduced only 25 years later by G. Stephenson) stood on the rails. The force of the steam engine was transmitted to the wheels by gear transmission and the running of the machine was balanced by a large flywheel. The steam engine was called *Invicta*. It amazed spectators with its clouds of steam. During the demonstration it hauled five wagons with their load of iron and 70 passengers who had climbed

47

47. Dr Church's steam coach of 1835 had spring-cushioned wheels

48. The Marquis of Statford behind the steering lever of the steam tricycle built in 1858 by Thomas Rickett, who is sitting next to him

48

aboard, and easily coped with a cargo of 26 tons. Trevithick was rewarded for his efforts to improve his mobile steam-carriages. However, as the cast-iron rails were cracking and breaking all the time under the weight of the *Invicta,* horses started being used again. As a result Trevithick tried to build his next steam-carriage—ordered by the owner of the Wylam Colliery—as light as possible. It could not start moving, however, because its wheels kept slipping. The inventor did not give up. In 1808 he constructed in London a circular rail track surrounded by a high fence. Those who paid a shilling entrance fee could watch the *Catch Me Who Can* locomotive running in circles. The speed of about 20 mph the engine attained seemed to the spectators a devilish one. The locomotive was finally wrecked by derailment.

After the experience with the locomotive in Wylam, Trevithick's followers no longer believed that the smooth wheels of the locomotive on smooth rails could transfer by friction a sufficient traction force. They therefore started looking for ways of solving this seeming impasse. John Blenkinsop and Matthew Murray built for the Middleton mine railway a 'rack' locomotive with a driving wheel which meshed with a toothed third rail laid alongside the track. In 1813, the English engineer Brunton provided his steam engine with a mechanism that pushed the locomotive with swivelling levers like the legs of a horse. The brothers Chapman manufactured a steam-carriage hauled by a wound chain located between the rails.

49

49. Trevithick's *Invicta* (1803—04) reached a speed of 5 mph hauling a 26-ton load

50. In London, in 1808, at a price of one shilling anyone could admire the *Catch Me Who Can* locomotive or even have a ride in the attached carriage

50

51

51. The 'rack' locomotive built by Blenkinsop and Murray in 1811

52. George Stephenson (1781—1848), inventor of the steam locomotive and builder of the first railways

52

Finally, the mine inspector of the Wylam Colliery, William Hedley, understood—and proved by experiments—that friction depended on the pressure of the wheels. He mechanically coupled the driving wheels. His locomotive, called for its noisy exhausts *Puffing Billy*, was the first one to have a boiler made of steel sheets. It was in use for nearly 50 years.

The most enthusiastic pioneer of the steam locomotive and the founder of the steam railway was, without doubt, George Stephenson (1781—1848). Stephenson, who learned to read and write at 15 years of age, and at 22 became an engineer and later a mining consultant, built many experimental locomotives, before developing the successful locomotive *Locomotion* for the first railway connecting Stockton and Darlington. On 27 September 1825, Stephenson's *Locomotion* hauled 21 wagons with 450 enthusiastic passengers. With another 12 cars loaded with coal and flour the train achieved a speed of 12 mph. At the end of its service, *Locomotion* became a railway monument in front of the oldest railway station in the world at Darlington.

After this success Stephenson was asked to measure and build a railway line from Liverpool to Manchester. Natural obstacles were tremendous: the same could be said about the resistance of the land owners. In the end the railway with a tunnel, sixty-three bridges and viaducts, bridging among other obstacles the swampy land of Chat Moss, was put into operation. At the same time a competition for the design of the fastest engine to serve the new railway line was declared.

On 6 October 1829, five locomotives met on a 2-mile section of the new railway line at Rainhill, near Liverpool. One of them called *Cycloped* was, however, immediately eliminated, since it turned out that it was driven by a horse hidden inside. Burstall's *The Perseverance* was too cumbersome and could not take part in the competition. Braithwaite's and Ericsson's *Novelty*, with an unusual shape, as well as Ha worth's *Sans Pareil*, suffered from constant failures and had to be hauled away. The winner was Stephenson's *Rocket*, which hauled a train with a $12^3/_4$-ton cargo at an average speed of 13 mph. With one car and 36 passengers it achieved a speed of 29 mph. Without any load it attained a speed of 35 mph: for many years it held this speed record against all types of transport. Stephenson handed over a part of his remuneration to his friend Booth. Following Booth's recommendation, Stephenson changed the usual way of heating under the boiler: flames from the furnace were led through twenty-five copper fire tubes inside the water space of the boiler. Connecting rods of two inclined steam cylinders directly turned the front driving wheels. The *Rocket* carried a reservoir of water and a coal container, predecessor of the tender.

A year later, Stephenson opened a regular service on the Liverpool & Manchester Railway with eight gala trains carrying 600 guests from all over the world.

The beginning of the 'coach' automobile

The first fuel used to set in motion a vehicle—a wooden cart—was the energy of burnt gas produced in a cylinder. The 'engine' was built in 1807 by a Swiss, Isaac de Rivaz in his shed in Vevey. Under a piston moving in a long cylinder he injected town gas from a small rubber ball, igniting it by an electric spark. The piston was to be pushed upwards and set a flywheel revolving. The flywheel would drive the front wheels of the cart by means of a rope. The energy from the explosion was greater than expected: the cart smashed through the shed gate and finished up a broken heap in the street. That night Rivaz wrote his patent application for the use of town gas as a source of engine power.

Seventy years later, thanks to the Frenchman Lenoir and the Germans Otto and Langen, the first practical internal-combustion engines were developed. They were improved within a short time, thus opening the way to a light and practical motor vehicle—the automobile.

The German, Karl Benz, is the man most entitled to be called 'inventor' of the motor car as he was the first to sell horseless carriages, made to a set pattern and not 'one-off' experiments, to the public. Other pioneer designers were: Gottlieb Daimler (also from Germany); Frenchmen Emile Levassor and René Panhard; the Lanchester brothers from the UK and the American, Henry Ford. There were, of course, other notable inventions which contributed to the successful development of the motor car, such as electromagnetic ignition (developed especially by the Austrian, Siegfried Markus) and the pneumatic tyre (invented by John Dunlop).

Karl Benz, manufacturer of petrol engines in Mannheim drove his tricycle in front of the public for the first time on 3 July 1886. Parts of the spring-cushioned 'horseless carriage' were based on bicycle design, having two large wire-spoke rear wheels and a smaller front wheel which could be steered; solid

53. Stephenson's *Locomotion* of 1825 was in service on the first railway line in the world, from Stockton to Darlington (*Science Museum, London*)

54. A reconstruction of Stephenson's *Rocket*, partly assembled from original parts. It can be seen in the Science Museum, London

54

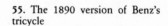

55. The 1890 version of Benz's tricycle

56. Layout of the horizontal single-cylinder engine on a Benz tricycle, showing the horizontal flywheel

57. Gottlieb Daimler (on the rear seat) in his 1886 petrol-engined coach

58. An automobile built by the Frenchmen Panhard and Levassor in 1891. The engine is located vertically at the front of the vehicle

59. A light automobile built by the American Duryea brothers in 1895

55

56

57

tyres were used. A water-cooled single-cylinder four-stroke engine located between the rear wheels drove the countershaft and differential gear by means of a flat belt. A chain drive transmitted the engine power to the two rear wheels.

The output of the engine was only 0·75 hp, but the light vehicle achieved a speed of about 9 mph. In his memoirs Benz mentions the capricious nature of his *Benzina* and the excellent assistance he received from his wife: 'I needed her for pushing the vehicle when I tried to start the engine, and I needed her even more on my return, when she had to push me to our house . . .'

One year later, thanks to the installation of an epicyclic gear, the vehicle acquired a second gear.

The Benz tricycle made the first long distance ride of a 'horseless carriage' in 1888, when Karl's wife and sons Eugen, 15, and Richard, 13, took off one summer evening without his knowledge to visit grandfather at Pforzheim, a distance of 70 miles. They bought motor spirit from the chemist, had blacksmiths take up the slack in the chains, and cobblers reline the brake shoes with leather.

Tricycles met with success especially in France. Later on Benz began to manufacture four-wheel automobiles, whose mechanism had, according to the wording of the patent, 'the steering circuits at the tangent of the steering mechanism' (meaning the steering pivots). Benz, happy that he had solved a number of technical problems, called the new vehicle *Viktoria*. In 1895 he sold 135 cars. Five years later he manufactured three-gear vehicles *Ideal, Tonneau, Duc, Phaeton* and even the four-gear car *Mylord-Coupe*. In all of them he installed horizontal cylinders.

Gottlieb Daimler, with the help of Wilhelm Maybach, developed and manufactured engines with vertical cylinders that gave higher revs and power outputs compared with the old stationary engines. In the beginning they used hot tube ignition but subsequently changed to electromagnetic ignition, which was more efficient. In 1885 they introduced the first motorcycle and later the same year installed a 1·5 hp engine in a modified coach; using a friction cone clutch with two gears, the vehicle reached a speed of 11 mph. A year later, Daimler built a double-cylinder engine with the cylinders arranged in the form of a V. The engine had a fin-type radiator cooler. At the world exhibition in 1889, held under the Eiffel tower, Daimler demonstrated an all-metal automobile as a symbol of the 'age of steel'. It had riveted sheets, tube chassis structure, a differential and a four-speed gearbox. Water was cooled during its passage through steel tubes. Daimler's engines were bought in large numbers by the French pioneers—Panhard, Levassor, Peugeot—for use in their own cars.

The first company set up in the United States to produce petrol motor cars was the Duryea Motor Wagon Company of Springfield, Mass., late in 1894. Frank and Charles Duryea had developed an experimental car in 1892—93, and was almost certainly

58

America's first four-wheeled 'gas car' to run on the roads, although it may have been antedated by a few months by Lambert's tricar. In later life, the brothers quarrelled and each claimed to have been the designer of the Duryea automobile. A Duryea won the 54-mile *Time-Herald* Race in 1895, averaging a speed of less than 8 mph, and two Duryeas took part in the London-to-Brighton Emancipation Day procession in 1896. Although early Duryea cars had many ingenious features, they were not a great commercial success.

During 1896, G.B. Selden took out a patent for a carriage driven by a Brayton-type two-stroke gas engine. In 1899 he sold manufacturing rights to a financial syndicate. This led to the formation of the Association of Licensed Automobile Manufacturers (forerunners of the SAE) who tried to mon-

59

60. The 12 hp internal-combustion engine which powered the flight of the first successful aircraft — the Wright brothers *Flyer*

60

61

opolise the automobile industry in the US, as Lawson had done in the UK, by forcing all manufacturers to join them and pay manufacturing licence fees. After many legal battles, the Selden patent was finally 'busted' on behalf of Henry Ford's company in 1911.

Henry Ford made his first crude, experimental, motor quadricycle in 1896 and followed it with improved versions. Later on, in partnership with Tom Cooper, he made two racing cars for publicity purposes, and with the financial backing they won him he formed the Ford Co. late in 1901. Horizontal-engined 'gas buggies' were made at first, followed by four-cylinder, vertical-engined cars, still with two-speed epicyclic gearing in 1904—05. The Model T was introduced in October 1908 (James Couzens

61. The *Flyer* which, with Orville Wright at the controls, made its first bumpy 12 second hop into the air on 17 December 1903

62. Wilhelm Maybach driving a motor boat in 1887, whose three air propellers are belt-driven by a Daimler four-cylinder engine

was the principal designer), and by dropping all other models so as to increase production of the T, unchanged, for many years at a constantly reducing price, Ford brought motoring to the masses. More than 15 million were made in a 19-year run.

62

I Demonstration in 1787 by the American John Fitch in Philadelphia of a boat with twelve oars propelled by Newcomen's steam engine

II Cartoon by Erich Lessing in 1842 depicting disasters to come, following the increase in the numbers of steam vehicles (steamers) on the road

III Section through a double-current electric locomotive: 1—pantograph for dc voltage feeding; 2—pantograph for ac voltage feeding; 3—main transformer; 4—voltage regulator; 5—semiconductor (quartz) rectifiers; 6—oil coolers; 7—series resistance; 8—main switch; 9—cooling fan for electric motor; 10—brake compressor; 11—start resistors; 12—traction motors; 13—main air reservoir; 14—control desk

IV Double-current electric locomotive SNCF, type CC 21000. Power output 7,750 hp, weight 120 tons, maximum speed 137 mph (manufacturer: Alsthom + Société MTE)

63. The first practical electric locomotive built in 1879 by W. Siemens. Although it was of restricted size (490 mm wheel spacing), its power output was 3·5 hp

Ersfe electr. Locomotive
Berliner Gewerbe Ausstellung
im Jahre 1879

63

Combustion engines for sea and air transport

Daimler and Maybach did not find a significant field of application for automobiles in Germany and therefore started to install their combustion engines in ships. By the beginning of August, 1886, they were already ploughing the waters of the river Neckar in the first motor boat. By means of belts, a four-cylinder engine drove three air propellers 3 feet in diameter. In ships the considerable weight of Daimler's engines did not matter and they were largely used in Europe for the manufacture of high-performance sport motor boats. They were so solid and robust that, for instance, the boat of a French engineer F. Forest performed reliably from 1891 to 1913. The power to weight ratio on these engines was 1·3 hp/110 lb.

Aircraft designers, however, wanted engines with the lowest possible weight while maintaining a high power output. For the first Zeppelin airship, Maybach designed two Daimler four-stroke engines which produced 16 hp each, their weight/power ratio being 33 lb/hp. By 1900 this ratio had been reduced to 14 lb/hp.

With the increasing development in aviation it became of paramount importance to reduce the power weight ratio even more. The first successful motor aircraft in the world, built by the brothers Wilbur and Orville Wright in 1903, was equipped with an Otto-type engine, which gave a power output of 16 hp and weighed about 170 lb (11 lb/hp). For comparison, present-day aircraft piston engines have a weight/power ratio of 0·66 lb/hp, while the latest prop-jet aircraft engines achieve a ratio of only 0·17 lb/hp.

The electric motor

This has played a restrictive role in the development of transport, although it runs smoothly and is easily controllable. This is because an electric motor for its source of power is handicapped by the need of heavy batteries or by the necessity to be electrically connected to the mains supply.

In spite of its limitations, there was an electric paddle-wheel ship sailing on the river Neva in Petersburgh in 1838. The designer B.S. Jakobi fed its electric motor with a power output of 1·3 hp by the current from a galvanic battery. The next battery-powered boat was not built until 50 years later by a Frenchman, G. Trouve, but this kind of driving power can never match either the petrol or diesel engine. One exception in marine use, however, is the submarine, where electric motors provide the main source of driving power; the current for these is obtained from banks of batteries which, themselves, are recharged by a generator driven by a diesel engine, when the submarine is on the surface.

In 1835, the American Davenport and Davidson from Scotland tried to build an electric locomotive driven by the current from galvanic cells.

In 1851, the American C.G. Page tried to feed an electric locomotive travelling the Washington-Bladensburg line from the electricity supply. In 1879 Werner Siemens demonstrated at the Berlin Industrial Exhibition a simple functioning electric locomotive fed with current by means of a sliding shoe from a conductor rail.

3 Railways

Ten years after the triumph of Stephenson's *Rocket* about 600 miles of railways were in operation. Industry and business flourished at places connected by tracks with the rest of the country. The coming of the railway in Canada and the United States made possible the rapid expansion and growth of these two countries in the nineteenth century. New towns grew up around the wooden railway stations. Stephenson's locomotives penetrated everywhere. Disassembled in parts, they crossed the sea in crates and were transported by wagons to places where the track line opened new horizons. Only later were they replaced by American-built locomotives.

Steam locomotives of the first railways

Stephenson provided the locomotives serving the historical Liverpool-Manchester line with four wheels only, one leading axle and one driving axle.

The engine driver, the stoker and the brakesman were exposed to the elements of the weather, as were the passengers travelling third and fourth class. The 'open air' passengers were also subjected to smoke and soot from the chimney. Only the first and second-class carriages were enclosed with windows. Although the carriages were not heated in winter, people were used to far more atrocious adversities when travelling by horse-drawn vehicles, and regarded rail transport as definite progress.

The United States did not want to lag behind. In 1828, Horatio Allen, engineer to the South Carolina Railroad, brought four locomotives from Europe and used them first on the original horse traction mine railway at Quincy. The first of them, the *Stourbridge Lion*, was put into operation in August, 1829. She left behind so many broken and cracked rails that her first journey became her last. The rails were then strengthened, but the boiler of the next locomotive, the *Best Friend of Charleston* which was welcomed in the city of the same name by gun salute and flags, exploded.

It was finally a locomotive from the Baltimore engineering works, the *Tom Thumb*, which undertook the first long-distance journey. She differed from European locomotives in many ways. In the middle of the platform chassis there was a vertical cylindrical boiler with a chimney; the steam engine was provided with vertical cylinders driving the shaft. A gear drive transmitted the power to the driving wheels. The engine driver stood on the front platform, the stoker on the rear one. An improved locomotive of this era, the *Atlantic*, ran on the first railway line from Baltimore to Ohio together with other European and American locomotives.

At high speeds the four-wheel locomotives suffered from unsmooth running. After a train was derailed in France near Versailles killing 57 persons,

Stephenson and other designers decided to add another axle. This type, classified by international convention 1 A 1 (the figures indicate the number of free axles, the alphabet order of the letters indicate the number of driving axles), survived for several decades. A new improved series of locomotives was called by Stephenson the 'Patentee'. The Patentee-type locomotive had a larger firebox surface area compared with the *Rocket* (the number of fire tubes were increased from 25 to 130), it weighed 9 tons and gave a power output of 40 hp. On 7 December 1835, one of them, *Der Adler,* opened the service on the first German railway connecting Nuremberg with Furth, 4 miles away. The legendary engine driver William Wilson drove the locomotive wearing a top hat, and his wages were said to be two and a half times the salary of the railway manager.

On 29 October 1838, a train decorated with flags and hauled by another Stephenson locomotive left Berlin for Potsdam. Wealthy passengers used to travel in the railway coaches, while the less fortunate ones had to be satisfied with hard benches in the *bankenwagens*. Horse-drawn coaches could be transported on the platform wagons attached to the end of the train. As was usual at that time, the train ran only during the day.

The Leipzig-Dresden line was put into service on 7 April 1839. It was built using flat-bottomed Vignoles rails. The tracks led through the 500-yard long Oberau tunnel. Stephenson's locomotives, as well as those imported from the USA, were joined by the first German locomotive *Saxonia*, type B 1, 1838, built by Professor Schubert at Übigau.

The power output of the steam engines had to be substantially increased, since the trains were becoming ever longer and the locomotives had to overcome sharp gradients of the new railway lines. This led to the 'long-boiler' locomotives being built after 1845. Their vertical firebox was topped by a steam dome. The firebox with the chimney was located at the other end of the long boiler. The first mountain railway between Zürich and Baden (called *Spanische Brödli Bahn,* since the curvature of the railway was similar to a popular Swiss pastry) was serviced by a new series of locomotives of the 2 A class. The locomotives had only one driving axle and at high speeds they were unsteady and quite dangerous. After a serious accident near Gütersloh in 1851 (the Crown Prince Friedrich Wilhelm was among the injured passengers), the designers of European locomotives preferred two coupled driving axles (series B). When, later on, the railway had to overcome the sharp Alpine gradients, a third coupled axle was added to the locomotives (series C).

Originally the railway had been designed for plains and valleys. According to Stephenson, sharp gradients could be overcome by means of ramps, and a steam engine at the top of the hill could haul the carriages by a rope winch. This solution was also proposed by some authors when designing the connection between Vienna and Trieste, where the Alpine mountain range formed a tremendous ob-

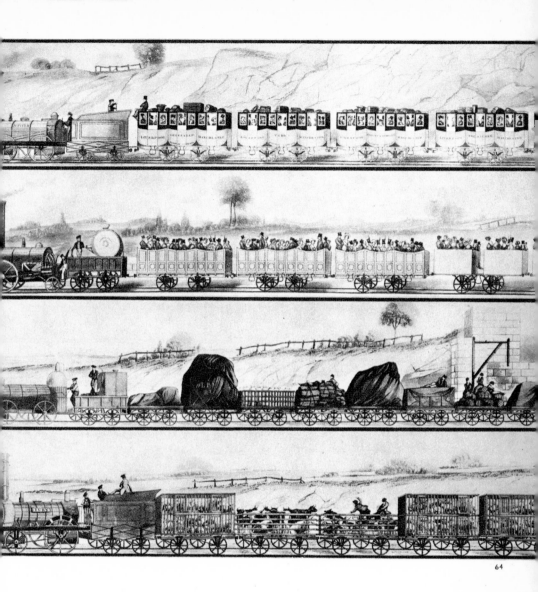

stacle. Charles von Ghega designed and built the first mountain railway worked by steam locomotives and on 12 April 1854, the first train climbed over the Semmering Pass, riding through five tunnels and over 135 bridges with an average gradient of 2·5 per cent. It was hauled by the locomotive *Mürzsteg* with three coupled axles. To increase her adhesion the weight of the tender was ingeniously utilised.

The coal and water container—the tender—used to be hauled right behind the locomotive. After the year 1860 short-distance locomotives appeared with water and coal in containers placed alongside the

64. Locomotives and carriages on the Liverpool—Manchester line
First drawing: 2nd and 1st-class carriages.
Second drawing: 3rd and 4th-class carriages—for standing passengers.
Third drawing: freight train.
Fourth drawing: cattle train
(*The Science Museum, London*)

65

66

54

65. Replica of the 1832 locomotive *Atlantic* with two carriages. This was used on the Baltimore and Ohio Railroad, the first North American railway line. *(Smithsonian Institution, Washington)*

66. In 1835, Stephenson's locomotive *Adler* opened a regular service on the first German railway line, from Nuremberg to Fürth

67. French long-boiler locomotive *Sezanne*, built in 1847 by A. Hallet in Arras

67

68
69

68. The first Swiss locomotive *Limmat* (1847) on the Spanish Brodli line *(Verkehrshaus der Schweiz, Luzern)*

69. Locomotive *Muldenthal* with a tender, built in 1861 by R. Hartmann in Chemnitz; speed 30 mph *(Verkehrsmuseum, Dresden)*

boiler. This type of locomotive had a better adhesion and was therefore especially useful on mountain railways. Thus the railway overcame the last obstacles.

The 'big-wheel' locomotive: The English engineer Crampton tried to achieve higher speeds by using a larger-diameter driving axle. The driving axle had to be located at the rear end of the boiler and consequently this type of locomotive had to be substantially longer. The steam pressure was increased and the firebox surface area enlarged. It was no surprise that in 1846 Crampton's locomotive broke the world record achieving a speed of 75 mph. Ten years later the British installed, in the middle of the locomotive, wheels of such a size that they reached the top of larger than usual boilers. They were called 'Big Wheels' and one of the most famous among them was *The Lady of the Lake* built in 1859 by John Ramsbottom for the London and North Western Railway.

American locomotives: These developed at a faster rate than European locomotives. Although they were heated in the beginning by wood only, their designers used two to three times more steam pressure, thereby increasing their power output. A typical feature of the Pacific locomotive from the era of the conquest of the West was a short cone-shaped and gradually widening chimney carrying an unusually large lamp, behind which a brass signal bell was fixed. This was subsequently replaced by a steam whistle. At the front the locomotive was provided with a cruciform frame, the 'cow catcher', capable of pushing aside anything that came in the way of a train running across a prairie. At a time

when European engine-drivers were exposed to rain and cold, their American colleagues were sitting on upholstered seats located in spacious cabins sometimes painted in bright colours. By the mid-nineteenth century, high-performance locomotives in the USA were already provided with four driving axles (series D).

Technological improvement of locomotives

The layout of Stephenson's valve gear had been replaced in 1844 by that of Walschaerts and in 1849 by Heusinger's arrangement which, with better steam expansion utilisation, reduced the consumption of steam and consequently that of the fuel by a quarter. By means of a steam injector invented by the Frenchman Giffard in 1858 water was pumped from the tenders.

By the end of the 1870s steam engines were built with an axle load of 14 tons and usually with two or three cylinders. Only the elegant British locomotives of the Victorian era had their steam cylinders inside the frame—like the Patentees. The compound locomotives especially contributed to a substantial improvement in performance and to a reduction in coal consumption. Steam from the superheater was led into the low-pressure compound cylinder after which it was blown out into the atmosphere. Such a locomotive was introduced for the first time in 1878 by a Swiss engineer Mallet. It was designed for heavy-duty mountain service on a line with sharp curves, so Mallet divided the locomotive into two parts: the forward swivelling bogie had a separate drive. These high-performance loco-

70. Crampton locomotive *No. 80* introduced in 1852 on the Paris—Strasbourg line

71. 2-C-2 locomotive from the end of the 1880s serving on the Pacific Line

72. An American 2-C locomotive manufactured in 1900 by the Richmond locomotive works

73

74

73. A French 2-C steam locomotive from 1914 with a cylindrical slide valve and Heusinger distribution

74. Austrian locomotive series 310·20, which had a tapering boiler, was kept in service until after the Second World War

75. Express train locomotive *SNCF* (Hudson series) from 1949, had a partly streamlined body; power output 3,350 hp, weight 212 tons. Its front part is provided with deflectors to disperse the chimney smoke

motives were developed for use on mountain lines and for pulling heavy freight trains. The heaviest Mallet articulated locomotive in the world had 6 + 6 coupled wheel sets and weighed 387 tons.

The mountainous, mainly narrow-gauge lines of South America, Africa and India — 2ft, 3 ft 3³/₈ in (metre-gauge), 3 ft 6 in — are served even today by Garrat articulated locomotives. This type of locomotive has a double boiler supported by two independently driven and swivelling bogies. The arrangement was patented as early as 1863 by the Englishman Robert Fairlie.

The theory of thermodynamics inspired the designers of locomotives to increase the steam parameters. A major contribution in that sense was

that of a German engineer W. Schmidt who, in 1898, completed the modern locomotive with a steam superheater. Since that time most locomotives superheat the steam leaving the boiler at a temperature of 190° C (406° F) in a superheater, thus achieving a temperature of 350—400° C (758—848° F). On the other hand the increased steam pressure necessitated rather complex designs and was not therefore accepted for general application. Neither the principle of coal dust combustion nor the attempts to drive each set of wheels independently from V-arranged steam-engine cylinders found any larger application in practice.

With the exception of early American and some Russian locomotives heated by wood, coal remained the main fuel of the steam locomotive. During an average journey, about 1,100 1b of coal is burnt on each square yard of the grate and even the most skilled stoker could not load more than 2¹/₂ tons of coal using a shovel. A screw feeder called the 'stoker' was invented to do this work. The 'stoker' takes coal from the bottom of the tender and distributes it evenly on the surface of the firebox with the help of steam nozzles.

A steam locomotive consumes all the water from its tender after covering a distance of about 125 miles. In Britain and the USA additional water supplies were obtained while running from a water chute located between the rails; the engine driver just lowered a feeding chute in the opposite direction of travel.

For lines leading across prairies and the deserts of Africa and Australia condenser locomotives were developed, where the condensers were in an attached carriage, which was longer than the locomotive itself. Steam from the cylinders was exhausted into air-cooled tube condensers and the condensed water conducted back into the boiler for reheating. Such a locomotive could cover a 600-mile journey.

Steam turbine locomotives: Although they had a higher efficiency, they were rather too complex. The first of them was built in 1908 by a Swedish engineer, Ljungström. In Germany these locomotives were manufactured by Kraus and Maffei, in the USA by the Baldwin company. The power output of the turbine was transmitted by gears to one set of wheels and through the coupling rod to the remaining driving axles. For the return travel the American locomotives had a second turbine.

Express steam locomotives: At a speed higher than 60 mph, air resistance plays an important role in the performance of a locomotive. By 1904 when the Henschel company in Germany started to build express steam locomotives, they took note of this fact and designed them with a streamlined body. In 1904 a three-cylinder 2-B-2 steam locomotive reached the highest speed of that time, 85 mph. Three years later, a locomotive with a conical forebody achieved a speed of 95 mph. The speed record competition then moved to the United States where long and straight lines enabled the locomotives of the 'Atlantic' type (series 2-B-1) to achieve speeds of 110 mph on the New York Central line. In Britain an LNER express train with a streamlined locomotive body, the *Silver Link,* reached a speed of 112·5 mph on the trial trip of the Silver Jubilee train in September 1935.

77

76. Mallet-type mountain locomotive for Brazilian railways; maximum power output 1,850 hp *(Rheinstahl)*

77. Henschel-type locomotive with high-speed double-cylinder steam engines in 1941 achieved a speed of 111 mph. Maximum power output 2,300 hp

78. A Garrat articulated locomotive, series 2+D+1+1+D+2 for Angola railways. Power output 1,600 hp, weight 150 tons *(Rheinstahl)*

79. A Henschel high-pressure freight train locomotive series 2+D+1 with pulverised coal fuel *(Rheinstahl)*

German streamlined locomotives, type 2-C-2, achieved a speed of 160 mph only 6 minutes after the start. In May 1935, the 4-6-4 No. 05.001, built by the Borsig Locomotive Works in Berlin, broke the world record with a speed of 124·8 mph. In July 1938 the British locomotive *Mallard,* type 'Pacific', reached a speed of 125·5 mph. None of the European locomotives, however, broke the world record claimed by Pennsylvania Railroad's Atlantic-type steam locomotive which in June 1905 reached a speed of 126·7 mph.

The end of the steam locomotive: The huge wheels of express steam locomotives with glistening rods served as a symbol of power and technology for many years. Designers, however, have calculated quite accurately that the overall efficiency of a steam locomotive cannot exceed 16 per cent and that only 5 to 6 per cent of the burnt coal energy can be exploited for useful work. Speed could not be increased above 127 mph — the unbalanced weights of the crank and piston mechanisms would not allow it. Moreover, the steam locomotive had to be serviced by two or three operators, its preparation for operation was extremely time-comsuming and its smoke polluted the railway and its surroundings.

Thus, at a time of its highest technological perfection, the steam locomotive had to give way to its electric, diesel and turbine rivals.

80

80. Condenser locomotive, series 2 + D + 2, which gives a power output of 3,000 hp. Still in service on the South African railways *(Rheinstahl)*

81. British LMS express train locomotive (Coronation series). Note the water trough between the rails so that locomotives could take on water at slow-down speed

81

Electric locomotives

If a modern electric freight locomotive with its relatively small wheels stands beside a steam locomotive, it certainly is not very impressive. But as soon as it starts to move, you can immediately see the difference. With the high power output of its electric motors (8,000 hp), the electric locomotive can get under way swiftly and with very little noise, hauling double the load of a steam locomotive which needs a long time to build up speed and is, furthermore, enveloped in clouds of steam and smoke. On comparing their performance, one electric locomotive can replace three steam locomotives. Instead of a three-member crew in a dirty cabin located inconveniently at the rear of the locomotive, one engine driver can control everything by himself. He sits in a closed cabin with a controller's wheel, control levers and an instrument board and has an excellent view of the line in front of him.

Direct-current electric locomotives: The history of direct-current electric locomotives began on 31 May 1879, at the Berlin Trades Exhibition. A smokeless and noiseless train hauled by an unbelievably simple locomotive without a chimney, conveyed passengers on a 300-yd long narrow-gauge line. It was driven by a direct current (dc) electric motor fed via a rheostat by the current from a third (centre) elevated rail. Its designer, Werner von Siemens, built a similar small locomotive in 1882, but with double the performance, for a Saxonian coal mine. It was called *Dorothea* and served reliably for 45 years.

At that period Edison in the USA was also experimenting with electric traction. His first locomotive ran at speeds up to 40 mph on narrow-gauge

82. Streamlined locomotive 2 + C + 2 put into operation in 1935 on the Berlin—Dresden line was capable of accelerating from 0 to 99 mph in 6 minutes. Power output was 1,600 hp

track specially laid for the purpose in 1880. Designers were not capable of parting company with convention; they covered the driving electric motor with a box shaped like a steam boiler.

The first electric locomotive in the USA in routine operation was called *Ampere* and was designed in 1883 by Leo Daft. It was fed by current from an auxiliary rail. This design has been maintained up to the present time in underground and elevated urban railways. The shoe sliding along the overhead power-supply cables appeared in 1895.

Very rapid and widespread development in electric traction took place in the years from 1890 to 1910. On 18 December 1890, the first underground electric railway in the world was opened by the City and South London Railway. The first length of line ran for 3 miles between Stockwell and King William Street. The trains were hauled by four-wheel electric locomotives which were driven from a 500 volt direct-current supply; the electricity was generated in the railway's own power station at Stockwell. The power output of the two motors of a City and South London locomotive was 100 hp.

The first conversion of a section of steam railway to electric working took place in the USA in 1895. Nearly 4 miles of the Baltimore and Ohio Railway were electrified where it ran in tunnel under the city of Baltimore. Power output of the four motors of a B & O locomotive was 1,080 hp.

Alternating current locomotives in Europe: The use of low-voltage (500-600 V) dc supplies prevented the development of high-speed electric locomotives. As a result the Swiss, who wanted to utilise their cheap electric power from their hydro-electric power stations, studied the possibilities of alternating current (ac) application. The Brown Boveri company chose for the line from Burgdorf to Thun a system with overhead mains supply, fed by an ac voltage of 750 V with a frequency of 40 Hz. On 19 July 1899, an electric locomotive called the 'Paddle Wheel Steamer' was put into operation. A circular cover was the only access to a low-speed electric motor of 295 hp located in the middle of the frame. The power output was transmitted by rods to stub axles. This system was used for a time in more powerful locomotives, although it was uneconomic and very clumsy, for the inertia weight of the rods had never been fully balanced. No doubt the electric locomotive designers were imitating the principle of the steam locomotive driving system. Cumbersome cranks and rods could be found as late as 1913 in one of the most powerful locomotives used by the Swiss for the Bern-Lötschberg-Simplon line. This line was fed by a single-phase voltage of 15,000 V with a frequency of 16·66 Hz. The maxi-

mum speed of the locomotive with an output of nearly 2,500 hp was 50 mph.

Siemens had divised improved three-phase asynchronous motors and, taking into account their simplicity, reliability and the possibility of electric braking, wanted to apply them in electric locomotives. For that purpose, however, three safely insulated mains were required. During his test of electric locomotives Siemens used three conductors, one above another, on the side of the test track. The locomotive had a high mast collector with three sliding shoes. The same arrangement was used on part

of the military Marienfelde-Zossen line near Berlin, where in 1902 tests of three-phase ac locomotives by Siemens and the AEG company were initiated. On 26 November 1903, the Siemens locomotive with two asynchronous motors of 270 hp reached a speed of 130 mph, which was not to be surpassed for 50 years.

This system of traction was convenient, especially for mountain railways. The feed in to locomotives was simplified; two phases were fed by two separate collectors from overhead mains, and a rail connected the locomotive with the third phase. This system, in its time widely used, was given up by Switzerland and in Spain fairly quickly; in Italy, however, it survived up to the 1960s.

The technical development of electric traction

86

83. Engine driver's cabin in an electric locomotive

84. The electric freight train locomotive *(left)* can haul three times the load of the steam locomotive *(right)*

85. During the four months of the Berlin Trades Exhibition (in 1879) 86,000 passengers tried the first electric train of the world *(Deutsches Museum, Munich)*

86. T.A. Edison, the American designer, at the controls of his electric locomotive on the Menlo Park track, 1880

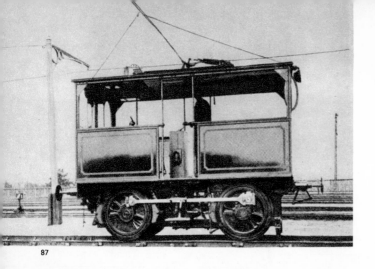

87. A small electric shunting locomotive provided with a sliding shoe was serving at the Potsdam station in 1894

88. A German test commission of 1903 headed by W. Siemens standing at an electric railway car which reached a speed of 130 mph—a world record. The two three-phase asynchronous motors ran off 12,000 V supplies *(Deutsches Museum, Munich)*

varied from country to country in Europe. The current systems were never unified.

In West Germany, East Germany, Switzerland and in Scandinavia a system has been preserved from before the Second World War; it is an alternating single-phase current with the frequency lowered to 16·66 Hz, the voltage being 15,000 V. These lines, however, have to be fed by their own power stations or by the railway frequency-converter stations.

Owing to exceptionally favourable traction pro-

perties of dc electric motors, some countries opted in favour of the direct-current system. The initial low voltage of 1,500 V was increased after the Second World War to 3,000 V. The disadvantage is that dc traction requires costly stations converting the alternating current from the public network into direct current. One such station has to be built every 12—15 miles along the line. This is economically justified only on lines with high density traffic where higher costs are compensated by savings due to the more simple design of dc locomotives.

V Italian electric articulated express train with tilting car bodies

VI American (Amtrac) electric locomotive type E—60. operating at 25,000 V ac, 60 Hertz *(General Electric)*

VII Section through a diesel-electric locomotive: 1—control desk; 2—main air tank; 3—diesel engine; 4—water cooler; 5—fans for cooler; 6—electric traction motor; 7—dynamo; 8—dynamo air-cooling ducting; 9—cooling fan for electric motor; 10—air filter; 11—air cleaner; 12—diesel engine supercharger

89. A circular cover protected the sixteen-pole motor of the first Swiss electric locomotive (1899)—known as the 'Paddle Wheel Steamer' because of this cover. It ran off a three-phase, 750 V supply *(Fotodienst SBB)*

90. A powerful Swiss locomotive, which reached a speed of 50 mph on a mountainous track in 1913. Operating off 15,000 V, 16·66 Hz, the single-phase ac motor gave an output of 2,400 hp

89

In 1955, the French demonstrated the capabilities of a dc electric locomotive during a carefully prepared test with a Co-Co locomotive (No. 7107). With three express carriages, it achieved a record speed of 205 mph. The current collectors, although pressed by the air to the roof of the locomotive, transmitted by spark discharge 4,000 A to the locomotive during the trial. (Note that in electric locomotive wheel arrangement notation, motored axles are denoted by a letter — B for 2, C for 3 and so on and non-motored axles by a number. When an axle is driven by its own motor, a small letter 'o' is added after the letter.)

The single-phase ac system of 16·66 Hz underwent further development as well. Some drawbacks of the ac electric motor were removed. The use of semiconductor elements and the wireless control of the magnetic field of the stator windings enabled ac motors to produce more power per unit than dc motors. The highlight of ac motor development is the thyristor locomotives, e.g. the German type E-103 locomotives with commutator motors which

90

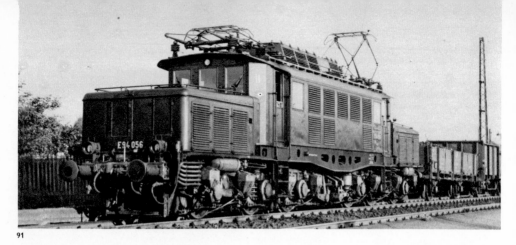

91

91. Heavy freight train electric locomotive of 4,200 hp in service before the Second World War; it had independently driven bogies

92. The fastest locomotive in the world, SNCF, type CC-7107, reached a speed of 205·6 mph in 1955

93. The so-called 'two-hundred-kilometre' locomotive of the West German railways fed by 15,000 V, single-phase current of 16·66 Hz, has a power output of 6,700 hp and weighs 115 tons

94. Modern electrically driven bogie connected with the carriage body of the ET 430 by two pneumatic rubber bags *(M.A.N.)*

95. Electric train unit for rapid transport used by the Swiss SBB railways *(Schlieren)*

92

93

can produce a permanent output of 1,675 hp. This means that a 115-ton locomotive with four driving axles can achieve an output of 4 × 1,675 hp = 6,700 hp. Each motor is individually cooled by air blown into its casing by a fan. Consequently, it can be overloaded during the start to 200 per cent.

After the Second World War, the French (on their lines in Savoy) and later nearly all European countries began to supply electric locomotives directly at the industrial frequency of 50 Hz, the voltage being 25,000 V. The advantages of an ac mains supply compared with dc distribution are the higher voltage requiring a smaller cross-section for the conductor wires, thus saving a considerable weight

94

95

of copper; because of their lighter weight, the catenary from which the conductors are suspended, with its support, could also be lighter.

In 1956, British Rail adopted the 25 kV, single-phase 50 Hz dc system for the electrification of certain main lines, the first to be converted being the London Midland Region.

With this system, each locomotive carries a transformer to control the voltage applied to the traction motors. Additionally, where dc traction motors are in use, a rectifier is connected between the transformer and motors to convert the ac supply into dc. Mercury-arc (lamp) rectifiers were first used for this purpose, subsequently semiconductor rectifiers

were introduced. In some ac locomotives, the traction rectifiers consist partly of thyristors developed by the Swedish company ASEA, which both rectify the ac input and allow the dc output voltage to be controlled electronically without using a motor-driven tap-changer. Thyristor control is much simpler than the conventional tap-changing process and varies the voltage so gradually that the system is often called 'stepless control'. Sudden increases in voltage as the driver increases power when starting a heavy train can cause wheelspin, and so the smooth build-up possible with thyristors enables the best use to be made of the adhesive weight of the locomotive. Besides the development of loco-

motives for the separate ac and dc systems, there has emerged in recent years locomotives able to work on both types of supply. This was made possible by ac locomotives with rectifiers, because they are 'half dc' anyway, and so when an ac locomotive reaches dc territory the supply is simply switched directly to the dc mains supply, bypassing the transformer and rectifiers. Germany, France and Belgium all have locomotives which can work on the two ac systems (low- and standard-frequency) and the two dc voltage (1,500 V and 3,000 V) used on the main lines of the European continent. Some countries have remained faithful to the systems of electrification they developed over many years, but the traveller in the international electric express trains of today passes from one system to another without being aware of it.

A section through a representative type of double-current locomotive is shown in Plate III. The current is collected from the overhead cable by a pantograph (1 or 2) through the main switch (8) to the transformer (3) located in an oil tank. The rectifier (5) for the traction motors (12) conducts the current from the voltage regulator (4) by means of a connection with start resistors in an air-cooled casing (11). Above each electric motor there is a cooling fan (9). The brake compressors (10) for supplying air to the main air reservoirs (13) for the

continuous train braking system are fed by current from the transformer.

In a modern locomotive, the driver sets the required speed within a range of 18 — 125 mph on the automatic acceleration instrument; electronic automatic equipment enables this speed to be reached without any undue overload and at the highest possible acceleration. A digital system controlling the revolutions of the driving axles prevents wheel slipping during starting or braking. At high speeds electric brakes are used, in which the motors are converted into generators and the current produced is either consumed by resistors or is recuperated back to the network. At lower speeds the continuous train brake is used. The latest locomotives are provided with disc brakes.

Electric motor train units: The very small outside dimensions of the driving bogies with two sets of wheels allow various arrangements of electric motor train units for suburban transport, express trains or special express units. Bodies of the carriages which used to be attached to bogies by means of spiral springs and shock absorbers, are nowadays connected to the bogies by pneumatic bags. Shocks cannot be transmitted to the light car bodies and in the case of the so-called swivelling suspension, the pressure in the bags quickly changes when the train enters a curve. The body of the carriage is inclined

in the curve by 9 ° and the passengers do not feel the disagreeable lateral effects. Moreover, the train can run in curves without slowing down. Only the pantographs of the locomotives have to swing out on the opposite side in order not to slide off the trolley. In Italy these trains are aptly called *pendolino*.

Development of electric traction in the world:
About 37,000 miles, or nearly 40 per cent, of all the main European railway lines are electrified. Even the Trans-Siberian line crossing Asia is electrified; it uses mainly a dc system of 3,000 V. Electric express trains on the Moscow—Leningrad line can reach a speed of 125 mph. Scandinavian railways are fully electrified. Between Kiruna and Narvik freight trains carrying iron ore are hauled by a 115-ft long locomotive with 12 sets of wheels and with a power output of 10,000 hp.

The United States have only recently discovered the advantages of electric traction on lines with a large density of traffic, especially in the New York corridor. An ac traction system is used, with either 25,000 V or 50,000 V at a frequency of 60 Hz. This same frequency, with a voltage of 20,000 V, is used also by the fastest railway in the world — the Japanese Tokaido.

The electrified railway is highly efficient and at the same time clean and noiseles.

96. This American urban electric transport double-decker unit carries 964 passengers

97. The Soviet aluminium express train ER-200 carries 816 passengers and can complete the Moscow to Leningrad run in 3·5 hours

Diesel locomotives and train units

Compared with the steam locomotive, the diesel locomotive can make a fairly quick start, has a twice or three times better fuel efficiency (30—35 per cent) and can cover a distance of many hundreds of miles without refuelling. In comparison with the electric locomotive, the diesel locomotive is more noisy and requires more maintenance but on the other hand it does not require the costly trolley network.

The first 'rail' vehicle driven by a petrol engine was designed by Gottlieb Daimler in 1887. Its place of origin was a wooden shed called solemnly and boastfully *Hauptbahnhof Cannstatt*. But the petrol engine was not destined to survive as a major motive power for railways. This was due to the cost of this highly-refined spirit, and the serious fire risk from the highly-inflammable fuel should a derailment or other mishap damage the fuel tanks. Three years later his collaborators tried out another rail car, this time driven by a diesel engine (run on oil).

In 1912, the Sulzer company of Winterthur tested a motor locomotive with a low-speed diesel engine producing 950 hp at 240 rpm. But this slow-speed engine was not suitable for railway use. On the other hand, five light coaches manufactured by Sulzer for the German railways succeeded. Each looked like a clumsy bus on rails. A four-cylinder cowled diesel of 200 hp drove an electric generator, which supplied current to the two traction motors driving the front and rear bogies. The last of these motor coaches ended service a few years ago as an auxiliary vehicle of the Swiss railways (SBB).

After the First World War diesel rail cars or motor coaches were used mainly on local European lines. In the beginning they looked like road buses — some of them were even built for mixed operation. These travelled by road from the nearest town to the railway station, and there, because of their light steel wheels coaxial to the tyres simply sat on the rails. Later the shape of the coach was adapted to suit the railway. Nowadays these small motor coaches are frequently used on secondary lines; usually they have a petrol or diesel engine of 140—220 hp. The power output is trasmitted by a mechanical gearbox, as in an automobile.

There are three methods of transmitting the power from the diesel engine to the driving wheels of locomotives and motor coaches: mechanical, hydraulic and electric. Direct drive is not suitable due to the high torque necessary for starting the train when the engine revolutions and power output are at their lowest. In mechanical transmission, a multi-speed mechanical gearbox is used — as in trucks — but the gear-changing is facilitated by an electric system. Mechanical transmission can be used up to power outputs of 550 hp and has a high efficiency. It is often employed in shunting locomotives.

In hydraulic power transmission, the diesel engine drives a rotary pump which transmits the pressure and kinetic energy of the oil to the blades of an adjacent turbine. The turbine revolutions, and thus the revolutions of the driving axle connected with the turbine by gear transmission and propeller shafts, can be controlled either by changing the filling of the oil circuit (Voith system) or by changing the position of the turbine blades (Lysholm-Smith system). Small and efficient units are capable of outputs from 270 to 2,000 hp. In the usual arrangement (see Fig. 102), the diesel engine (1) drives the propeller shaft by means of a hydrodynamic gearbox (2) on the bogie, and its own cooling fan (4). From the gearbox power take-off (3) the power is transmitted by propeller shafts and bevel gearing (or differentials) to individual sets of wheels. In order to improve efficiency, the hydraulic system is switched off as soon as the locomotive reaches its travelling speed and the individual shafts are connected mechanically.

Diesel-electric locomotive traction is suitable for power outputs above 1,800 hp. Both diesel-electric and diesel-hydraulic traction have made an impact

98

98. The 1887 Daimler petrol vehicle at the Cannstatt station

99. The second Daimler motor carriage of 1888 looks like the present-day diesel rail cars on local lines, except for the open driver's position

100. The diesel rail car *Sulzer* from 1914 resembles a rail bus. The company applied diesel-electric drive here for the first time

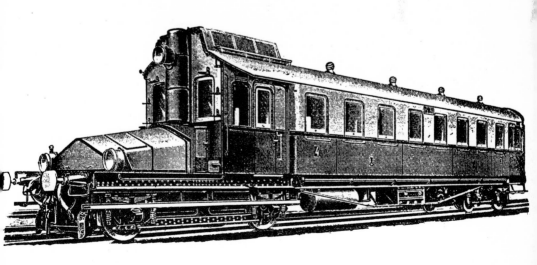

in Britain, while in the USA, apart from the limited mileage of electrified lines, the entire United States rail traffic is now handled by diesel-electric power. A representative type of diesel-electric locomotive is shown in Plate VII. Here, a low-speed diesel engine (3) drives a dc generator or dynamo (7), the (controlled) current output being fed to the dc series traction motors (6) on the bogies. Another type of diesel-electric locomotive is the Henschel BBC series DE-2500. In these locomotives a 2,400 hp diesel drives a three-phase alternator (ac generator). After the alternating current is rectified to direct current, the rectified current is converted by a controlled thyristor alternator to an alternating current with variable frequency and voltage. This ac current feeds simple, cheap and reliable asynchronous driving motors on the bogies. By a continuous and smooth frequency change — independently of the diesel engine revolutions — it is possible to directly control, without contacts and with minimum losses, the revolutions of the traction motors. This system prevents wheel slip and achieves the highest possible engagement moment in the wheels. The forward travel can be immediately switched over to very efficient electrodynamic braking by means of the traction motors which, as soon as the synchronous revolutions are exceeded, immediately pass over to the generating mode.

Locotractors with power outputs up to 1,000 hp

101. A diesel-hydraulic shunting locomotive with a 830 hp diesel engine and a Voith gearbox (*Werkfoto Krauss-Maffei*)

and with a maximum speed of about 25 mph have been designed for shunting or service on factory sidings. The driver's cabin is located in the middle of the machine to give the operator a good view of the two opposite directions, which alternate rather frequently during such a type of service. Remote radio control of these locomotives by a dispatcher has been recently developed, so the cabins will remain without any operator.

Freight diesel locomotives are designed for heavy-duty service on all the railways of the world. They have either a diesel-hydraulic (Plate IX) or diesel-electric power transmission; some of the larger locomotives give power outputs of 8,000 hp.

The basis of USA freight trains is represented by using combined diesel-electric locomotives, which are jointly controlled from one cabin. In extremely long freight trains one driver can control up to six locomotives. The USA holds a world record in this field. On 11 November 1967, the Norfolk and Western Railway Company ran a freight train carrying 40,000 tons of coal in 500 wagons. In the front it

VIII West German four-unit electric express train Intercity, type ET 403; it can reach a speed of over 125 mph *(MBB)*

IX Krauss-Maffei diesel-hydraulic, remote-controlled locomotive. Engine power output: 1,100 hp at 1,200 rpm *(Krauss-Maffei)*

X A TEE (Trans Europe Express) series VT 11·5, with five carriages, is driven by diesel-hydraulic units, each of 1,100 hp. Maximum speed 94 mph *(Werkfoto M.A.N.)*

XI One engine driver controls three diesel-electric freight locomotives at the head of a heavy freight train on the Seabord Coast Line, USA *(G.E.)*

XII Experimental Canadian diesel-electric express train LRC, which has achieved a maximum speed of 156 mph. Carriages have tilting bodies.

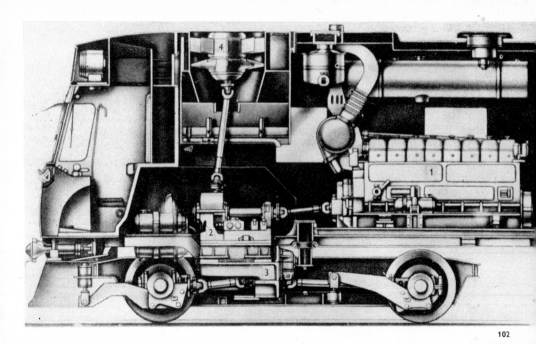

102. Diesel-hydraulic power transmission in the TEE express train locomotive. 1 — Diesel engine 2 — Hydrodynamic gearbox 3 — Gearbox power take-off 4 — Engine cooling fan

103. This French (SNCF) diesel-hydraulic locomotive for express trains has two engines which give a total power output of 4,730 hp and can reach a speed of 93 mph

104

105

106

104. Henschel BBC type DE-2500 diesel-electric locomotives with alternating power transmission (*Rheinstahl*)

105. One of the heaviest present-day eight-axle diesel-electric locomotives for Union Pacific. Its power output is 8,000 hp

106. Passenger motor train of the Spanish railway (*M.A.N.*)

107. The motor radiator of this 1934 American diesel-electric locomotive was located in the front, behind a grille

107

was hauled by three diesel-electric locomotives of 2,680 hp each, and three other locomotives were attached after the 250th wagon. The length of the train was 3·72 miles and when more than 1,000 couplings were stretched out during the starting manoeuvre, the length of the train was extended by another 656 ft.

Light motor express trains usually consist of a front and rear motor coach with passenger dining and sleeping cars in-between. In Europe it was the German high-speed diesel train *Fliegender Hamburger* which opened the era of light motor trains in 1932. The double set of wagons with two diesel locomotives, of 470 hp each, reached speeds of over 100 mph. Light and fast motor trains are nowadays the most widespread means of passenger transport in South America, Africa, India and Australia. Ex-

clusive fast and comfortable trains began to be built in the USA in 1930 for long-distance lines.

The Americans came up with quite a new conception of aluminium express trains. They were called *Aerotrain* and *Jet Rocket* and they were partially designed by aircraft designers. As a result, express trains appeared which had an unusual streamlined shape to the locomotive face. They were half as light as express trains and carried the same number of passengers. The aluminium *Aerotrain* with 400 passengers reached a speed of 102·5 mph, although it was driven by only one diesel engine with a power output of 1,300 hp. For the first time pneumatically-cushioned carriages were used. First-class cars were air-conditioned and tilting seats of the aircraft type were oriented in the direction of travel as in aircrraft.

108. ASEA diesel-electric locomotives, serving since 1968 on the Stockholm—Malmö line, are provided with a scenic superstructure for passengers, located above the motor unit of the first and last carriages

109. This streamlined Aerotrain connecting Chicago, Denver and Colorado Springs consists of four three-part carriages for 400 passengers

110. The British High Speed Train (HST) with diesel-electric power transmission achieves a speed of 110—136 mph

108

The 50-year-old idea of the American H. N. Gresley to couple the faces of cars on one common bogie was utilised by the Spanish designer Goicoechea in articulated express trains (Talgo) serving on the Spanish National Railways (RENFE). The abbreviation Talgo originates from the full Spanish name of the train—Tren articulado ligero Goicoechea-Oriol. In this type of train all the vehicles except the first, which has two axles, are carried on a single pair of wheels only, and the wheels are independently suspended with no solid rotating axles linking each pair. The leading end of each coach is supported by the rear end of the vehicle ahead. The major advantage of a Talgo articulated train is the drastically reduced weight, while one disadvantage is the difficulty of altering the formation of a set to meet varying traffic demands. The Mark III stock introduced in 1965 has a standard train of fifteen vehicles (including a diesel-hydraulic locomotive, two kitchen/bar units and one luggage van) taking 96 first-class and 256 second-class passengers.

The Trans Europ Express (TEE for short) is the most luxurious and comfortable way to travel by train in daytime in Europe. The characteristics of TEE are high speed, short stops at commercially important stations, passage of frontier stations without stopping (or with minimal stops) and formalities conducted in the train. TEE trains have their own livery of red below and cream above the waist and are listed separately in all European railway timetables. While diesel multiple units were initially used when the first TEEs started to run in 1957, the trend has been to replace the diesels by trains hauled by electric locomotives (Plate X).

On British Railways HST (High Speed Train), seven air-conditioned passenger carriages are put between two diesel-electric locomotives (each diesel engine gives an output of 2,250 hp and the most up-to-date ac transmission is used). At the very first test in 1973 this train broke the world speed record in the field of diesel traction reaching 144 mph.

Canadian railways have introduced an express set whose designation LRC expresses the properties of this unusual train: Light—Rapid—Comfortable. In the shorter version the diesel-electric locomotive of 2,800 hp hauls five 108-ft long carriages with tilting duraluminum bodies; in the long-distance version ten carriages are put between two locomotives. Carriages with different designs—from comfortable family compartments to carriages with free access and adjustable seats—can each serve 84 passengers.

The design of these super-express trains enables speeds up to 180 mph—the existing diesel engines, however, are now powerful enough to reach it, and here the field for the internal combustion turbine is wide open.

109
110

Turbine express trains

In 1941 the first gas-turbine-electric locomotive using heavy oil was submitted to its first test. It was built by the Swiss company Brown Boveri and the trials lasted for 13 years. The locomotive successfully covered a distance of 237,500 miles and confirmed that the internal-combustion turbine represented the best type of engine for high unit performance, unattainable by other engines. The development of electrification and short European lines, however, did not provide favourable conditions for its use. Nevertheless, the Renault company in France built several direct-drive gas-turbine locomotives.

Great Britain tested turbine locomotives with pulverised coal combustion, but noise problems and difficulties with the high turbine revolutions (up to 30,000 rpm) hindered their development.

High-performance turbo-electric locomotives were put into service for the first time on the Pacific lines in the USA and on the long-distance Canadian lines just after the end of the Second World War. A turbine locomotive of 7,400 hp, with electric power transmission, is now used to transport loads of 5,000 tons.

In the USA, efforts to compete with air transport on medium and long-distance lines led to the production of light express trains driven by aircraft turbines with low rpm. Three- to seven-car units of the Budd and Garret company, or the Turbotrain for 150—250 passengers, reach a speed of 155 mph on the Boston—New York line. The turbines are switched off when entering New York due to strict regulations about noise level, and the trains reach their destination driven by electric current. Electric motors are fed by current from a third auxiliary rail.

In the 1970s trains driven by aircraft turbine traction were tested in the USA and in the USSR. The turbines, with a power output of more than 6,500 hp, were placed on the roof which clearly showed the exceptionally favourable ratio of the weight of these engines to their power. The cars reached speeds of up to 185 mph.

French turbotrains: The French decided to use the well-proven compound turbines designed for helicopters for driving fast express trains. The driving machinery consists of two 'Turmo' turbines with a power output of 1,250 or 1,475 hp coupled with an ac electric generator of 200 Hz frequency. This driving arrangement can be easily assembled on the floor of the turbine train.

In 1970 the ETG express trains *(Elément a Turbine Gaz)* were put in service between Paris and Cherbourg. With four cars, they achieved a speed of 100 mph and thus cut the travel time by an hour. Contrary to practice elsewhere, the passengers in these express trains did not pay any extra fare. Two years later, because of the large interest of the public, sixteen improved RTG turbotrains with air-conditioned cars for 280 passengers and with a maximum speed of 125 mph were put into service. The turbines were improved to such an extent that they required a short, four-hour service only after 400 operation hours. A major overhaul was required after 5,000 hours.

The most successful unit from the point of view of speed, economy and comfort, the TGV-001 *(Turbine a Grande Vitesse)*, was put into service in France on 4 April 1972. On 8 December 1972, the

111

111. Experimental American turbine unit M-497 carries on its roof a pair of aircraft turbines

112. *Turmo* turbine drive unit, which produces 3,015 hp and weighs only 5 tons

113. The first test run of the British turbine express train APT, which is to serve on Canadian and North American railways as well

112

TGV-001 reached a record speed of 197·6 mph. The air-conditioned TGV consists of ten cars for 382 passengers. The output of the four turbines is 5,890 hp. Large scale tests with a train of half the usual length demonstrated that on a good track it could reach a speed of 187 mph. The streamlining of the train was so well designed that the airflow of a train at a speed of 162 mph is the same as that produced by the classical express train passing at a speed of 80 mph. The train has double-walled sound-insulated cars; even at the highest speeds the noise level inside amounts to only 60 decibels. This is in sharp contrast to modern turbo-prop aircraft where the noise level inside the fuselage cannot be reduced to below 78 decibels.

The train is provided with four kinds of brakes. The main one is an electric resistor brake. In case of its failure an eddy-current brake can be activated. At lower speeds the classical block brake is applied, though it will be replaced by disc brakes. At a speed of 135 mph the stopping distance of the train is 1,837 yards and at 186 mph the braking distance is extended to 4,165 yards.

British turbotrains: The British APT turbotrains (Advanced Passenger Train) are intended to form the basis of the future express train network of Britain. They were put into service for the first time on the London—Glasgow line. They consist of four to ten coaches. Four-coach sets are 288 ft long, but their weight is only 145 tons. They are driven by four Leyland turbines. On the Derby test track a speed of 195 mph has been reached.

It can be expected that by the end of the 1970s turbine trains will serve all the long-distance non-

113

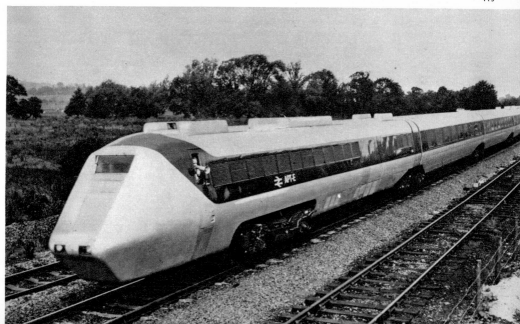

electrified lines of between 250 and 600 miles and will possibly replace the smaller airlines which sometimes have insufficient passenger capacity and which are not always reliable.

Passenger carriages

The development of carriages happened in four stages of approximately 50 years each. First-class carriages of the early trains were very similar to horse-drawn carriages and stage-coaches. They were upholstered and provided with leaf springs. Passengers in the second class, however, travelled in a roofed carriage with wooden benches, and passengers in the third class stood in open carriages without any suspension, exposed to wind, rain, snow and soot.

Fifty years later all the carriages more or less resembled present-day ones, at least in outward appearance. Usually a carriage was divided into several compartments, each of them provided with individual side doors. Wooden steps to facilitate the entry of passengers were fixed to the side of the carriage as a kind of walkway. The conductor had a very difficult task, because he had to walk along these walkways passing from one compartment to another while the train was running. The wooden and later steel-riveted frames of the carriages ran on two or three sets of wheels, provided with hard springs. It is nearly unbelievable that carriages of this conception have survived to this day in Europe. However, one hundred years ago the predecessor of the present-day express train coach appeared. Its long frame was supported at both ends by swivelling bogies. The individual compartments were connected by a corridor located either in the middle or at one side of the carriage.

Entry platforms in vestibules at both ends of the carriage appeared first in America and later in Europe as well. By the end of the 1890s, platforms between carriages were bridged by small covered gangways. After another 50 years passenger carriages were provided with nearly all the accessories seen at the present-day, but real comfort could be expected only in the first class.

From the 1930s onwards, new steel-panelled stock began to make its appearance in Britain. This form—a wooden-framed body covered with steel plates and mounted on a steel under-frame—was very light and withstood shocks well.

Our present-day carriages are now usually interconnecting and passengers can pass easily from one to another. With the use of aluminium and duralumin, carriages are now half the weight of earlier ones. They move on bogies with pneumatic suspension and with their wheels turning in anti-friction bearings. Using incombustible plastic materials for upholstery, the architect-designed carriages offer a comfort that until recently could only be found in ship cabins.

Heating in ordinary carriages was non-existent in the early days. The only warmth passengers could

114. Four stages in the 150 years of development of passenger trains

enjoy was provided by oblong metal footwarmers which were filled with hot water or heated sand and hawked at railway stations. The footwarmers were reputed to keep their warmth for only two hours. The Pullman cars which were later introduced from America provided oil-fired hot-water heating from a boiler in each carriage but it was rather complicated. Steam heating, adopted in Britain at the end of the nineteenth century, finally provided the necessary warmth for winter travelling. Steam was distributed by pipes from the locomotive boiler, the pressure being suitably reduced.

Carriages were first lit, very inadequately, by pot lamps burning oil. In America the Pullman cars introduced excellent lighting provided by kerosene lamps suspended from the ceiling. In England and later on all over Europe gas lighting became popular. Originally, rubber bags on the roofs of the carriages were filled with gas and acted as reservoirs. In 1867 a Berlin engineer Pintsch developed an efficient oil burning gas generator. Consequently, vent chimneys above each individual burner appeared on carriage roofs.

Dynamos for electric lighting began to be installed under the frames of carriages at the beginning of this century. They were driven from the train wheels and linked with lead or iron-nickel storage batteries.

Before the 1880s brakemen used to sit on the carriage roofs although later they were given brakemen's cabins. Following a whistle signal, they tightened or released the brakes manually. In 1866 an English engineer named Kendall tried to replace the manual brake shoe application with one operated by air. Each carriage had to have not only its own air reservoir, but also a compressor driven by a belt from the wheels. In the end the compressed-air brake invented by the American engineer Westinghouse became the one most widely used on railways. In 1872 he developed it so that it acted automatically if a train broke apart. It was adapted for European use by the engineer Knorr in 1908 and by a number of other inventors such as Kunze, Bozic, etc. Modern light express trains have dropped the principle of a radially thrust brake shoe and replaced it with disc brakes. During braking, a polished disc, with interior ribbing for better cooling, is gripped from each side by brake shoes which have a special friction lining. The effect is more powerful, the brake is more reliable and the wear on the wheels is reduced.

Sleeping and dining cars: These will always be associated with the name of G. M. Pullman, originally a Chicago craftsman. His first sleeping car appeared on the American railways in 1859. With travel on American long-distance lines taking up to a week, it is not surprising that the new comfortable cars gained immediate popularity. Pullman cars

1830

114 A

1880

114 B

1930

114 C

114 D

1980

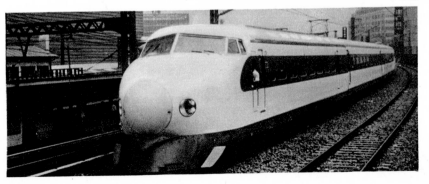

115

were heavy and needed to be supported by bogies with six or even eight wheels. The enterprising Pullman was constantly improving his cars: he provided them with a lavatory and a bar. In 1867 the first Pullman dining car, the *Delmonico,* equipped with a kitchen, was put into service. On the main lines, express trains consisted only of Pullman sleeping and dining cars. The Belgian, Nagelmackers, introduced the sleeping cars to Europe in 1872. It was the *Compagnie Internationale des Wagons-Lits* (later the German MITROPA) which must take credit for the development of the sleeping cars on various services in Europe.

Present-day carriages: All carriages are built in agreement with the safety regulations and size standards of the International Railway Union (UIC). They are 75—88 ft long and their weight of 30—40 tons is carried by bogies with two sets of wheels. The suspension is provided by leaf or spiral springs with rubber noise-absorbing blocks. Hydraulic shock-absorbers take care of any tendency towards pitching and rolling. Carrriages are connected with short flexible tunnels so that passengers can pass from one to another.

For short-distance travelling carriages divided into two large second-class compartments are used. As a rule these carriages have two rows of seats on either side with room for 84 passengers. Heavy express train carriages have either ten compartments for 60 first-class passengers, or 12 compartments for 72 second-class passengers. Seats are cushioned with incombustible foam materials and are anatomically shaped. Heating is based either on the principle of high steam pressure or on electricity, with the possibility of temperature control.

The latest carriages, whose production is co-ordinated in Europe by the company Eurofima, are built for speeds of up to 125 mph. They are equipped with disc brakes—in electric trains with magnetic brakes as well—and are air-conditioned.

In light super-express trains the equipment of carriages is similar to that provided for planes. Tilting seats face the direction of travel; luggage and coats can be put into lockers in the entry vestibule.

During long-distance travel passengers need to be able to move around freely and possibly enjoy some form of entertainment. For that purpose social carriages are included in the trains. In these a passenger can usually find tables with mobile or swivelling seats, a cocktail bar, and conferences or a film screening can be organised.

Dining car design has also progressed. In the 1930s they looked rather like showy restaurants. The interior of present-day dining cars is more simple but at the same time more practical. The catering area consists of three floors: the sales counter and the bar are located at carriage floor level, on a higher level there is an electric kitchen with cookers, grills and microwave heaters, which can be supplied by a current collector on the roof, and in the lowest part of the carriage is the food store and dish-washing facilities. But the interest in self-service buffet cars is growing. In Europe the 'Quick-Pick' cars are popular.

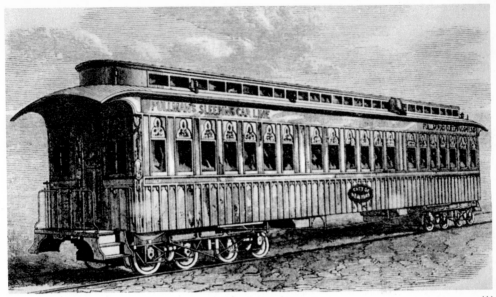

115. British passenger and mail carriage from 1842. It served on the Junction Railways between London and Lancashire

116. The original eight-axle Pullman sleeper of 1869

117. Two opposite seats *(right)* could be folded to form beds separated by a curtain *(left)*

118

Train radio or TV did not meet with great success. Designers are now trying to build loudspeakers into seat-headrests.

Modern sleeping cars offer comfort of different levels, from the cheapest *couchette* cars (compartments for six persons with night adaptation from the normal day seating arrangement), and three-bed, twin-bed and single-bed compartments with small wardrobes, washbasins and sockets for electric shavers, to air-conditioned compartments with tables, chairs, wardrobes and an adjacent lavatory. The simpler accommodation units are called roomettes, the de luxe class, compartments. The highest hotel-level comfort is offered by the American railways with their master-rooms which, in addition to sleeping arrangements provide chairs, a table, a lavatory, shower and a desk complete with a telephone for ordering meals and other services from the train stewards.

The special coaches of royalty and presidents of the last century are nowadays the pride of museums. Presidents and other notables, such as managers of big companies now use short private trains specially equipped with a radio, telephone and teleprint communications. Showy luxury has given way to light and practical equipment.

Carriages of the future: With the exception of those for light super-express trains, these will be mainly double-deckers. The Canadian branch of the Hawker-Siddeley company proposes a modular carriage, 84$^1/_2$ ft long and 15$^1/_2$ ft high. Pneumatically-controlled sliding doors open giving access to vesti-

119

118. Carriage with unconnected transverse compartments accessible from a wooden walkway. It ended its service on German railways only after the Second World War

119. Disc brake on the axle of a modern bogie of an express train carriage

120. Carriages of the French express train (TEE) *Le Capitole*, with air conditioning, window blinds and with a body made of stainless sheet metal *(SNCF)*

121. Laminated aircraft-type tilting seats in the 1st class carriages of the French express train *TGV-001* *(SNCF)*

121

122

122. Queen Victoria's saloon carriage of 1869 with gas and electric lighting, yellow roof upholstery and walls and seat covers decorated in blue

123. Private conference compartment of the Rank-Xerox company with offices behind the bar

124. Spanish railway dining-car of the 1930s

125. Bar compartment of the French express train *Mistral* *(Compagnie Internationale des Wagons-Lits)*

bules in which a display indicates which of the 160 seats are vacant. The front and rear of the carriages can be modified (Fig 130) depending on whether they are to be used for long-distance travel or local transport, or whether they are to be self-propelled or make use of a diesel-electric or electric unit.

Large carriages with a scenic deck at the top, and with saloons and buffets downstairs, will represent a revolution in travelling (Plate XIX). They would necessitate, however, tripling the track gauge to nearly 15 ft, which is still financially unacceptable.

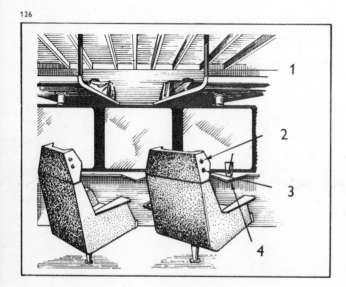

126. Swivelling seats and refreshment tables in a self-service buffet carriage. 1 — handbag shelf; 2 — radio volume knob; 3 — tilting seats; 4 — triangular table

XIII American Turbotrain for 144 passengers is driven by six turbines each producing 550 hp. Maximum speed is 130 mph.

XIV The French turbine-driven express train TGV-001 has opened regular service on the European continent. *(Creusot-Loire)*

XV Modern European second-class carriage with twelve compartments, air conditioning and magnetic brakes is designed for speeds of 125 mph *(Linke-Hofmann-Busch)*

XVI Interior of the self-service dining car 'Quick-Pick' *(Wegmann-Werkfoto)*

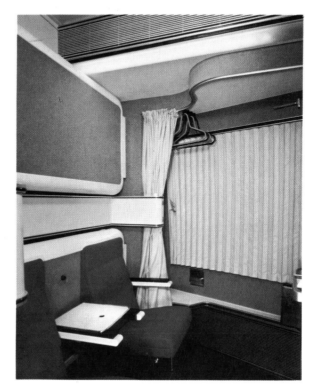

XVII Interior of a saloon carriage with movable seats (Société Industrielle Suisse)

XVIII By folding two beds located one above another in a compartment of the Catalán-Talgo express train space is provided for two chairs and a table between them (Patentes Talgo S.A.)

XIX Futuristic view through a double-decker broad-gauge carriage

127. European Pullmans of 1878 with transversely arranged sleeping compartments, a wash-basin in the ante-room and gas lighting

128. Cutaway view of a two-passenger compartment showing a sofa on the floor and beds under the roof *(Compagnie Internationale des Wagons-Lits)*

Wagons of freight trains

At the beginning of railway transport short, unsprung double-axle wooden wagons were used, which were coupled together by chain links. Goods were held in place on wagons by rope or chain and were covered by a tarpaulin. Cattle wagons had grill-like sides covered by a roof. Later wooden wagons were provided with spoke wheels and had transverse metal buffers. The sides of the wagons hinged downwards for loading. The maximum carrying capacity of such a train was 3 to 4 tons. By the end of the nineteenth century spoke wheels had been replaced by solid wheels with metal tyres and leaf springing. A screw coupling replaced the chain link and the wood or steel underframe of the wagons

130

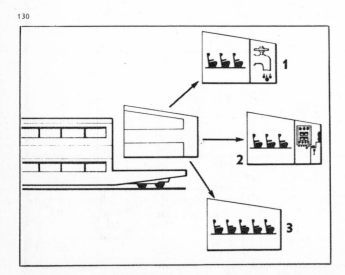

129. A carriage of the future—double-decker module from Hawker-Siddeley, Canada

130. For long-distance journeys the module with washrooms (1) or with dining-rooms (2) is used. The driving system can be changed by using a modulus with a pantograph and transformers for electric drive, a modulus with diesel-electric or one with turbine drive. In suburban transport modulus (3) with seats is used

had two pairs of buffers, one at each end. These were either round or oval and those at one end of the wagon had a flat face, while the ones at the other end were concave. When two wagons were coupled, a flat buffer impinged on a curved one and prevented breakage at the circumference when rounding curves. The carrying capacity of the wagons was 10 to 20 tons and the number of covered wagons capable of transporting soldiers and horses in the case of war, was rising quickly.

After the First World War goods wagon stock in Europe underwent a gradual unification process. Following the example of passenger carriages, long-bogie wagons appeared, their carrying capacity ranging up to 50 tons. They began to be specialised: covered wagons for perishable goods; open wagons for the transport of coal, ores, gravel and sand; platform wagons for timber and large machinery transport; and tank wagons for liquids.

Present-day wagon stock is not only designed for different kinds of freight, it is also equipped to save time and labour and facilitate mechanised or automated loading or unloading. Wagons have pneumatic brakes automatically adapted to the type of load. The average carrying capacity has risen to 50 to 60 tons (in the USA 80 to 100 tons). The average freight train speed in Europe is about 50 mph, in the USA over 60 mph, and in Japan, on the Tokaido line it rises to 85 mph.

Closed wagons are adaptable. As a rule they are fitted with single or double sliding doors giving access for fork-lift trucks entering from a loading platform and moving the freight in crates or on standardised pallets. In some large wagons the whole side can be slid back or removed, speeding up mechanical loading so that it takes less than one hour. Two workers loading the wagon manually would have to work for ten hours to complete the job. In order to make possible loading of closed wagons from the top by means of cranes, some are equipped with a sliding roof.

Open wagons: Some of these have hinged sides which can be opened. The wagons can thus be loaded or unloaded from the side. Open wagons of the gondola type are popular for the transport of loose material such as sand. They are shaped like a tub, are filled from the top and emptied usually by tilting. Large gondola wagons are often made of

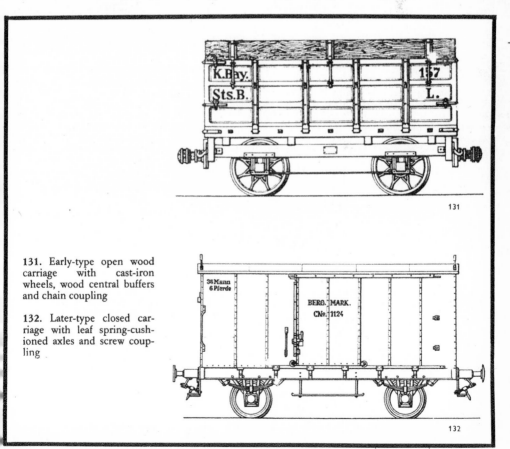

131. Early-type open wood carriage with cast-iron wheels, wood central buffers and chain coupling

132. Later-type closed carriage with leaf spring-cushioned axles and screw coupling

131

132

133

welded aluminium. At the highest permissible axle load the use of aluminium allows the quantity of material to be carried to be increased by 10 per cent.

Automatic-discharge wagons carry their cargoes in angular, funnel-shaped compartments, closed at the narrow base by a slide. When this is opened the contents (coke, gravel, coal, sand or other such materials) run out under their own weight usually into hoppers located directly under the rails. Nowadays these wagons are provided with a hinged or sliding roof for loading.

Platform wagons are still popular because of their simple design and versatile character. They have a wooden floor and can be provided with stan-

133. 1970 goods marshalling yard showing the diversity of wagon types and styles

134. Large-capacity, 92-ft long, closed wagon with removable walls and sliding roof. Weight 26 tons

135. Closed four-axle wagon with sliding roof and sliding doors

136. This gondola aluminium wagon with automatic couplers can carry 75 tons of loose materials

134

135
136

137. Three diesel-motor loco-motives hauling a coal train carrying 5,000 tons of coal

138. Cars entering a platform train for transportation through the Alpine tunnels

139. This three-deck Canadian National Railways wagon can transport 18 automobiles

chions, for the support of loads of timber, pipes, rails, etc. And the container era would be unthinkable without them.

Two thousand metal **tank wagons** in the shape of horizontal barrels with a maximum capacity of 10 tons were ordered in 1875 by the inventor of dynamite, Alfred Nobel. He used them for importing Caucasian crude oil. Present-day large-volume welded tanks can each carry 60 tons of liquid.

Refrigerator wagons are even older than tank wagons. In September, 1852, the *Eastern Express* came to Chicago bringing fresh fruit and vegetables from the South in a refrigerator wagon. The cooling installation was driven by a steam engine using steam from the locomotive.

Refrigerator wagons and refrigerating warehouses are controlled in Europe by the international company INTERFRIGO. The insulation of wagon bodies is designed so that a temperature of −10 °C (50 °F) can be maintained in a refrigerating area lined with dry ice for five days, provided that external temperature is normal. Otherwise these wagons have electric refrigerating systems fed from an alternator located on the bogie. Sometimes a whole re-

frigerator train has a central refrigerating system in one of the wagons.

Wagons for automobile transport are used extensively in Alpine tunnels. Cars are loaded onto platform wagons with a light load-bearing guard-rail at the sides and with a protective roof. The drivers save time and fuel and do not have to undertake a tiring journey across the Alpine passes. For car transport direct from the manufacturer, the French SNAV double-decker wagons are mainly used in Europe. These are three-bogie double-decker wagons with loading ramps and accommodate ten large or twenty-two small cars on each wagon. Canadian and USA railways use even longer wagons with three tiers which can be reached by special ramps. On some railways in the USA, automobiles are transported in two parallel rows in a vertical position — the 'Vert-a-pack' system (Plate XXI).

Wagons for loose materials, filled pneumatically, use the principle that fine-grain materials can be converted by aeration into an easily flowing mixture. In a matter of minutes, nearly 80 tons of loose material can be transferred like this into a special road vehicle. A compressor in the truck is activated and starts blowing air through a hose under a finely-meshed screen under the load. The air penetrates the material, separating its grains, and it acquires the properties of a fluid. After opening a gate-valve to a second hose, the load, by a combination of its own weight and moderate additional air pressure in the closed container, begins flowing into the truck.

Special wagons are adapted for the transport of various kinds of freight. Pontoon wagons with up to 32-axle bogies can transport loads of up to 400 tons, things like heavy containers and transformers. One of the most interesting types of wagon is the kind used for carrying molten cast iron from a blast furnace to steel-making furnaces. In this, two sixteen wheel bogies support a torpedo-shaped container with a refractory lining filled through an opening at the top with up to 300 tons of cast iron. On arrival at a steel plant, an engine at the rear of the wagon is started, and begins to tilt this huge, ladle-like wagon so that the molten iron flows out.

Wagon turn-round and its control

On West German lines alone about 400,000 wagons are under daily operation. The average interval between loading and unloading varies between 4 and 5 days. If this could be reduced only by several hours, it would mean a thousand wagons less could be used. To ensure that wagons crossing from one country to another do not have to return empty, the turn-round is controlled in Western European countries by the EUROP organisation, and in the socialist countries by the OPW organisation. To facilitate automatic turn-round control the International Railway Union (UIC) devised a unified system of wagon designation. Specialists in electronics have developed sensors recording this designation. Coding on the wagons is in the form of stripes with

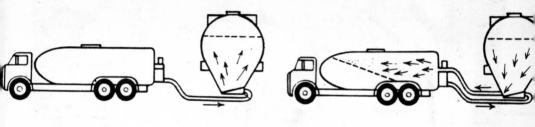

140. The Rheinhausen metallurgical works use twelve mobile ladles with a capacity of 300 tons each to transport liquid pig iron to steel works

141. Loose materials filling and discharge by compressed air: 1—compressed air; 2—compressed-air hose; 3—railway wagon; 4—grille; 5—materials 'flow' hose; 6—air-release valve

142. Train with wagons for loose material transport passing a code-sensing unit

different reflectant properties located in predetermined places on the side of the wagons. When a train passes the control point, laser or photo-electric sensors record the number, even if the speed of the train is as much as 85 mph. The data about each wagon is then transmitted immediately to the computer used for freight traffic control.

In order to accelerate the marshalling of wagons according to their destination, all of them in the future will have to be provided with automated couplers. Coupling heads protruding from the ends of the wagons will make contact so that they are not

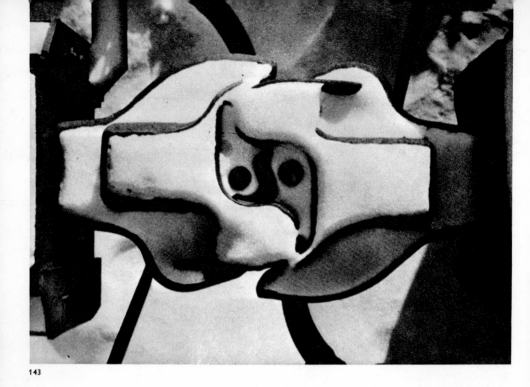

143

only coupled, but the pneumatic brake and electrical systems are connected inside the coupler as well. The wagon stock of some countries—USA, USSR, France, and in part Britain, West Germany and Japan—is already equipped with universal couplings so that they can pass freely from one country to the other with no link-up problems.

Containers and terminals

A container can be a very large metal box that can be opened or easily dismantled, or it can also be a tank or a refrigerator box fixed to a frame and of standard dimensions. It gives protection to goods which need not be specially packed, it is easy to store, and it can be handled mechanically as one unit through all stages of trans-shipment without its contents being touched, even during journeys combining road, water and rail, and possibly air, travel.
Containerisation: Railway containerisation has something of a history. As far back as 1842 the bodies of mail coaches carrying people, mail and parcels were lifted bodily by crane on to platform wagons to be taken from Paris to Orleans and return in the same way. However, the stimulus for the birth of modern container transport came from the American SeaLand shipping company which discovered in the 1960s that the transport of large metal boxes between the East and West coasts of the USA was cheaper by ship than by road. This was

143. Automatic couplers of two wagons connected up (G. L. Thorp)

144. Loading of a coach superstructure on to a platform wagon, Paris, 1842 (PTT-Museum, Bern)

in spite of a roundabout journey via the Panama Canal; the boxes were carried to the port by truck, transferred on to a ship by crane and unloaded in the same way at Los Angeles. Special container ships brought the first containers to Rotterdam and Bremen in 1966. The International Standard Organisation (ISO) immediately assumed the task of working out a draft proposal for a world container standard. They based their proposals on certain facts: the wooden pallets widely used for goods transport have dimensions of 800 × 1,200 mm (31·5 × 47·25 in), a total width of 2,500 mm (98·5 in) must not be exceeded on the road and for rail travel 2,600 mm (102 in) is the maximum. The basic dimension for container width and height was settled as 2,438 mm (8 feet). The length of the container can be varied according to the load, which can vary from 5 to 30 tons gross weight.

A container is not cheap—the type 1C costs approximately the same as the average motorcar

Basically it is made up from a steel frame of standard dimensions, with either fixed or removable side walls, which can be sealed when in place. The corners of the container are provided with openings to give access to lifting and anchoring points, the latter used to hold the container in position on a wagon or ship. Containers are treated with anticorrosive paint which will protect them from the effects of sea air. **Tank containers** have a welded tank anchored to the main frame and have standard-sized openings for filling and discharge. They carry various liquids, from milk and beer, to heavy oil and tar.

Refrigerator containers consist of a refrigerating unit mounted on the frame and using current either from the railway network or generated by its own diesel engine.

Recently **lattice containers** of size 1A capable of holding up to three automobiles have been introduced.

Containers are usually handled by light mobile equipment: by fork-lift trucks with a high load-bearing capacity; by portal-type lift trucks; by stacking trucks or by mobile cranes. Containers are usually stacked in three tiers one above another although their robust frames can support up to eight tiers even when fully loaded. The main container trans-shipment points—(railway stations and ports)—are equipped with heavy lifting machinery,

especially new types of overhead travelling cranes, gantries and luffing cranes (Plate XXVII) with a lifting capacity up to 40 tons. Instead of the traditional crane hook they have telescopic spreaders, which can be adapted to the length of the container and locked in place through the container openings. Containers need not be protected against weather and therefore the terminals do not need large, roofed buildings. The concrete areas where the containers are stored in multi-tier rows are as large as small fields.

The use of container transport throughout the world increases dramatically every year. It is expected that in the future containers will be transporting about 80 per cent of all goods. In 1976 the main container shipping lines carried a quarter of a million 1C containers, and railway container transport across the USA and USSR is continually expanding. Using this route the cost of taking goods from Britain to Japan could be a third less than by a container ship covering the same distance. Containers mean that ports are no longer overloaded, goods are well protected and not damaged in transit and considerable additional savings are made since many of the boxes, covers and packing materials inside the containers can be salvaged. Containerisation has, of course, contributed to very close international cooperation between different countries.

Combined transport systems accelerate container

145

146

Container designation	Height (mm)	Width (mm)	Length (mm)	Length (feet)	Max. gross load-bearing capacity (kg)	Max. gross load-bearing capacity (tons)
1A	2,438	2,438	12,192	40	30,480	30
1AA	2,591	2,438	12,192	40	30,480	30
1B	2,438	2,438	9,144	30	25,400	25
1C	2,438	2,438	6,096	20	20,320	20
1D	2,438	2,438	3,048	10	10,160	10
1E	2,438	2,438	1,981	6.5	7,110	7
1F	2,438	2,438	1,219	4	5,080	5

145. The ISO 1C container is the most widely used type in railway and road transport. Its capacity is 1,155 ft³ of material or goods with a weight up to 18 tons. The container's weight is 2 tons

146. The ISO 1C tank container has a capacity of 4,400 gallons

147. Refrigerating container used on South African railways. Even in a hot climate the temperature inside the box is maintained at −30°C (−22°F)

trans-shipment. Superstructures of present-day lorries are built as containers, and trailers can be driven up a ramp right on to a platform railway wagon. Very low platform wagons have to be used, since the maximum permissible height on the road is greater than that on the railway. In the USA and Canada where the height of rail cars is not limited as much as in Europe, the 'Piggyback' type of transport and the 'Flexi-van' type for loose materials has been widely used. France uses the 'Kangourou' system, in which a special tractor pushes the trailers on to the platform wagon. On the wagon there are special guides for the tyres as well as for the central steel wheel at the front of the trailer. In West Germany the 'Hucke-Pack' system is gaining increasing popularity. An interesting variant is the transport of trucks and their trailers in one. This system is called 'Rollende Strasse'; the trucks drive on to special low wagons from a loading platform. Only 14-in diameter wagon wheels are used, so that the floor itself is just 16 in above the level of the rails. In 20 to 25 minutes a train can take aboard 20 such combinations. The train carries the driverless trucks, to their place of destination covering perhaps 300—600 miles in a night. Local truck drivers, waiting at the unloading platform, take them over and continue the journey to the final destination.

147

148

148. Containers are suitable for carrying by all means of transport. Trans-shipment is rapid and cheap.

149. A mobile double-portal crane with a spreader trans-shipping the largest ISO container 1A *(Valmet)*

150. Heavy-duty jib crane placing a Seatrain 1A container on a wagon

149

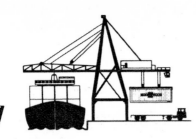

150

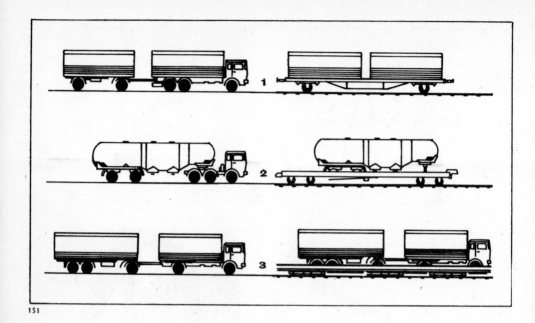

Goods stations and their operation

From railway sidings and loading platforms the loaded wagons are gathered and taken to a marshalling yard. There trains are assembled from them according to the known destination of the various wagons. For more than a hundred years marshalling involved complicated shunting, with directions to the drivers of the shunting engines given by flags and whistle signals. As early as 1846, however, operators of the goods station Dresden-Neustadt in Germany proposed a new idea: the utilisation of the weight of the wagons during marshalling. Wagons were pushed one by one to the top of a slightly inclined ramp. From there they would roll towards a network of sidings, guided by the changing of points to the appropriate place.

Present-day dispatching areas are fully automated. The projected date of despatch of individual wagons and their destinations are fed into the memory bank of a central processing unit. Uncoupled wagons in the right order are pushed to the top of the ramp. According to the data supplied to it the computer sets the points for the descending wagons so that they end up on the right track and in their correct order to make up the trains. Before the wagons reach the end of their runs, the computer automatically operates a brake so that they come in contact with the wagons already at the end of the line at a speed not exceeding 3·3 ft per second, when automatic couplers are activated.

The length of such an automated marshalling yard is sometimes as much as 2 miles. The

151. Three basic ways of combined transport: 1 — interchangeable truck superstructures transshipped by a crane; 2 — the 'Piggyback' system; 3 — transport of a whole truck train—the so-called *Rollende Strasse* (rolling street) system

152. Heavy double-axle 'Piggyback' semi-trailer on a platform wagon of the Canadian National Railways *(CN)*

153. Thirty-nine foot long 'Piggyback' semi-trailer with a towing vehicle bringing the freight from the consigner to the railway

dispatcher and the controller (Plate XXVIII) work in the computer tower usually located in the incline itself to ensure good visibility. From 5,000 to 10,000 wagons can be marshalled in a day. Data about a newly assembled train is transmitted by the marshalling computer to a second computer controlling operation of the trains once they reach the main lines. Each wagon is thus routed to reach its destination without loss of time and by the shortest possible route. The data supplied by the computer can be used for transport tariff calculation. Within ten years these fully-automated systems, controlling the day by day turn-round of tens of thousands of wagons over a large territory, will be installed all over the world. In the USA and especially in Britain the TOPS (Total Operations Processing System) is

154

155

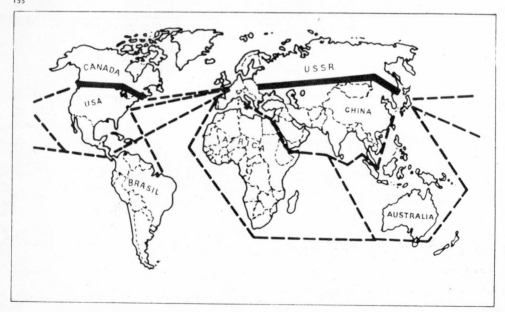

widely used. In the control computers all the necessary data about locomotives, their repairs and about the different types of wagons is stored. Information about train marshalling is transmitted to the computer by means of a keyboard. From that moment the system records all data about the movement of any individual wagon, even about damage if this should occur and about the repair target date. It also provides advance information for the prospective customer of the transported goods.

Passenger stations — past and present

Until the 1850s railway stations were situated on the outskirts of cities. Railway stations of that time looked like dwelling houses. An uncovered platform was built adjacent to a two or three-storey station building. However, during the following decades railway stations began to be moved to the centre of big cities and had magnificent new station buildings. Many of those which have been preserved have a neo-gothic, neo-renaissance, romantic, or other eclectic style of architecture. New hotels, restaurants and shops were built along the streets leading to the railway stations. Early tram and omnibus routes were also directed along these streets. Thus the street in which the railway station lay became the main artery of a town or city. An ever-increasing number of tracks passing through many stations had to be protected from rain, snow

and bad weather in general, at least where the passenger boarded the trains. The main buildings therefore took the form of big covered halls. It was not an easy task for the builders. The initial wooden structures were replaced by high, cast iron or steel glass-covered arches. The largest railway station in the world, the Grand Central Station in New York, was built between 1903 and 1913. The surface area of the two levels amounts to 48 acres. The 41 tracks in the upper level and the 26 tracks on the lower level can serve 600 trains carrying 200,000 passengers daily.

The architecture of today's railway stations is similar to that of many public buildings, being based mainly on prefabricated panels or steel and aluminium structures with plenty of glass. Passenger halls are usually topped by offices for station administration. Only a few countries still preserve a traditional style for their station buildings (Plate XXX). In modern stations entrances and exits are as a rule on different floors, access to platforms being provided by subways. A post office, restaurant or hotel sometimes forms part of the station. Passenger halls are equipped with escalators from one floor to another, slot machines for ticket sale and cybernetic information indicators. And even small village stations have changed their idyllic character. They are being replaced by glass structures with automatic left-luggage systems and with slot machines for ticket, food, book and magazine sales.

156

154. Loading of semi-trailers on wagons by the French *Kangourou* system

155. The main container routes of the world.

156. Pneumatic track brake on a hump

The highest railway station in the world, at 15,610 feet, is that of Ticlio junction in Peru. The largest waiting-rooms in the world, accommodating 14,000 people, can be found in Peking Station. The densest traffic is that entering and leaving Tokyo Central Station, which serves about 2,500 trains and about 2 million passengers daily.

Railway construction and maintenance

Although no modern track-laying machines and equipment were available, the construction of historically important transcontinental lines in the USA and Canada—when not slowed down by natural obstacles—went on at an amazing pace. The Central Pacific Line broke a world record on 28 April 1869, when a team of Irish workers laid five pairs of rails in a minute—short rails nailed to sleepers—and by evening had laid 3,500 rails corresponding to 10 miles of track.

Manual labour during construction, repair and possible reconstruction of railways has been replaced nowadays by highly-efficient machinery. During the initial construction of a permanent track, bulldozers and other machines prepare the ground and cover it with gravel ballast, on which a special crane lays long track sections, assembled complete with sleepers. After these have been joined, mechanical packing machines tamp the sleepers to ensure correct alignment. The level of the track, the accuracy of the gauge and the degree of bank on curves is checked by a special carriage equipped with automatic recording instruments. It is capable of operating at a speed of 50 mph.

In railway reconstruction and rail replacement, welded sections with a length of up to nearly one mile, are used. The gravel cleaner is an example of railway technical ingenuity. It looks like a movable bridge, holding up sections of track complete with sleepers by means of pulleys. A special rake conveyer belt sweeps out the old gravel. This is cleaned in a drum mounted on a wagon and then spread over the ground again to form ballast. The bridge then moves forward re-laying the tracks on the ballast.

The king of heavy railway construction machinery is, without doubt, the railway reconstruction train. The wagons that make up the train carry different types of machinery driven independently by diesel engines. This 'factory' moves along an old track carrying sections of new rails which are laid beside the old at a speed of 984 ft/h. Special machines unscrew the bolted joints of the old rails and their sleepers are moved aside. Next the gravel cleaner goes into action and then the first wagon of a second group moves the new rails and another the sleepers. Track assembly and tamping follows.

157

157. Potsdam railway station in 1848

158. Brignole station in Genoa, built from 1902-05

159. Charing Cross station, completed in 1864, had underground ramps for coaches leading to the platform *(British Railways)*

160

160. The new Braunschweig station with entry hall in front

161. This modern small railway station in Troisdorf, West Germany, is surrounded by slot-machines of all kinds

161

For speeds above 125 mph the mounting of heavy rails on concrete slabs is being tested. The rail is not supported by transverse sleepers. The concrete is laid so that it runs along under the rails. Fixing bolts are replaced by steel springs.

Remarkable railways of the world

Pioneer railway lines: By the end of the second half of the nineteenth century, the railways were facing the problem of opening up the unpopulated parts of the USA, Canada and Siberia. The objective was to exploit the tremendous natural resources and to ensure the development of industry and the economy in general, and at the same time to ease communication between one side of a continent and another.

The Pacific Railroad was built in record time in the years 1863—1869. It connected San Francisco and Omaha, Nebraska which was already in railway communication with New York. The total length of the Pacific line was 3,305 miles. Near the Missouri River an army of mainly Irish and Mexican workers, employed by the Union Pacific company, began the conquest of the prairies and the Rocky Mountains. Working from the other side of the continent, Chinese coolies hired by the Central Pacific company met with more serious difficulties when trying to penetrate from the West Coast near Sacramento, and crossing the mountain ranges of the Sierra Nevada. In spite of snow storms, a shortage of building materials, lack of water in the deserts, and the constant danger of attack by Indians, workers from the two companies, thanks to the excellent organisation of the work, met and confronted each other on 10 May 1869, at Promontory Point, the 'end of track'. In celebration, the governor of California drove the last spike made of pure gold into the last sleeper, using a silver sledge-hammer. The wreathed and festooned locomotive *Jupiter* from the east stood face to face with locomotive *N.119* from the west. The foremen of the two companies, together with their teams of workers, had their photographs taken and all over the United States bells started ringing. The Atlantic Ocean was connected by railway with the Pacific. In the years 1884—1888, the North American continent was partly bridged by another long line (1,935 miles). This was the Northern Pacific Railroad from Minnesota to Washington, while a third line, the Southern Pacific Railroad, 2,614 miles long, was built shortly after.

162. Welded sections of rails for track reconstruction

163

163. Pacific Line construction near Ogden (1869)

164. Part of a track reconstruction train placing new sleepers on cleaned gravel and then laying new welded rails

164

'From ocean to ocean' was the slogan of the builders of the 2,918 mile long Canadian Pacific Railway from Montreal to Vancouver. This daring construction had to surmount the Rocky Mountains and in the years 1881—1885 it opened up the territory of the Yukon for gold prospectors. At the same time it became a kind of link in the shortest combined ship and railway route from Europe to China.

In 1892 the construction of the longest railway line in the world, the Trans-Siberian Railway, was begun. The two starting points, one at each end, were the towns of Vladivostok and Tchelyabinsk, and the total distance to be covered was 4,651 miles. It had to cross many large rivers, circumvent Lake Baikal and cross vast unpopulated forest lands. On its completion in 1905, the construction of the northern Amur branch was started. Here another obstacle besides the forests appeared: eternally frozen soil. Further on, swamps and moorlands teaming with mosquitoes slowed down the construction, so that the railway was only finally opened in 1916. The track gauge is 5 ft. At present this line is fully electrified from Moscow to beyond Irkutsk and the Moscow—Vladivostok journey on the Trans-Siberian Express takes nine days.

165. The historic meeting of the Union Pacific and Central Pacific companies at Promontory Point, 10 May 1869

Railway bridges

Wooden bridges could meet the requirements of the railways only at the very beginning of their development. In order to accelerate the advance of the Pacific line, for instance, 'match' bridges were erected and viaducts supported by timber piers and braced against side winds by steel cables. Bolted wooden girder bridges, invented by the American Howe, were of special value in wartime since they provided a temporary but quickly-built means of communication.

Iron bridges had an unfortunate beginning because cast iron was used in their structure. When one of the first and longest lattice-girder bridges collapsed in a storm on December 28, 1879, and a train plunged into the waters of the stormy Tay estuary in Great Britain, killing all 78 passengers, cast iron was replaced by steel. When very large spans above estuaries and wide rivers were required, suspension bridges with the deck suspended by chains and later by cables were designed with success. As viaducts over deep valleys, arch bridges serve very well. Nowadays steel lattice girder construction is mainly used, supported by stone or concrete piers.

The world's first successful railway suspension-bridge was completed in 1855 by the American John Roebling. He added an upper deck to a bridge which had been built in 1848 over the Niagara Gorge below the Falls. The upper deck carried a double-track railway with a road and footpath beneath. Roebling later achieved an even more striking success by building the famous Brooklyn Bridge

165

166

over the East River in New York. It has a main span
of 1,595 ft and two side spans of 930 ft. In Great
Britain the famous railway and ship builder I. K.
Brunel designed a bridge crossing the River Tamar
with the deck suspended from chains fixed to
a concave arched girder. When a train crossed the
bridge, the suspensions stretched and the arch flat-
tened slightly. This idea is utilised even today in
large span bridges. Arched spans are formed from
welded plate girders or are made of reinforced concrete. For a while all-metal lattice-girder bridges
were designed in such a way that a cantilever structure was carried between the two piers. An example
of this design is the famous Forth Bridge in Scotland which crosses the Firth of Forth. The two
main spans are 1,710 ft and it was opened in 1890.
But the 1,800-ft main span of the Quebec Bridge
over the St. Lawrence River in Canada makes it the
largest cantilever span in the world. All together 85
people lost their lives during the construction of
this bridge.

The bridge arch sometimes supports the roadway
on tiers. The well-known Sydney Harbour Bridge is
an example. The span of its steel arch is 1,650 ft and
it was opened on 19 March 1932. The longest
bridge in the world of this type is the Bayonne
Bridge over the Kill Van Kull, connecting Bayonne,
New Jersey, with Staten Island, where the span of
the steel arch measures 1,675 ft; the bridge was
opened in November 1931. An alternative con-

166. The 230-yd long wooden girder bridge across
the Dale Creek on the Union Pacific Line

167. Rescue teams looking for survivors in the water near the collapsed spans of the 3,600-yd long,
cast iron bridge across the Tay estuary, built in 1878
by Thomas Bouch.

168. The 776-ft long stone viaduct built in 1908 by
Séjourné on the French narrow-gauge Cerdagne
railway line. The central pier is supported by an
arch built into the walls of the ravine

struction was used by the French engineer Eiffel
when building the Garabit Viaduct in the South of
France (Fig. 169), which was completed in 1884.
France has, however, still preserved the historic
stone railway bridges built by the engineer Séjourné at the beginning of this century.

The Great Salt Lake trestle bridge in Utah, USA,
was one of the most impressive trestle viaducts ever
conceived. When it was opened in March 1904 it
was 27$\frac{1}{2}$ miles long, nearly 16 of which consisted
of embankment. It was abandoned in 1942.

169. The sickle-shaped arch of Eiffel's viaduct Garabit (1886) has a 540-ft span supporting the bridge deck 399 ft above the valley.

170. The plate-girder welded bridge across Fehmarsund has an elevated part suspended from arches of caisson profile

171. Through the northern mouth of the Wattinger tunnel on the St. Gotthard line the spiral climb of the railway on two levels can be seen

171

Longest tunnels of the world

Passengers regarded the first railway tunnel in the world, built by Stephenson in 1830 on the Liverpool — Manchester line, as an unbelievable achievement, though it was only a few yards long. Twenty-seven years later, French and Italian workers started to struggle through the rocky core of the Alps in an attempt to build the Mont Cenis tunnel, which was to be over 8 miles long. Primitive boring units and gunpowder enabled the teams to advance by only 3—5 yards daily. Forty thousand wagons of rock had to be evacuated from the tunnel before workers advancing from the opposite sides of the mountains could shake hands on 26 December 1870. Immediately after that another and even more daring venture was begun, the construction of the St. Gotthard tunnel, which would connect Switzerland with Italy. Two-and-a-half thousand workers drove the 9-mile tunnel through solid rock, continually plagued by landslides and flooding. When it was opened in 1880, there had been three hundred and fifty victims among the workers. Later on, the Lötschberg tunnel was built, in which the axis had to be changed to avoid constant flooding by hot water from below ground, but it was finally opened in 1913. The two Simplon tunnels, at 12 miles 537 yds and 12 miles 559 yds, are still some of the longest in the world. In order to avoid difficulties with underground hot springs while operating in them and to accelerate the evacuation of materials and im-

prove the gallery ventilation, the chief engineer, Brandt, decided to build two single-track tunnels about 56 ft apart. These were transversely interconnected. He began by driving the first tunnel only. After overcoming tremendous obstacles this was completed on 24 February, 1905. The construction of the second tunnel was delayed by the 1914—1918 war, but it was put into operation in 1922.

During the reconstruction of the Pacific line, the Huntington Lake Tunnel in the Sierra Nevada was built. With its 13^1/$_2$-mile length it outdid the European tunnels. It was hoped that the length record would return to Europe with the construction of the Channel Tunnel.

The history of this project began in the days of Napoleon III. As early as 1881 the project was solemnly launched in England and in France simultaneously with the first token excavations, but for a number of reasons in 1883 work was suspended. It was not till 1973 before the two countries signed an agreement to re-start work on the Tunnel. It was planned that by 1980 electric trains with passengers and cars were to begin running at a speed of 88 mph in two one-way tunnels about 328 ft below sea level. The 30-mile tunnel was to cut the Paris—London journey to 2 hours 40 minutes. Between the two tunnels a third service tunnel was to be built. Its task would be to ventilate and service the main tunnels, being connected with them every 240 yards. The Priestley subaqueous shields that were to be used in the construction and would advance by

172

over half a mile a month were delivered and the preparatory work was begun. Owing to inflation of costs, however, Britain withdrew its participation.

The longest submarine tunnel will very likely be the 34-mile Seikan tunnel. When completed in 1980 it will connect the Japanese islands of Honshu and Hokkaido, passing 330 ft under the bottom of Cugar Bay. This double-track tunnel consists of one concrete tube of 36 ft inner diameter. There are also service tunnels which will ventilate the main tunnel and evacuate water for in spite of special insulation, water does percolate through the 32-inch thick concrete wall of the main tunnel. When the first electric express trains of the New Tokaido Line start running, thus cutting the present 18-hour journey from Tokyo to Saporro by one third, the lengths of the ten longest tunnels in the world (including the Channel Tunnel which one day might be still built) will be as given in the accompanying table.

172. About 60 trains a day, running at a speed of up to 77·6 mph, pass through the Simplon tunnels, one of them being the well-known Simplon Express (Paris to Istamboul)

173. A cross-section of the triple tunnel under the Channel (top), the beginning of construction works on the French side in 1973 (centre), and 'Chunnel' coast stations for passenger coaches (bottom)

Major tunnels of the world

Tunnel	Location	Length	
		miles	yards
1. (Seikan)	Honshu—Hokkaido, Japan	(approx. 34 miles)	
2. (Channel Tunnel)	France—England	(approx. 30 miles)	
3. Huntingdon Lake	USA	13	960
4. Simplon	Switzerland—Italy	12	559
5. Apennines	Italy	11	879
6. St. Gotthard	Switzerland	9	547
7. Lötschberg	Switzerland	9	132
8. Mont Cenis	Italy—France	8	868
9. Cascade	USA	7	1,387
10. Arlberg	Austria	6	639

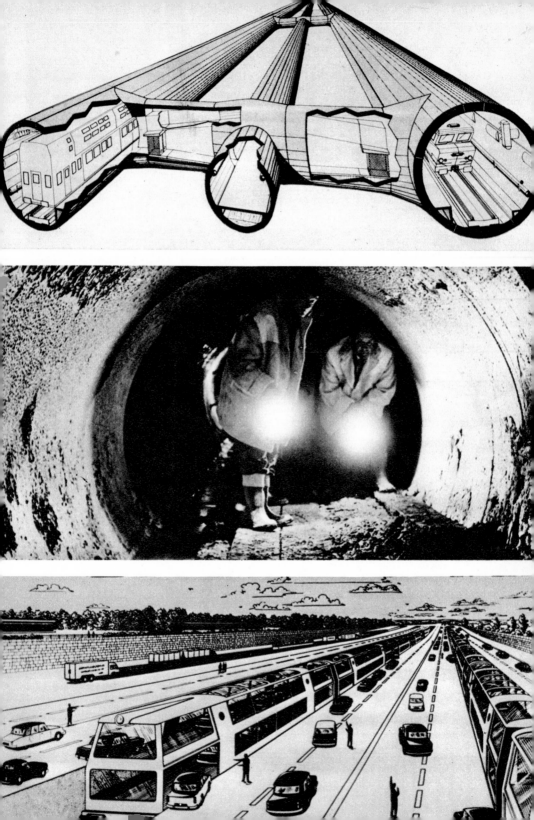

174. The fast automated BART line is integrated within the motorway network in the vicinity of San Francisco

175. View of the Central Berkeley station within the BART railway network

XX British Procor large-volume gondola wagon with a capacity of 110 tons

XXI Car loading using the American Vert-a-pack system

XXII A twelve-axle pontoon wagon for heavy freight up to 250 tons *(Werkfoto SIG-Nauhausen)*

XXIII Mechanised trans-shipping of loose materials by the fluid technique *(Whitting-USA)*

XXIV A Plasser-Duomatic packing machine

XXV A Spanish articulated motor express train, the Talgo *(RENFE)*

XXVI The famous *Blue Train* leaving Cape Town

Unusual railways

Out of a total of $1\frac{1}{4}$ million miles of track in the
world (of various gauges) one can only single out for
special mention those railways which stand out
either for the daring of their design or for some
other unusual feature. The total length of the North
American railways is about 250,000 miles. Ninety-
five per cent of the traction is by diesel locomotive,
but there is some electrification. For instance, they
decided to use the BART system in the San Francisco area and in the north-east corridor between
Washington and Boston.

BART (Bay Area Rapid Transit), put into service
in 1972, is an example of an excellent network of
fast electric trains with automated operation in the

176. A broad-gauge electric express train in the
Tchitin Valley on the Trans-Baikal Section of the
Trans-Siberian railway

San Francisco Bay area, where about 5 million inhabitants are concentrated. A network of double-
track lines, directly connected with the modern motorway network, was put into operation at a cost of
1·5 milliard dollars. It serves the city agglomeration
with its numerous and deep bays. Twenty-two miles
of track go through tunnels, 30 miles over bridges
and elevated railways and 25 miles along high railway embankments. Computers control the continuous movement of light articulated electric trains

with two to ten carriages, fed by direct current from a lateral rail as in an underground railway. Passenger comfort was improved by using a large track-gauge. The coaches are 10 ft wide and 69 ft long, each of them having 75 seats.

In rush hours trains arrive in the modern, multi-storey stations at intervals of $1^1/_2$ minutes, and during the night, 16 minutes. In every train a minicomputer accurately controls the stopping of the train and doors are automaticaly closed and opened. At a speed of 50 mph, which can be increased if need be up to 85 mph, the BART capacity is 30,000 passengers per hour in both directions.

The north-east corridor along the 500-mile coast, from Washington to New York to Boston, serves an area with 40 million inhabitants. When the motorways proved to be inadequate, the railway lines were reconstructed (in the first place straightened) and adapted for speeds up to 156 mph. Fifty Budd-Westinghouse electric express trains cut the journey from Washington to Boston from the original $8^1/_2$ hours to 5 hours. Plans are for superfast turbine express trains to be used on this line, capable of competing sucessfully with the overloaded air transport.

In 1982 the new Baikal-Amur Trans-Siberian line (BAM) will complete the present Soviet railway network of 85,000 miles of track. The original Trans-Siberian railway has been reconstructed and electric express trains from Moscow via Baikal, running along the Amur branch, transport passengers for a distance of 5,810 miles. In the past a journey from Moscow to Vladivostok undertaken by horse-drawn coach took three months; nowadays the time is cut to less than a week. At present the BAM is being constructed several hundreds of miles to the north of the original Trans-Siberian line. It leads from Lake Baikal to the port of Nakhodka and will be 2,000 miles long. It will accelerate the ever-increasing freight transport between Europe and Japan and will enable the exploitation of the tremendous natural resources of Siberia. Twenty thousand people using the latest mechanised equipment (e.g. 10,000 tipping trucks) have begun work on the line. The problems of railway construction in areas with eternally frozen soil are being overcome with new technology. Already under construction are 142 big bridges and a number of tunnels, and the length of one of them under the Muysker mountains will exceed 9 miles.

The New Tokaido line and the Sanyo line are at present the fastest railways in the world. They are the pride of Japan. Although the tracks pass through hills and valleys, they are as straight as possible and built largely on embankments and concrete bridges. Electric express trains reach a speed of 130 mph, which will be increased to 156 mph when the line is extended. This speed was reached in 1973 on the first line.

The New Tokaido line connects Tokyo and Osaka, a distance of 322 miles. Electric motor units consist of twelve carriages with 132 seats in the first class and 855 seats in the second class. The power output of 15,000 hp is divided among 48 dc electric motors fed by quartz rectifiers from a trolley with a voltage of 25 kV and frequency of 60 Hz. The traffic is controlled from the central control room in Tokyo, where a signal panel representing the movement of the trains along the whole line allows coded pulses to be transmitted from the control room via the rails to each train. The speed of trains can thus be controlled in steps of 18 mph. The engine-driver controls only the stopping of trains at the stations. The concave laminated nose-covers of the locomotives accomodate radar for sensing obstacles. Carriages have pneumatic suspension. During the journey passengers can make phone calls. The 'Hikari' super-express trains, stopping at only two out of the ten stations between Tokyo and Osaka, cover the distance between the two cities in 3 hours. From Osaka the New Sanyo line, 103 miles long, proceeds through a submarine tunnel to the Hakato station on the island of Kyushu. Railway ferries connect this line with the two remaining main islands of Japan. The Seikan tunnel will eventually connect it with the island of Honshu. The total length of Japanese railways is now 25,000 miles.

The Trans-Africa line, which was planned by that untiring coloniser Cecil Rhodes to link Cape Town with Alexandria, a distance of nearly 6,250 miles, was one major railway project which remained uncompleted.

The railways of South Africa have a standard gauge of 3 ft 6 in. The line which runs from Cape Town to Kimberley on to Bulawayo in Rhodesia, branches off to Victoria Falls station, where the passengers can admire the unique waterfalls on the Zambezi river. Over 2,000 miles from Cape Town the train joins the Congo railway network which will bring it to the Atlantic coast at Kinshasa. At the other end of Africa the railway from Alexandria runs by the side of the Pyramids, passes by the Cataracts of the Nile and ends at El Obeid in the Sudan. But still over 2,000 miles of Rhodes' original concept are missing to connect it with the Southern African network. Another railway which is still incomplete is the Trans-Sahara line planned by the French. It was to connect Dakar with Sekondi and the coast of Ghana. And Africa, split into small independent states, has not found the necessary financial sources for a complete railway network.

The Trans-Australia line connects Sydney on the Pacific ocean with Perth on the Indian Ocean. Its worst sections are 450 miles through the waterless desert of the Nullarbor Plain and 50 miles across the Ooldea sandhills. It holds a very specific record: for a distance of 297 miles it has the longest straight

177. The express train *Hikari* leaving Tokyo station

stretch of track in the world. It was completed in 1917 and during the construction three different track gauges were used which slows down its operation. Freight trains carrying wheat, meat and wool have to trans-ship the goods several times. Although the total length of the Australian railway network is nearly 44,000 miles, the interior of Australia has not yet been touched by the railway. The attempt to cross Central Australia from the south to the north ended in the line from Adelaide at Alice Springs at the foot of the Macdonnel mountains in the Northern Territory. From the opposite direction the interior is approached by a line from Darwin reaching as far as Birdum. However, the 603-mile gap in a region without a drop of water still has to be bridged by motor transport.

178. India still remains the paradise of steam locomotives

179. A Trans-Australian motor express train on its way to Perth

180. Mechanical semaphores can be found on local lines even today

181. Light-signalling device of a three-sign automatic block

179

180

181

At the end of the last century the Transandine Railway outdid all the mountain railways of the world. These lines were designed and built by the engineer Henry Maiggs, who died there. The railways were to transport minerals from the Peruvian mountains to the Pacific ports.

Nowadays, the passenger train *El Rapido,* with a standard track gauge, undertakes the break-neck journey from Lima to Huancayo in the Andes. Every day, the train climbs up the sharp zig-zag gradient. At an altitude of 13,000 ft the passengers are offered oxygen bags, since the pressure drops to 415 millibars compared with the 765 millibars at the point of departure. On the second branch of the same line the railway achieves, near La Cima, the record altitude of 15,808 ft.

From the Chilean-Bolivian port of Antofagasta a narrow metre-gauge line climbs up to reach the saltpetre fields of Potosi at an altitude of 15,705 ft.

There are still many places in the world waiting for the railway to make their treasures accessible to commerce. Prospective plans are very daring. One of them, for instance, is to connect the USA and USSR by a broad-gauge line running across a bridge or a dam across the Bering Strait.

Signalling and automated systems

From the very beginning of their operation railways introduced various safety measures to avoid collisions. For example, the engine driver in single-line operation could set his locomotive in motion only if he had received his 'token', usually a tablet or a staff. At the next station he handed over the token to the engine driver of a stationary locomotive coming from the opposite direction. In that way it was ensured that only one train could be running on the section of line between the two stations in question.

182

183

182. Arm-signalling devices of the American automatic block system of 1913 were connected directly with the track and would stop a train ignoring a warning signal

183. Control tower of an automatic-signal railway station

184. The control panel of the entry gate system of Duisburg station allows for 'blind' control of the train movements at the station

185. Various conductor arrangements positioned at intervals of 7·46 miles and fed by electric current enable the locomotive sensor to sense (A) the speed signal, while the sensor (B) issues instructions for a change of speed

Elsewhere the line was divided into sections by signal posts. At a determined time, for instance five minutes after a train had passed, the linesman swung the signal to 'clear', which meant that the following train could proceed. But unexpected obstacles on the track encountered by the first train could well cause a fatal collision if it had to stop because of them. A new safety system was introduced dividing the line into sections protected by mechanical semaphores with signalboxes all along the line in contact by telegraph and later on by telephone. A train could enter the section only after the signal was given that the next section was free. But human errors still caused serious accidents from time to time and the unreliable human factor

had to be replaced by automation. This was initiated in 1870 by the American W. Robinson, the inventor of the electric track circuit. If the circuit was occupied by a train, the track circuit controlled the position of the semaphore. From that time, railway safety automation developed in several inter-related stages.

The automatic block divides the line into approximately half-mile-long electric circuits. The right and left rails are electrically insulated. As soon as the wheels of a locomotive or of any other railway vehicle enters a section of track, a short circuit occurs. This causes a signal to be transferred to the section semaphore, which in turn closes the entry of the section to any following train. The former

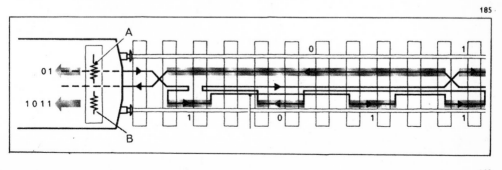

186

186. Aerial view of the accident caused by the derailment of the Swedish *North Arrow* express train in the village of Alby in 1964

187

mechanical semaphore has now been replaced by colour-light signals with three to four signs. A red light protects a section, prohibiting the entry of other trains. An amber light shows the driver that he is approaching an occupied section. A green light, on the other hand, permits him to carry on at full speed. The circuit of the automatic block includes warning systems for crossings and automatic swing gates. On a 60-mile section the employment of the 60 linesmen of the past could thus be avoided. Trains may follow each other at four-minute intervals.

However, despite these safeguards it was still possible for an engine driver either to overlook a signal or to ignore it. The system was therefore completed by the so-called train safe-guard device, transmitting signals directly into the driver's cabin. Pulses coded according to the colour signal, are transmitted from the signals to the track. A sensor carried by the locomotive and close to the top of the rail, senses the pulses by induction. These are amplified and processed by an installation in the locomotive. Should the engine driver ignore these visual warning signals or not be vigilant enough to see them, an automatic brake is activated.

Fully automated systems have been introduced on present-day main lines for the protection and control of the trains. A point-to-point communication between the train, the line and the control centre is ensured. The engine driver receives detailed information about everything that happens ahead of him on the line. He obtains data about the time-

187. Wrecked bogies of a Belgian express train which was derailed while entering a bridge, both bridge and train being completely destroyed. *(CTK)*

schedule situation and has, moreover, direct communication with the controller. Since the track itself is not capable of transmitting a large number of signals, a system of conductors laid between the rails is used instead. Signals are received by induction sensors fixed under the locomotive or the train. The principles of the systems introduced in West Germany, Britain, the USA and France differ slightly, but their function is identical. In the most simple arrangement one conductor is straight, parallel to the track, and the second one is in zig-zag form. The locomotive sensor responds in varying ways when it runs over the zig-zag loops at different speeds. The locomotive control system is thus informed about its position on the line and about the immediate speed of the train. Pulses in the cable circuit caused by the running of the train are also transmitted to the control centre, where a light signal model displays the movement of the train along the whole line.

In a system applied for instance on the Tokaido line the controller follows the train continuously; from his control panel he transmits instructions to the train to change speed, to brake, etc. In other systems, however, the train instruments are automatic. The control computer compares the speed of

the train with the programme of optimum speed and modifies it accordingly. More simple is a system where the programme of the journey—information about gradients and descents, about prescribed speeds on individual sections—is transmitted directly to the locomotive. A conductor in the form of rectangular loops is laid between the rails; according to the polarity of the current another locomotive sensor reads the necessary information from the binary coil elements.

In railway stations the original manual changing of the points is nowadays carried out by remote-control electro-mechanical point operating apparatus. The control room is located in the control tower of a station. By depressing a push-button a programme is activated, automatically opening the track for an arriving train to reach the correct platform and safeguarding it at the same time against other trains.

Track and station systems will eventually be integrated within a complex automated system controlled by a computer. The system will be protected against any hazards even at the highest speeds. But already the railways are much safer than road transport, although from time to time a technical failure or human error can cause a spectacular railway catastrophe. The French SNCF calculated for the benefit of its passengers, that if they wanted to be killed in a railway accident, they would have to spend 1,280 years in a train according to the statistical average.

Innovational railways

Few people realise that each of the 50 million sets of railway wheels running all over the world incorporate the invention of a genius. The conic cant of the tyre of 1 : 10 or 1 : 20, and the rail being inclined towards the centre of the track avoids friction and the flanges protect the train from derailment. The wheels can easily carry either a heavy freight train or a light express, up to speeds of 155 mph. The necessity to reduce train speed in curves of a comparatively small radius has been eliminated in an unexpected way — by tipping the carriages and locomotives. As soon as a sensor of transversal centrifugal acceleration detects a curve, a servo-mechanism immediately inclines the carriages pneumatically by 9 to 10 degrees towards the centre of the curve and thus reduces unpleasant centrifugal acceleration for the passengers.

Further express train speed development depends on full automation of the operation, on train weight reduction and on the selection of a perfect streamlined body. Otherwise the necessary driving energy sharply increases. A train with a 1,100-lb weight would require:

input power 3,752 hp for 125 mph
input power 10,720 hp for 187 mph
input power 21,440 hp for 250 mph
input power 53,600 hp for 312 mph

After 1945, a solution for the future of fast trains was looked for in the so-called monorails.

The suspended monorail railway was based on the historical concept of the well-proven urban suspended monorail track in Wuppertal. In order to achieve higher acceleration, higher speeds and a lower noise level, steel wheels were replaced by pneumatic ones. The suspended structure was built in a box girder, containing the motor supply systems and signalling linkage. The first of these railways, called Skyway, was put into operation on a short section of line in Houston, USA. The 12-ton aluminium car for 110 passengers could only reach a speed of 20 mph in such a short distance, although the designer calculated for a speed of up to 250 mph. A more perfect system was realised by the French Safege company in Chateauneuf sur Loire. Eighteen-metre long trains, pneumatically suspended and provided with disc brakes on two

four-wheel bogies (plus guiding bogies) achieved a speed of 50 mph without any noise. The Japanese applied this system on a 4-mile line in Tokyo where sets of coaches for 165 passengers overcome a gradient of up to 3 in 4 and pass round curves with a radius of only 164 ft.

Saddle railways move along the top part of a concrete girder. In order to maintain stability, they are provided with lateral guide wheels running along the sides of the girder. The most widespread is the 'Alweg' system. The name was derived from the initials of the Swedish inventor Axel Lennert Wenner Green. The design was inspired by the example of the steam saddle monorail invented by Charles Lartique which, as a kind of curiosity, connected the Irish towns of Listowel and Ballybunion, a distance of 9 miles, from 1888 to 1924. Nowadays the Alweg monorails transport visitors to various entertainment parks and world exhibitions. They were put into permanent operation first of all on a 1-mile line in Cologne on the Rhine. In Seattle, USA, a $1^1/_4$-mile double-track line using four carriage sets with a capacity of 10,000 passengers, is in operation. The longest existing Alweg system transports passengers from the centre of Tokyo to Haneda airport on an 8-mile concrete line. The trains have up to nine articulated carriages. They were found to lack, however, the necessary stability and the capability of maintaining adhesive force at higher speeds. Re-

188. Within 1·5 seconds after entering a curve, the electromagnetic servo system tilts the carriages of the ETR 0160 locomotive in such a way as to prevent the outward thrust exceeding 0·04 g

189. The suspended railway, *Safege,* at Chateauneuf sur Loire has 59-ft long carriages for 32 sitting and 91 standing passengers

189

190. Two four-section Alweg units passing on the concrete girders of the double-track line in Seattle, USA

191. Bertin's Aerotrain on an 11-mile long concrete track between Cartottes and Château Gaillard

search therefore centred on systems without wheels, and bogies hovering on an air cushion or on magnetic fields. Their design was facilitated by the discovery of linear electric motors without rotating parts.

Linear electric motors of the present-day, designed by the English professor Laithwaith, have only two parts. A strong aluminium strip is installed on a railway line, usually between the rails. It performs the function of the rotor in an asynchronous electric motor. The strip is surrounded on two sides—with the necessary $^3/_8$-in clearance maintained—by an air-cooled stator winding mounted on the bottom of the vehicle. When the stator is fed with current, it is attracted (together with the vehicle) forward or repelled backward. If the current direction in the coils is reversed, the electric motor brakes intensively. The weight/power ratio of a linear motor is 13 lb/hp compared with the 65 lb/hp of a conventional electric driving system.

Hovercraft trains were not successful. For 15 years teams of scientists in France, Britain and in the USA were developing trains moving on an air cushion created by fans between the guiding part of

192. The British experimental hovercraft train RTV-31 'riding' on a caisson-profile track. Using a linear electric motor it reached a speed of 297 mph. The experiments, however, were given up, because the air cushion suspension was very uneconomic

the train and a concrete rail. The most advanced design was that of the French engineer Jean Berthin. His *Aerotrain*, with 80 passengers, reached a speed of 156 mph on a test track near Orleans. The noise of the turbopropeller drive, however, exceeded the permissible limit, and moreover there were braking problems. Braking was carried out by a readjustment of the propeller blades, by pressure of jaws against the guiding track and by brake parachutes for emergencies. The British Hovercraft company therefore equipped its hovercraft *RTV-31* with a linear electric motor. The noise was substantially reduced, but the system as such remained surprisingly uneconomic. For a 1-ton carrying capacity a power output of 30 hp minimum was needed, ten times as much as in a system using magnetic hovering.

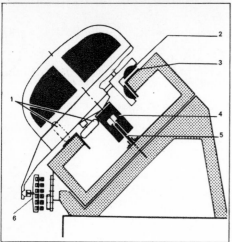

193. On a circular test track at Erlangen, West Germany, the AEG-BBC and the Siemens companies test an electrodynamically hovering train with a maximum speed of 124 mph

194. A cross-section of a banked curve in the track of an experimental EDS system magnetic train: 1—auxiliary wheels used when the train is stationary and for guiding it on curves; 2—superconductive magnet; 3—conductive plate combining the roles of a rail and of a repelling magnet; 4—linear electric motor stator: 5—rotor aluminium strip—a part of the track; 6—current collector for high speeds

195. A 9·8-ft long linear electric motor producing an efficient traction of 50 hp weighs 7,053 lb including the cooling system with a fan

193
194

195

Three concepts of magnetic hovercraft trains:
It took 40 years before the patent for magnetic hovering registered in 1934 by the German engineer Hermann Kemper was put to practical use. The first and apparently most simple theory—to provide the bottom of the vehicle and the surface of the track with permanent ferrite magnets in order to obtain the necessary power—cannot be realised with existing magnets. The second alternative of magnetic sliding, called the EMS system (Elektromagnetisches Schwebe system), has been successfully developed by the Munich industrial corporation, Transrapid. The vehicles have super-conducting magnets: the train carries its own cryogenic station supplying the magnets with liquid helium at a temperature of −269 °C (−452 °F). Due to the effect of its powerful magnetic field, the vehicle hovers (or is attracted in the case of a bottom circuit) above the coils fed with electric current. The close-on 11-ton *Transrapid 02* with 16 magnets reached a speed of 102 mph in 1971. The 18-ton *Transrapid 04* developed a speed of 125 mph on the Munich-Allach test track, and in February 1976 the experimental metering car *Komet*—accelerated by jets—reached a speed of 223 mph. In Japan

196. In 1970, on a test track in Pueblo, the Americans were trying out a car with a linear electric motor fed by current from its own generator, which was driven by a gas turbine

a magnetic Hitachi hovercraft vehicle is being tested. It should achieve a speed of 275 mph. EMS vehicles have to be equipped with a complex autopilot system maintaining, by changing the magnetic field, a permanent and constant distance of the vehicle from the surface of the track.

The third system, the so-called 'electrodynamic system' of hovering (EDS), is more simple. During the movement of the vehicle superconductive magnets induce the current in conductor strips on the track, bringing about a repellent effect. Experiments of the German BBC and AEG-Telefunken companies on a circular track in Erlangen show that for 4 to 6 inches hovering height only, 2·7 to 4 hp output is needed per 1 ton of weight.

In 1980, all the types of magnetic hovercraft trains are to be run in competition on a test track at

197. A three-part magnetic Transrapid-EMS train for 300 passengers with a linear electric motor *(MBB)*

198. The Inter-city Express Train is planned to be the main element for rapid railway transport in West Germany. For speeds up to 300 mph, magnetically suspended or hover-trains will be used

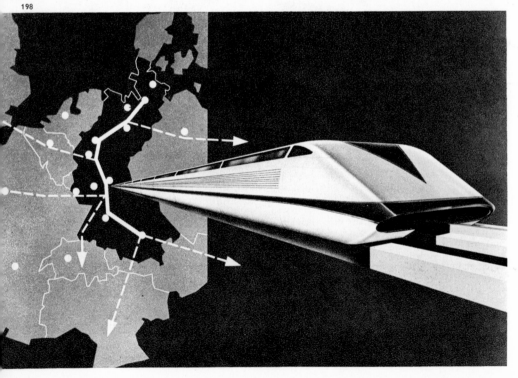

XXVII An overhead travelling crane with spreader, for trans-shipment of all ISO standardised containers

XXVIII Automated control of Southern Pacific freight wagons (top). Control computer (centre). Terminals for checking marshalled trains (bottom)

XXIX Automated tracks branching into a 40-track gridiron at d'Hourcade station near Bordeaux *(SNCF)*

XXX The modern architecture of the main railway station in Madrid is adapted to the Spanish tradition
(RENFE)

Donauried in West Germany. The system that proves the best will be used for a network of fast railways, which should, by about 1990, ensure express train connection of Hamburg, via Hannover, Düsseldorf, Cologne and Mannheim with Munich. Intercity magnetic trains should reach a speed of 275 mph, fully replacing internal airline connections between all the economic centres in West Germany. A similar plan is being studied by Japan and the USA for the most densely populated areas.

199. A copy of Stevens' rack locomotive from 1825 proved that it was reliable

Rack railways

When the railways started penetrating into the Alps in the 1850s, the human desire of time immemorial to conquer the mountain peaks seemed to be approaching fulfilment. But the adhesion of the smooth locomotive wheels made it impossible safely to overcome gradients steeper than 1 in 40. The technicians therefore began studying the possibility of using rack drive, developed by Blenkinsop in England as well as by Colonel John Stevens in the USA who, in 1825, built a railway with a rack between the rails in the garden of his house. A toothed wheel driven by a steam engine via a shaft enmeshed with the rack.

The first rack railway on the Madison-Indianapolis line, built in 1847, overcame a 1 in 12 gradient using a locomotive with all axles driven. In sections with especially steep gradients a second steam engine was used to drive a cog-wheel which meshed with a rack. In 1869 Sylvester Marsh built the first mountain rack railway in the USA. On a 3-mile track it carried passengers to the 6,293 ft summit of Mount Washington in New Hampshire. On this, on gradients up to 1 in 3, a locomotive with a vertical boiler pushed a carriage for 50 passengers. For de-

200

scents Marsh used an air brake; steam cylinders used air instead of steam and thus were transformed into compressors. The engine driver released the compressed air to control the braking.

Kaspar Wettli in Switzerland used a different system in his attempt to climb the Alps. His 25-ton locomotive had a cylinder with profiled flanges instead of a cog-wheel. These enmeshed with ribs between the rails, arranged in arrow formation. The outcome of the experiment on the Wädenswille-Einsiedel line ended, however, fatally. On 11 November 1876, just before reaching the peak, the flanges of the cylinder broke and the locomotive rolled down the slope. Later, on exactly the same section, another catastrophe occurred. After a brake failure a locomotive ran down a 1 in 20 gradient hitting the buffer stop at the terminal, and twenty-one people died. This accident happened on 22 February 1948.

For his mountain line from Vitznau to the summit of the Rigi, the Swiss mechanical engineer N. Riggenbach designed racks with trapezoidal teeth between stiffening angles. There were 69,000 teeth in the 4-mile track, which overcame gradients of 1 in 4. Opened in 1871, it gave access to a spectacular view in one of the main tourist centres of Switzerland. It met with such success that two years later the summit of the Rigi was reached by another rail-

way built from the east with the Arth-Goldau station as its starting point. The original 16-ton Riggenbach locomotive, which used to push a carriage with 54 passengers, is admired nowadays by visitors to the Museum of Transport in Lucerne. If the Rigi railway is the oldest one, then another Swiss rack railway, opened in 1889 and leading to Mount Pilatus, is the steepest. Leaving from the Alpnachstadt station the 3-mile rack climbs up to an altitude of 6,500 ft overcoming gradients of nearly 1 in 2. The designer, Dr. Locher, used a pair of racks with vertical teeth which meshed with the pinions of the locomotive. In the beginning, geared steam locomotives with a short transverse steam boiler used to be used on this railway.

Before the Second World War, however, the steam locomotives on these two lines were replaced by comfortable electric rack railway units. Under the peak of the Rigi blue trains from Goldau meet with the red trains from Vitznau.

The European rack railway altitude record is held by the Jungfrau line. From the starting station of Kleine Scheidegg at an altitude of 6,762 ft the metre-gauge track runs through continuous tunnels in the Alpine slopes and ends at the tunnel station of Jungfraujoch at an altitude of 11,332 ft, below the peaks of the Jungfrau (13,642 ft) and Münch (13,448 ft).

201
202

200. The historical steam locomotive of the oldest rack railway, to Pilatus, built in 1889 *(Verkehrshaus, Lucern)*

201. This blue-and-white rack unit climbs from Arth to Rigi in 35 minutes *(Swiss National Tourist Office)*

202. The terminal station of this rack railway is hidden in a rock tunnel at an altitude of 11,330 ft *(Swiss National Tourist Office)*

203

Numerous rack railways in Switzerland, in West Germany, Austria, Yugoslavia and in the USA make the beauty of mountains accessible even under the most difficult conditions. The highest of them, in Colorado, ends at Pikes Peak at an altitude of 14,110 ft.

Cable railways

Carts hauled by a cable along girder tracks up sharp gradients can be found in medieval engravings. However, they were only put into routine transport operation comparatively recently.
Funicular railways: These were first built at the end of the last century to reach the tops of scenic hills in or near towns, and occasionally to ascend mountains. Very steep slopes were served by cable lifts: these, however, could only reach a height of 328 ft.

Single-track or double-track funiculars were more practical. Carriages were linked together by cables and in some rare cases did not need an engine to drive them. In one instance, for example, cars had tanks fitted underneath them. At the upper station the tanks were filled with water and, when the brakes were released, the car descended due to its weight, at the same time hauling up the car from the lower station attached to the other end of the cabel with empty tanks. The water-filled tanks of

203. The rope railway up Vesuvius, dating from 1880

204. This old lattice girder lift to Bürgenstock still carries tourists to see this wonderful view of Lucerr and its surroundings (*Swiss National Tourist Office*)

the first car were evacuated at the lower station. The only mechanical parts were the brakes.

One of the oldest steam-driven funiculars is the railway to the top of Vesuvius built in 1880. The double-track funicular to Leopoldsberg near Vienna, built in 1885, was driven by electricity, reaching a speed of nearly 2 mph. By 1914 about twenty-five funicular railways had been built in European mountains giving easy access to different tourist centres.

Today the funicular railway cabins are arranged stepwise. The lines themselves are usually and with advantage built as single-track railways. In the middle of the track the cars automatically avoid each other, because the wheels on one side are guided by a rail, while the wheels on the other side are in the shape of a cylinder running over the tips of the points. The car is fixed to a hauling cable and to an additional safety one. The driving system uses

205

206

205. A rope railway to Engelberg and a suspended cabin ropeway transport passengers to Titlis (altitude 9,907 ft)

206. KAPRUN 2, the most efficient and the fastest rope railway in the Alps, can transport 1,220 passengers in one hour

dc variable-speed electric motors to ensure smooth and continuous starting and braking. In case of cable failure, the cabins are provided with a safety push-type spring collet which, in an emergency, automatically grips the tops of the rails.

Between the two wars the development of funicular railways stopped completely. They were too slow and could not be adapted to changing profiles of surface. However the present-day invasion of tourists and especially of skiers to the mountains called for a return of interest in the progress of funicular design, which had been abandoned for many decades. New experience and knowledge allowed their capacity to increase to a considerable extent. The fastest and most powerful funicular rail-

way so far was put into operation in 1974 in the Alps, in the area of the Kaprun dam system. A double-section carriage for 180 passengers leaves a valley station, running first across a steel bridge and then proceeding through a 2-mile circular tunnel to the upper station of Alpin-Zentrum. It has an input power of 3,300 hp. On a straight and covered track the two cars run at a speed of 33 ft per second. When meeting each other in the tunnel their speed is 45 mph. The driver of the funicular has a point-to-point induction communication with the centre via a 2-in diameter hauling rope and a ballast rope. In full operation the funicular can transport 1,220 passengers to the top.

Aerial ropeways

First produced at the beginning of this century, these were a natural evolution from military and freight mono-cable or bi-cable ropeways. The oldest design, consisting of cabins hauled by a cable fixed to posts, can be found in the Gdansk museum. The old ropeway for the port of Gdansk was designed in 1644 by the builder Adam Wybe.

The construction of the Alpine tunnels, during which they were used, contributed to the development of aerial ropeway design. After the completion

207

207. The first big suspended ropeway, dating from 1912, connected Rio de Janeiro with the Sugarloaf Mountain

208. 3-km long French suspended ropeway to Bourg St. Maurice, with a cabin for 70 passengers

of the tunnels many aerial ropeways remained in operation. The platforms used for loads of building materials were replaced by open or closed tourist cabins. The German designer J. Pohling figured prominently in the development of aerial ropeways. He built the first 2,854-ft long passenger aerial ropeway in 1908 in Hong Kong to transport workers to a railway construction site. In 1912—19 he built a double-section cabin aerial ropeway to the Sugar-Loaf Mountain above Rio de Janeiro. His design was very close to the present-day concept. Cabins for 18 passengers moved at a speed of 8 ft per second on two track cables 8 in apart.

Nowadays the aerial ropeways have one- or two-track cables, and the cabins are usually closed. A 2-in diameter cable can bear a maximum load of 1,000 tons. Cabins for 45—120 passengers, made of aluminium and laminated plastic, move in gradients up to 1 in 2 and at a speed of up to 33 ft per second. The Squaw Valley ropeway in California has the biggest cabin in the world for 125 passengers. The largest span between two posts — 2¹/₂ miles — is that of the ropeway to Mount San Jacinto in California. The longest ropeway in the world, also reaching the highest altitude, is the Teleférico Mérida in Venezuela which has cabins for 45 persons. The journey takes 1 hour; passengers have to change

cabins three times, the ropeway track having four sections. The terminal station Pico Espejo is at an altitude of 15,630 ft.

Self-propelled ropeway cabins are a revolutionary innovation in the construction of ropeways. The top and bottom stations are connected by one-track cable and engine rooms and complicated systems of hauling ropes are no longer necessary. At the bottom of the cabin there is an automobile engine operated by the driver. The power output is hydraulically transmitted to a suspension device above the cabin. A system of collets grips the track cable so reliably that even gradients of nearly 1 : 3 can be overcome.

Sportsmen use ski lifts, chair or cabin lifts. Mono-cable chair lifts have a limited speed and a limited permissable height above the ground. Nowadays, passengers have a comfortable seat on a chair or in a gondola cabin (usually for four people), the cabin being suspended on an endless rope. At the top station the cabin is automatically released, stops, and passengers can get off safely.

Ropeways as an urban means of transport, forming in effect a suspended tramway or bus route, are at present of great interest to transport experts; they are noiseless and do not produce pollution. If, however, the cars are to travel in a horizontal direction, rope sag has to be eliminated, since it prevents high cabin speed. The Swiss engineer G. Müller solved this problem by means of a special rope suspension of the track cable, which, when not under load, is slightly dished upwards. When the cabin passes over it, it straightens so perfectly that it is as even as a rail. In 1975 in Mannheim, Müller demonstrated his Aerobus on a 2-mile track crossing the Neckar river. Three-element vehicles with twelve driving pulleys reached a speed of 25—38 mph. On the East Side of New York City an urban ropeway on high posts has been built which crosses the East River, providing a comfortable connection for 5,000 families living on Roosevelt Island.

The submarine funicular railway near Marseilles offering up to six passengers a remarkable half-hour journey at a depth of 33 ft under the water should be mentioned only as a curiosity. At present about 40,000 ropeways of all kinds are operated in the world, one half of them serving for passenger transport. They are very safe. According to the UNO statistics far more people die in automobiles when trying to reach the valley ropeway stations than in the ropeways themselves, where accidents are extremely rare.

209. A gondola ropeway built on Col de Menouve made the peaks of St Bernhard accessible to skiers and tourists *(Swiss National Tourist Office)*

210. This self-propelled cabin of the Austrian Reisch company is driven by an air-cooled VW engine

211. In 1975 a three-part Müller Aerobus unit carried 4,000 people an hour over the Neckar at the time of the Garden and Flower Exhibition in Mannheim

212. A submarine ropeway built in 1967 near Marseille, with a scenic cabin for 6 passengers

4. Road Transport

Development of the bicycle

The first really popular means of transport of this kind was a vehicle designed at the beginning of the nineteenth century by the German K. L. Draise. His *Laufmaschine* had two wheels connected by a wooden beam provided with a saddle. The rider, sitting on the saddle, propelled the vehicle by pushing on the ground with his feet. Although Draise's vehicle was far from being perfect, the inventor several times covered the journey from Mannheim to Karlsruhe in four hours, about a quarter of the time it took a pedestrian to cover the same distance. Draise's experiments took place in the years 1813—1817. After his start, various mechanical engineers tried to improve his design. The French locksmith P. E. Michaux takes the credit for transforming Draise's vehicle into a real bicycle. In 1855 he provided the front wheel with treadles, so that the tiring foot drive was no longer required. Together with the Englishman, Lallement, Michaux founded the first bicycle factory. Although the first bicycles were not sprung in any way so that they were generally called 'boneshakers', they soon became popular. Rate of development was fastest in Britain. Frames were soon made of steel tubes and the wheels had wire spokes. The Englishman, Cowper, replaced the original radial arrangement of the wires with a tangential one, distributing the stress more advantageously. In 1867 the wheels were provided for the

first time with anti-friction bearings, and two years later the English manufactured the first bicycle with narrow rubber tyres. Coventry became the production centre, and in an attempt to increase speed the designers opted in favour of larger diameter front wheels with foot pedals. Finally, however, the front wheel dimensions grew too great. Just to mount such a high bicycle required acrobatic talent. To ride was an adventure and falls were dangerous, so that in the years 1885—1890 these bicycles were mainly reserved for sportsmen only. For older gentlemen and ladies the safer tricycles began to be manufactured. On one tricycle, the *Sociable*, two riders sat between large wheels, driving them by pedalling and steering with a small front wheel. Another tricycle, called the *Rotary*, resembled a bicycle but had a small-diameter side wheel. Tricycles could not compete with bicycles, because they were heavier and slower, and as soon as smaller-wheeled low bicycles appeared, tricycles were soon forgotten. The true predecessor of the modern bicycles was the very safe *Kangaroo*, where the propelling force was transmitted to the axle of the front wheel from the pedals by means of two chains. When the foot pedals were thus separated from the wheel axle, the position of the rider could be lowered. This improved stability considerably and mounting and dismounting was much easier. The chain transmission enabled higher wheel revolutions without tiresome fast pedalling. This, together with improvements to the frame, led to the final replacement of high bicycles by low ones.

In 1873, the Englishman H. Lawson designed a bicycle with foot pedals located on the lower part

213

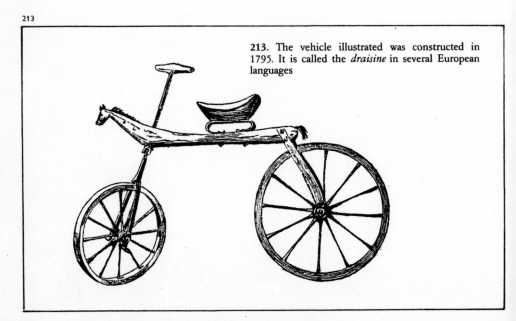

213. The vehicle illustrated was constructed in 1795. It is called the *draisine* in several European languages

214. Acrobatic mounting of the high Rudge bicycle in 1884

215. The Kangaroo bicycle was driven by two chains from foot pedals mounted at the end of the front forks

of the frame between the wheels. The pedalling effort was transmitted by a chain to a sprocket connected with the rear wheel. In 1885 James Starley manufactured a frame nearly identical with the present-day one, while reducing the wheel size at the same time to approximately the present dimension — 28 in. His bicycles began winning one race after another and proved to be excellent for ordinary everyday use. The Humber bicycle of that time weighed about 48 lb.

The invention of the British physician J. B. Dunlop who, in 1888, fitted his small son's tricycle with the first pneumatic tyre, represented another advance in rider comfort. It was really an air-filled hose, fixed into the rim of the wheel. Other countries did not recognise Dunlop's patent, as it had been already granted in 1854 to another Englishman R. W. Thomson. However, tyres of his type, although their rubber was cured according to the method established by C. Goodyear, were too expensive and were soon forgotten. But the Dunlop Pneumatic Tyre Company quickly improved things by using Wood's invention of a tyre valve and, under Welch's patent, the tyres were divided into a soft inner tube and a stronger profiled tyre casing with a stiffened rim.

Inventors and designers tried various ways of improving the pedalling mechanism and transmission and reducing the weight of the bicycle. As early as 1898 the *Hirondelle* with double-ratio drive and

216

with two chains appeared. Neither the Cardan transmission nor the lever systems for oscillating pedalling, both of which were tried, achieved such good results as the modern, light roller chains together with the installation of roller bearings in all the rotating parts of the bicycle.

While hub and back-pedalling brakes are still used, the majority of present-day brakes are applied at the wheel rim. On the older upright kind of roadster bicycle stirrup brakes pull up on the inner face of the rim, whereas modern block brakes operate against the side faces.

The modern bicycle, ridden for such purposes as shopping and journeys to work, is still widely used in India, China and Holland. It weighs 15 — 22 lb, can have lighting provided by a dynamo, and a luggage carrier in the rear. In central Europe the bicycle is more often used for sport and entertainment. Light sport bicycles weigh only 11 — 13 lb. By means of a shifting lever, the chain can be moved from one sprocket wheel to another. The sprocket wheels have a different number of teeth so that three to ten gear ratios can be chosen.

For tourism and recreation collapsible bicycles with small diameter wheels proved to have advantages. They were called mini-bicycles. The height of the saddle could be adjusted in order to achieve an economically convenient position while pedalling. Rubber suspension of the front wheel in various ways was a real innovation.

In an attempt to reduce the weight as much as possible, the English Reynolds company manufacture frames made of high-strength manganese-molybdenum steel, the thickness of the frame wall being only 0·3 mm. The frames weigh less than 4½

216. Tricycle *Sociable* for two people (1884)

lb and there are 15 different gear ratios. Rims are rolled from aluminium and the Michelin company offers an innovation, a tyre weighing together with the inner tube only 12 oz. Americans are testing shell frames, including a glass-laminate cycle fork. For young people a number of interesting accessories are available: electric horns, headlights with built-in transistor radios, saddles with high backrests, speedometers and electric tachometers.

The bicycle was the first mass-produced popular vehicle and a number of its components and elements were used in the development of the motorcycle and in the first automobiles.

Development of the motorcycle

As with all other means of early transport, the bicycle inspired designers to try and replace human force with mechanical power. In 1869, an American locksmith, Sylvester H. Roper, tried to drive the rear wheel of a bicycle with a small steam engine; the piston rods were connected with the cranks of the rear wheel. In 1880, however, he and his fellow-countryman, Lucius Copeland, came to the conclusion that the steam engine was totally inadequate to drive the light bicycle. The bicycle finally obtained a more or less satisfactory engine in Germany, where Gottlieb Daimler built into the structure of a wooden bicycle a single-cylinder petrol engine

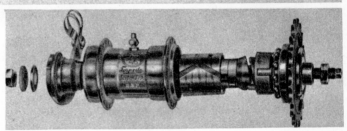

217. (a) A man's tourist bicycle, the Premier, of 1960, with a Torpedo drum brake. (b) Detail of idling system and Torpedo brake

217

218

which gave an output of 0·4 hp. Daimler and his machine made their first appearance in 1885, in the streets of Cannstatt. The wheels were provided with steel tyres. The engine with a fire tube was located under a saddle that was so high it looked as if the driver was standing. A transmission with two belts and a pinion in mesh with the gear rim of the rear wheel gave a speed of 6 — 12 mph.

In 1893 a predecessor of the motorcycle appeared simultaneously in France and in Germany. The Frenchman Millet built a five-cylinder, 0·75 hp radial engine directly into the rear wheel. The engine was equipped with electric ignition, had an air cleaner, and the speed was controlled by turning a grip. The motorcycle of Munich engineers H. Hildebrand and A. Wolfmüller was even more successful in Europe. Connecting rods of its double-cylinder horizontal four-stroke engine were in direct mesh with cranks at the rear wheel, which had the

218. An English Moulton minibike with an adjustable saddle and a shopping basket (1975)

219

supplementary function of a flywheel. This vehicle was called a 'motor bicycle' (*Motorrad*). Its running was a bit unpredictable, but the simplicity of the structure and comfortable travelling on broad pneumatic tyres won popularity. The manufacturers sold about a thousand of these machines, but there were problems with the driving system which remained unsolved and starting by means of fire lamps set several of the machines on fire. Eventually Hildebrand and Wolfmüller were obliged to stop production. About the year 1900 public interest centred on motor tricycles.

In 1897 two Russian emigrants, the brothers Michael and Eugene Werner, produced a design which became the basis of all future motorcycles *la Motocyclette*. It looked like the bicycles of that time; the front wheel, however, was driven by a belt from an auxiliary engine mounted on the handlebars, and the well-known French company Solex returned to this principle 50 years later. Others in the early days, mainly British designers, located an air-cooled engine on the frame, where the pedals had previously been mounted. G. Hendel applied this concept in the USA when designing his Indian motorbike, but in general, due to engine vibrations, the bicycle structure only had a short life. As a result, between 1898 and 1904 the Czechs V. Laurin and

V. Klement began producing Slavie motorcycles (exported to Britain under the trade mark Hewetson) with a stiffened frame suitable for engine mounting. The rear wheel was driven by a flat leather belt. Concentration of all the engine controls and brakes on the handlebars was also a useful contribution to the development of motorcycles, most of which took place in Britain. In 1904 the magazine *Motor Cycle* established that about 25,000 motorcycles were running in the UK.

In 1905 motorcycles—until then pushed in order to start the engines—were provided with kick starters. In 1910 they were equipped with gearboxes, separate at first, although about a quarter of a century later they were built in one with the engine. Just before the First World War engine capacities had increased up to 1000 cc and spring-cushioned front wheels were in use. During this war motorcycles were much used in military operations, their improved engines enabling speeds up to 50 mph to be reached. Designers of the German BMW

219. Daimler's historical bicycle of 1886

XXXI The control panel and desk of the fastest railway in the world, the Tokaido in Tokyo *(Hitachi)*

XXXII A Japanese experiment with magnets on the track and superconductive magnets in the vehicle (*JNR*)

XXXIII The magnetically suspended *Transrapid 02* driven by a linear electric motor on test track (*Krauss-Maffei*)

XXXIV The rack locomotive designed by Nicholas Riggenbach in 1873 for the Vitznau-Rigi line *(Verkehrshaus Luzern)*

XXXV The Alpine ropeway to Fellhorn with a double-track cable. Cabin for 80 passengers *(Leichbau-Zagres)*

220. A motor bicycle constructed by Hildebrand and Wolfmüller in 1893

221. The Slavie motorcycle of the Laurin and Klement company (1902) with belt transmission and a stiffened frame

222

223

224

222. An American Indian motorcycle from 1902 with an air-cooled four-stroke engine of 1·75 hp

223. An English A.J.S. sports motorcycle with a four-stroke OHC engine and chain transmission

224. A record-breaking BMW motorcycle with a twin-cylinder four-stroke engine, capacity 750 ccs, and with a special body, reached a speed of 137·4 mph in 1930

225

company came up with many innovations. In 1923 they introduced flat twin cylinders with power transmission to the rear wheel and in 1935 they incorporated telescopic front forks. Three years later they had telescopic rear forks as well. Electric starters were used first of all for the most powerful engines, the pioneer being the Harley-Davidson motorbike with a 1,200-cc engine capacity.

Present-day motorcycles are used in technically developed countries mainly for tourism, sport and entertainment. In less developed countries, however, they represent the basic means of transport. At present about 50 million motorcycles are running all over the world.

226

225. The Premier motorcycle with a two-stroke Fichtel and Sachs engine of 100 ccs (1937)

226. Italian Vespa 50 scooter (1965)

227

Small capacity motorcycles—scooters, mopeds, mini-mopeds: Scooters are small-wheeled motorcycles with an engine capacity of 125—175 cc. Their design gives the rider extra protection from bad weather and mud. Their predecessor was a low-built ladies' motorcycle, the Scott, manufactured in Britain as early as 1911. In the 1960s scooters were very popular, expecially in Italy and France.

Mopeds, with engine capacities up to 50 cc and with an output of 1·3—2·6 hp, are popular among young people. They follow the pre-war tradition of the popular European motor bicycles made by DKW and Fichtel and Sachs. They are manufactured in a wide range of styles from bicycles with an auxiliary engine to mopeds looking almost like real racing bikes.

Mini-mopeds are collapsible, have a weight of 66—110 lb, and are usually provided with an automatic clutch. They can be folded up to the size of a suitcase and can be transported in the boot of a car.

Electric mini-mopeds have very good prospects for use in towns (Plate XXXVI). They are noiseless, do not produce exhaust gases and can achieve speeds of 18—25 mph. However, their range of 25 miles per battery charge is still unsatisfactory.

Touring motorcycles: These are usually manufactured in a range of engine capacities from 250—500 cc. The two-stroke or four-stroke, single or multi-cylinder engines are usually cooled by air, and have power outputs of 20—30 hp. They easily reach speeds over 90 mph, their petrol consumption being about 70 mpg. Front and rear telescopic, hydraulic suspension forms part of standard equipment. The driving chain is usually covered. Classical drum brakes are on the way out, giving way to hydraulic disc brakes. An increasing number of designs use automatic clutch controls or automatic gearboxes. Wire wheels have lost their dominating position and spoke wheels cast from light alloys appear ever more frequently.

Big capacity motorcycles: Recent years have witnessed the development of very powerful machines. For instance, the BMW company increased engine capacities from 500 cc to 900 cc. Some air- or water-cooled multi-cylinder engines give an output of more than 80 hp. As far as the number of cylinders is concerned, the Italian Benelli 750 Sei, with a six-cylinder engine and transverse arrangement of cylinders, maintains a leading position. These Super-

227. Collapsible Honda mini-moped of 50 cc and 5 hp with a maximum speed of 37·28 mph

228. The Jawa tourist motorcycle with twin-cylinder two-stroke engine of 350 ccs and 18 hp. Front and rear telescopic suspension (1970)

228
229

229. A tourist twin-seat motorcycle, the Hercules Wankel 2000. Power output 27 hp at 6,500 rpm, six-speed gearbox, weight 397 lbs, max. speed 87 mph

230

bikes which have engine capacities corresponding to small car engines, weigh up to 660 lb. Some can accelerate from 0—60 mph in 5 seconds and are capable of speeds of 140 mph.

Italian sports motorcycles are well-known for their all-round qualities: the Benelli 750 Sei and the Benelli Quattro or Guzzi 250TS and MV-Agusta 350 Sport are among the best designed motorcycles in the world.

One quite recent innovation is the use of the Wankel engine. The German Hercules W 2000 and the Japanese Suzuki RE-5 and the Yamaha RZ 201 were joined in 1976 by a powerful motorcycle from Holland, the Van Veen OCR-1000, with an engine of this type, a capacity of 998 cc and an output of 100 hp. Its price was fantastic as well, corresponding to the price of three small cars.

In recent years Japan has become an important manufacturer of motorcycles. Among their more powerful machines, one of the most comfortable motorcycles is the Honda 1000GL, otherwise called the Gold Wing. The world speed record is held by a Yamaha with streamlined fairings and two engines. In 1974, Don Vesco riding this machine reached a speed of 280 mph.

230. The liquid-cooled, four-stroke Honda 1000 GL Gold Wing, power output 90 hp, cardan shaft drive, disc brakes, and max. speed 142·9 mph

231. A steam tractor of the Case Company of Racine, Wisconsin, from 1886

The era of the steam automobile

While in Britain the 'Red Flag' Act of 1865 virtually stopped the use of passenger steam vehicles, their development in France and in the USA went on. Poor roads, however, did not allow for much speed and, consequently, designers became more interested in steam tractors. Their most typical feature was a horizontal boiler with one or two cylinders behind the chimney. Their pistons were driven by a large flywheel via a crosshead and a rod. The flywheel could be used to drive mechanical saws or agricultural machines by means of a belt or, by installing a clutch, the power output could be transmitted by gears to large-diameter, steel driving wheels. Historical evidence proves that these machines, designed by English engineers for use in India, e.g. Crompton's *Blue Belle* from 1860, were very successful even under the difficult working conditions found in the East.

The development of road tractors and portable steam engines continued until 1920. Several years ago a group of British students showed what these clumsy machines, weighing several tons, could do. They used an ancient traction engine to tow a camping caravan, and at a speed of 12 mph undertook a tour of the world. During that time their *Britania* consumed 65 tons of coal and nearly 12,000 gallons of water.

Unlike those in locomotives, tractors and portable steam engines, the engine itself and the flywheel could not be seen in steam cars, these parts being covered by a coach body. In 1873, the Frenchman Amédée Bollée built quite a remarkable steam car, *L'Obéissante,* in Le Mans. He introduced a number of innovations. The two front wheels used horizontal stub axles as in present-day cars. All the control levers could be easily reached by the driver when seated; the boiler was served by a stoker standing behind him. The output of this steam engine was about 16 hp and the vehicle with 12 passengers could reach a speed of up to 25 mph. After several attempts to build steam omnibuses and tractors, Bollée designed in 1878 a lighter vehicle, *La Mancelle,* with the steam engine at the front. Eventually, Amédée Bollée introduced a concept which has survived to the present day: the power output was transmitted from the engine by a shaft to the rear wheels.

He demonstrated his vehicle in Vienna and everywhere his speed of 22 mph was an object of admiration and surprise. Towards the end of his life — he died in 1916 — Bollée appreciated the advantages of petrol engines in light cars and fully supported their development.

An interest in mechanical engineering joined the French Comte de Dion with the locksmith Georges Bouton; after their success with the steam tricycle

232

232. Bollé's *La Mancelle* from 1878

233. A De Dion-Bouton steam tractor in the Paris—Rouen race, 1894

233

234. Serpollet's tricycle with the so-called lightning boiler, Paris, 1887

235. A steam tricycle constructed by the American L. Copeland in 1884, with automatic water-level control in the boiler and with a combustion controller

Rudge in 1883 they founded a company which, later on, manufactured a number of four-wheel steam cars. Before they turned their attention to the petrol engine, their efforts with steam culminated in the building of a tow vehicle for coaches which in 1894 won the famous race from Paris to Rouen, a distance of 80 miles.

The third most important personality of the European steam car era was a Paris mechanic, Léon Serpollet. Besides building his first famous steam tricycle in 1887, he took his place in the history of motoring by obtaining the first driver's licence in the world. The licence authorised him 'to drive in all the Paris streets without any exception'.

For his three-wheel and later on four-wheel automobiles, Serpollet developed a kerosene-heated steam generator enabling him to outdo the power outputs of the petrol engines of the time. His cars were popular in aristocratic circles because they were very elegant and extremely reliable. He was also successful in various races for which he built steam cars with a streamlined body. In the 1901 Nice race he achieved a speed of 56 mph and only a year later 75 mph. Another vehicle, called 'Easter

236. A successful steam automobile constructed by the Stanley brothers in 1886, driven by a twin-cylinder engine of 6 hp

237. The Stanley Runabout family steam automobile of 1910

238. The Delling de luxe with a twin-cylinder high-pressure steam engine was manufactured in the United States up to 1927

Egg' because of its shape, reached a record speed of 82 mph, which remained unbeaten for a long time.

At that time the USA was already manufacturing and producing thousands of light steam vehicles with kerosene heating under the boilers. The American pioneer of steam tricycles was Lucius Copeland. His tricycles, built in 1884, had a boiler heated by coke. A miniaturised steam engine drove the wheels by friction gearing. The brothers F.E. and F.O. Stanley produced the largest number of steam

237
238

239

cars in the USA. From 1896 the boilers of their cars were, for safety reasons, wrapped in steel wires. A regulator controlled the kerosene fed to the burners so that steam pressure in the boiler could be controlled. The Locomobile Co., founded by the Stanley brothers, for many years manufactured popular light steam cars with an output of 14 — 28 hp. The car could start four minutes after ignition of the kerosene burners. The engines condensed the spent steam in a condenser and automatically pumped the water back to the boiler. The last Stanley car, the 1910 Runabout, is the pride of the Henry Ford museum.

Until 1927 the American Delling Motors Co. used to manufacture luxury steam cars, rather as a curiosity. Their price was 3,500 dollars. They were popular because of their noiseless operation. The last steam car to be manufactured in series production was the American Doble of 1931. The steam drive of these vehicles achieved a high level of technological perfection. Only two minutes after ignition of the burners the steam pressure reached an operating pressure. The vehicles had no clutch or gearbox and their service life was five times longer than that of petrol cars.

Renaissance of the steam car

In recent times, strict measures against air pollution caused by combustion engine exhausts centred attention once again on the steam car. Several years of experiments carried out by the Boston Thermo Electron company, subsidised by the General Motors and Ford companies, resulted in the construction of experimental high-pressure boiler steam cars. Electronically controlled oil burning reduced noxious combustion products to the minimum. In 100 hp cars the fuel consumption dropped to 35 mpg of oil. In their new six-seater steam car the

239. A racing steam car designed by the Australian Gene van Grecken and built by the Sydney Motor Show company in 1970

240. Harry Lawson and his wife in a Panhard and Levassor in front of the London Metropol at the start of the emancipation demonstration on November 14, 1896

American designers W. P. Lear and V. L. Minto use an engine with pistons arranged in a triangular configuration and water replaced by freon. Fifteen seconds after depressing the push-button igniting the burners the vehicle can start to move.

An Australian architect, Gene van Grecken, has constructed a sports car *GVANG* with a steam engine of 400 hp output at 3,500 rpm.

The research and development department of the Swedish Saab-Scania car factory is working on a revolutionary change in the design of the steam car. Their single-piston passenger car engine has an output of 280 hp and a weight of only 55 lb (Plate XXXVII). The boiler with 0·04-in diameter tubes delivers steam 5 seconds after ignition of the burners. Since the engine revolutions change continuously while running, the car is provided with another miniature steam engine driving the alternator, fuel pump and the boiler feed pump. In order to prevent the water circuit freezing in winter, an automatic installation activates the steam generator from time to time, even if the car is parked and without a driver. In an outdoor temperature of 0 °F, the fuel consumption necessary for this additional heating does not exceed 3½ pints of fuel for a one-month period when the car is not being used.

Work goes on and no-one should jump to the conclusion that steam cars are things of the past.

Development of cars in the early twentieth century

World museums and private collectors classify old cars in main categories according to the year of production.

The oldest and most valued cars come from the period before 1905, when the car started to take on its own identity and look less like a coach provided with an engine. Cars that were manufactured all over the world until the end of the First World War are classified as *veterans*. During this period it was France, Britain and Germany especially that contributed most to improved car design. The USA, however, led the way in producing a car capable of winning the world markets because of its low price. Cars from the period between 1919 and 1930 come into the *vintage* category, a period of the 'best years' of the car. At that time the car was recognised as a practical, reliable and efficient means of individual transport. Since 1930 — according to the thinking of the vintage period fans — car development has brought only efforts towards economies of manufacture to the detriment of car design.

Emancipation in England

The Motor Car Club decided to celebrate the repeal of the shameful 'Red Flag' Act by a demonstration of cars driving from London to Brighton, a distance of 53 miles. On 14 November 1896. 33 wreathed and festooned cars met in front of the London Metropole Hotel. At 10.30 Harry Lawson, the founder of the club, together with his wife, was the first to start in this historic procession, driving his heavy Panhard-Levassor. He was followed by a dozen other Panhards, by some Daimlers, by four Benz cars and by four light cars, the so-called *voiturettes* of Léon Bollée. They were accompanied by sundry electromobiles and steam cars, but the light *voitu-*

241

242

241. Peugeot's quadricycle of 1890 with a Daimler engine and a four-speed gearbox. The weight was 1,212 lb

242. The Canstatt-Daimler from 1889, power output 28 hp and a weight of 3,967 lb

243. The first Mercedes of 1901. Four-cylinder engine, 35 hp, weight 2,204 lb

rettes were the best performers and covered the distance to Brighton in less than four hours. Having overcome various difficulties, another ten cars reached Brighton before night fell. The rest could not make it, falling by the wayside for one reason or another. Except during the war years, this famous run has been organised regularly every year up to the present time. The Veteran Car Club of Great Britain has 2,000 members owning approximately the same number of carefully maintained 'old timers'.

The history of French cars

This begins with the successful car concept of Emile Levassor who died of injuries suffered during a race accident, one year after the emancipation demonstration in Britain. His company Panhard and Levassor developed the production of heavy cars with four-cylinder engines. The public, how-

ever, became gradually more interested in the light and economic *voiturettes* built since 1899 by De Dion and Bouton. Their water-cooled single-cylinder engines with an output of 8 hp were so reliable that fifty-one other manufacturers installed them in their cars. The *voiturettes* manufactured by Armand Peugeot also had a good reputation, and on a 750 mile run from Paris to Brest and back they maintained an average speed of 9 mph. Heavier types of Peugeot cars (Plate XXXVIII) were also well known for their reliability. In 1895 the mayor of the mountain town of Andermatt issued a certificate declaring that 'the Comte and Comtesse de Cognard, driving a Peugeot petrol car with its quadricycle engine, conquered the St. Gotthard Pass'. In 1897 A. Peugeot began series production of his cars in his two factories at Lille and Audincourt.

The history of Renault cars began in 1898 in the garden shed of the Renaults' home in Billancourt — carefully preserved to the present day. Among the 184 makes manufactured in France in 1900, Renaults very soon acquired a leading position. The 21-year-old Louis Renault improved a De Dion-Bouton tricycle by adding another road wheel and replacing its belt transmission with a three-speed gearbox provided with a reverse gear. In his light car, equipped with a 40-hp engine, Renault reached racing speeds of up to 78 mph. Later on, Renault introduced cars with lateral radiators. After the tragic death of his brother, who was killed in the 1903 Paris-Madrid race, Louis Renault gave up racing and went on improving the design of his cars. He provided them with sparking plugs that could be

244

dismantled, with hydraulic shock-absorbers and with a starter using compressed gas. In 1907 Renault began series production of roofed-in cars — *berlines* — used mainly as taxis. He also invented mileometers and fare counters for the taxis.

The history of German cars

After the death of G. Daimler in 1900, his son Paul, assisted by his father's long-time collaborator W. Maybach, went on developing the heavier Canstatt-Daimler car types. In 1901 the first representative of a classic, robust line of cars, called Mercedes—the Christian name of the daughter of the factory sales representative and future manager — left its workshops.

244. An Opel-Darracq from 1902. Single-cylinder engine of $8^1/_2$ hp and speed of 25—28 mph

245. The deluxe Berline Renault X of 1907. Four-cylinder engine, capacity 3,051 cc, power output 14 hp, weight 1,984 lb, speed 40·3 mph

245

The Mercedes with four broad pneumatic tyres and with a four-cylinder, 35-hp engine, weighed only 625 lb, only one half the weight of the Canstatt-Daimlers which had less powerful engines. It is worth mentioning here that in 1929 the two main German car manufacturers Daimler and Benz merged to form the Mercedes-Benz company which still plays a leading role in the technological development of European high class cars.

The very first Mercedes cars were famous for their outstanding reliability. Just before the start of the Gordon-Bennett race in 1903, the garage holding all the special Mercedes racing cars was destroyed by fire. So the drivers took part in the race driving production Mercedes models, not only finishing, but actually winning the race.

A year before, in 1902, another well-known German car factory was founded — that of Adam Opel at Rüsselsheim. Their first cars, manufactured under Darracq licence, were offered in four types and sold as Opel-Darracqs. A new feature was a convertible top. The gear lever was located under the steering wheel and the single-cylinder engine enabled a speed of 28 mph to be reached.

Thanks to German designers cars were further improved by Maybach carburettors and by a more advanced electric ignition system from Robert Bosch. In the town of Zwickau, mechanical engineer Horch began manufacturing noiseless gearboxes with gears in permanent mesh. He was also the first to use a propeller shaft.

246

247

246. A Renault from 1910, the type AX, with a twin-cylinder engine of 1,205 cc capacity, power output of 8·5 hp, and speed of 40·4 mph

247. The British Hutton sports car by Napier from 1908. Engine capacity was 5,900 cc

248. Henry Ford demonstrating his first quadricycle in 1892. The clutch was operated by a pressure roller on a belt.

The history of British cars

British engineers were not willing to copy the French light cars. From the very beginning they concentrated on the development of large-capacity engines, very successful in races. An early purely British car was the Napier. With S. F. Edge behind the wheel this car won the Gordon-Bennett Cup in 1902. Another outstanding British designer, Sir Herbert Austin, worked at first for the Wolseley company, and in 1900 his four-wheel *voiturette*

reached the finish of a 1,000-mile race without any difficulties. Shortly after this he founded the Austin Motor Company and by 1908 was offering 17 different models with engines from 14—50 hp. With his single-cylinder Austin Seven two-seater he opened the era of simple and inexpensive cars in Britain. Cars of this make were constantly improved. Various models were manufactured in different countries, inspired by the successful design of the 1922 Austin version.

F. W. Lanchester was a pioneer contributor to the development of British cars. His first designs from 1899 were characterised by torsion bar suspension and by magnetic needle ignition installed in his 10 hp engines.

The British Daimler company, founded in 1869, decided from the very beginning to manufacture expensive luxury cars. One of these Daimler cars was chosen by the king of England, Edward VII, to serve as his personal royal automobile. During further development, the British Daimler factory introduced the Knight valve which substantially increased the engine power output. Eventually the Daimler and Lanchester companies merged.

A car with a very reliable and silent engine was

249

250

249. Car bodies being assembled on their chassis — early mass-production introduced by Ford in 1912

250. One of the last Model-T Fords from 1927 — out of a series of more than 15 million

251. Opel's Laubfrosch, 1924. Four-stroke engine, 12 hp, with natural water circulation cooling and with pressure lubrication. Max. speed 43·5 mph

the outcome of the work of F. H. Royce in association with C. S. Rolls. In 1906 the two partners surprised the world with their Rolls-Royce Silver Ghost. By 1925, without any substantial modifications, 6,200 of these cars, with an elegant silver body and with an absolutely reliable SV 48-hp engine, had been manufactured for wealthy clients.

European pioneer motoring is not represented only by French, English and German makes. Among the other well-known names is the Fabbrica Italiana de Automobili Torino, founded in 1899 by Giovanni Agnelli with the co-operation of a group of wealthy car enthusiasts wishing to make Italy independent of foreign companies. The initials of this company — FIAT — are nowadays to be seen on millions of excellent cars.

In 1897, in the monarchy of Austria-Hungary, the car factory Tatra began the production of technically highly developed cars. In Spain the Hispano-Suiza make was born, and in Russia the first car factory was established in Riga in 1907.

Cars of that time were not yet provided with synchronised gearboxes. They were started by cranking a handle and brakes were usually applied on two wheels only. These technical drawbacks, however, did not constitute such an obstacle for their large-scale production as their relatively high price. This could be cut only by mass production. The first to implement this new type of car production was Henry Ford in the USA.

The history of American cars

The first car built by Henry Ford in 1896 in his small, rented workshop in Detroit, looked like a farm cart. A double-cylinder petrol engine with an output of approximately 4 hp drove a countershaft by means of a belt, and the countershaft, in turn, drove the rear wheels by means of a chain — as in the case of the Benz tricycle. Speeds between 10 and 20 mph could be achieved by shifting the belt. As a young university graduate Ford began his career as a driver, winning several races. Thanks to their racing performance the Ford cars acquired a very good name, which helped the cars manufactured by the Ford Motor Company in the reconstructed Detroit wagon works. When he had successfully sold 8,500 Model Bs, Ford extended his factory, ensuring at the same time a first-class service for his clients. Ford continued to develop his models and in October 1908 presented his Model T — the legendary Tin Lizzie. According to legend, the customer could choose any colour he liked for his car, provided it was black! With an engine capacity of 2,892 cc and with an output of 20 hp, the car was light, reliable and satisfactory even in the most difficult off-the-road conditions American farmers had to contend with. It had an epicyclic gear and instead of having a gear lever, was controlled only by pedals. This car was manufactured on an assembly line. In the final assembly line sector completely equipped bodies passed along an inclined platform onto chassis already equipped with an engine. Gradually Ford began to manufacture his own sheet steel and pneumatic tyres, founded his own glass works, and with the rationalisation of his production methods was able to cut down the price of the Model T to 500 dollars. By 1927, when production stopped, 15,007,033 Model T cars, without any major change being made to the original specification, had left the assembly lines.

The establishment of another major car company — the General Motors — was organised by an extremely capable financier, W. C. Durant, who

252

252. The Dixi-mobil, type DA-1, manufactured in 1928 in the Wartburg car factory in Eisenach under licence from the Austin company. Power output 16 hp, speed 46·6 mph, weight only 826 lb

253. The instrument panel with the steering wheel and gear lever of a car of the early 1930s

253

brought several smaller manufacturers together to form a big company. The most important assets of the company were F. Olds (Oldsmobile), H. Leland (Cadillac) and L. Chevrolet. Thanks to Durant the latter succeeded in cutting down the price of the popular Chevrolet to 490 dollars. After the First World War Ford and General Motors achieved an annual peak production of 5 million cars which was more than the total car production of · all other countries combined.

Development of cars from 1919—1939

The USA led Europe not only in mass production technology, but also in many of the technical innovations. With only a short delay, however, all the basic American developments soon appeared in the European car factories as well.

In the years 1919—1925 cars began to be equipped with brakes applied to all four wheels. W. P. Chrysler, whose achievements in the field of car development allowed him to found the third major American car company, introduced his concept of hydraulically-controlled brakes. By combining balloon tyres with lever-type dampers (shock absorbers) and subsequently hydraulic dampers, the ride became much softer and smoother. Competition also led to improvements in the surface protection

254. Rumpler's streamlined car from 1921

of bodywork. In the USA in 1924, Du Pont was the first to introduce nitrocellulose lacquer spraying. Instead of using the traditional nickel plating for radiator grilles and other external embellishments, Oldsmobile introduced chromium plating for these parts. Cadillacs were provided with panoramic splinter-proof glass windows.

Electricity found an ever-increasing field of application. R. Bosch, who had introduced high-voltage ignition in European cars, installed the first horn, in 1921, but the electric windscreen wiper only appeared in 1935, as did the first car radio.

'A car for the poor and a car for the millionaire': this wording could best express car availability in the 1930s. At the lowest level were the German Phänomobil tricycles with the front wheels driven by an air-cooled engine and an output of 8 hp, or the small Hanomags, output 10 hp, christened with the derisory nickname of 'Kommisbrot' (war bread).

Other predecessors of good quality, cheap popular cars were the British Austin Seven with an engine capacity of 747 cc — manufactured in Germany under licence as the BMW-Dixi — or the economic Opel Laufbrosch, with a petrol consumption of only 56 mpg.

Cars of larger engine capacities and luxury equipment included a range from Mercedes and Rolls-Royce in Europe, and American super de luxe cars such as Stutz, Pierce-Arrow and Duesenberg (Plate

XL). This last has even now hardly been matched in many respects. For instance, each of the 650 Duesenbergs manufactured had an interior arranged according to the individual wishes of the prospective owners. The eight-cylinder engine, with a capacity of 6,882 cc, had an output of 260 hp. The car had an automatic system of tyre inflation and its instrument panel looked like that of new era aircraft cockpits. Correct functioning of the engine was indicated by a series of warning lights. The car became an object of awe and admiration even on the part of authorities. Owners were not 'harassed' by police even for breaches of road traffic regulations.

Efforts to build a streamlined car to reduce air resistance at higher speeds had been made since 1913 when, in Italy, an Alfa-Romeo chassis with an engine of 30 hp was provided with a body shaped like a rain-drop. Dr. Rumpler in Germany used a similar shape in his experimental car in 1921. Ten years later a streamlined car with a totally smooth body and rear-mounted 80 hp engine was produced by the British airship designer D. Burney. At the same time (1932—33) an American architect,

255. Ledwinka's streamlined Tatra V-570 with the rear axle driven by an air-cooled four-cylinder engine

256. The two-door Opel Kadett limousine from 1936. Engine capacity 1,066 cc, power output 25 hp, rigid steel sheet body, max. speed 61 mph

256

257. The Citroen 2 CV from the 1930s, with a single headlight and water-cooled engine, was called 'the ugliest car in the world'

258. The two-door 1950 VW Beetle, with a sunshine roof

B. Fuller, demonstrated a three-wheel streamlined Dymaxion car, the first in the world designed with safety mainly in mind.

A more sober, and for the future development of cars a more important, streamlined concept was proposed in 1934 by Ledwinka, senior designer of the Tatra company. He demonstrated his idea in the Tatra V-570 car. His chassis frame-cum-body with an inclined back was supported by a tube structure. Located at the rear was either an air-cooled V8 or flat four-cylinder engine with rear axle drive.

Development of European popular cars

An efficient assembly line became the main prerequisite of cheap popular car production. The first company to implement it in Europe was Opel of Germany. By 1940 the Rüsselsheim assembly lines of the company had manufactured millions of cars —mainly the constantly developed models Olympia, Kadett, Kapitän and Admiral.

In the mid-1930s the mechanical engineer Ferdinand Porsche, a German designer of some 350 dif-

259. Three different Studebaker models from the time shortly after the Second World War

260. The Peugeot 104 engine of 1975. A transverse four-cylinder unit, it incorporates the clutch, gearbox and final drive to the front wheels. The wheels have independent suspension and are provided with disc brakes

ferent models, was commissioned to develop a popular car. The outcome was the legendary 'Käfer' (Beetle) of the Volkswagen (VW) company with an air-cooled flat-four cylinder engine. In its basic version this had a capacity of 1,200 cc, running at low revolutions (the maximum being 3,000 rpm) and was outstanding for its smooth and flexible running and for its long service life even if used in rough conditions or on motorways. As soon as production had been set up, the Second World War broke out, and the assembly lines in the reconstructed Wolfsburg factory only started to produce cars after 1948. On 12 February 1972, the Volkswagen Beetle broke the existing Ford Model T world record output of 15,007,033 cars. By 1977, when their production in Europe was discontinued, more than 19 million Beetles had left the factory. The Beetle had become the most popular car in the history of the automobile.

In France the production of the popular car was pioneered by A. Citroën. Designed just before the outbreak of the Second World War, the 2 CV with front-wheel drive, acquired tremendous popularity. Because of its simple body made of profiled metal sheet it was given the nickname 'The Ugly Duckling'. With a special suspension system incorporating swivelling arms, this cheap automobile could offer unusual comfort for its size. According to its publicity it was the only car that could carry a basket of eggs over rough country without breaking any. The original flat-twin cylinder, 375 cc engine, with an output of only 8 hp, was replaced after the war by a 425 cc capacity engine, with double the power output. Because of the sound basic design the car is manufactured even today—in a modified version—as the 2CV4 model.

The companies Renault, Morris and Fiat also played their part in the mass-production of popular cars. Developments in Europe included engines at the rear and front-wheel drive. Generally speaking the cars were small or of medium size and totally distinct from those of America. The Americans preferred big cars with engines from 130—260 hp.

Present-day passenger cars

The millions of cars on the roads of the world present such a large range of makes, types, powers and comfort that only the basic concept remains common. Most cars have a body; all have brakes and steerable front wheels. All cars have an engine and a gearbox, sometimes automatic. The engine can be located at the front, at the rear or in the middle and can be water or air cooled. Developments of refinements of these basics continue from year to year.

The car engine: Since its conception over a hundred years ago, the car engine has changed so much that neither Otto, Benz nor Daimler would recognise it today. More than 97 per cent of car engines work on the four-stroke cycle. The most widely used is the water-cooled four-cylinder unit; the eight-cylinder 'V' configuration is used mainly in America. In small cars flat engines with horizontally-opposed cylinders are the ideal solution, since they can be easily located under the car's floor.

The engine, with the clutch and gearbox, are usually mounted together and are made of cast iron or light alloys, or a combination of the two. The combustion chamber of the engine has been the subject of much scientific study to determine the best combination of efficient yet economic combustion and the most effective design of the ports. Compression ratios have gone through many changes. The tendency towards gradual increase was halted because the necessary fuels increased air pollution. Nowadays compression ratios vary between 8·5 and 9·5, making possible the use of petrol with-

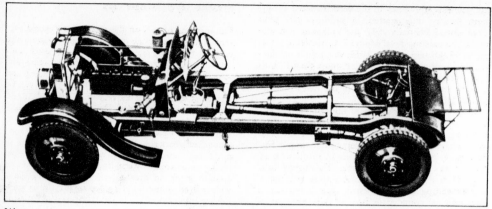

261

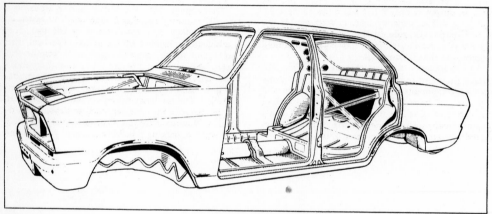

262

out noxious lead additives. In most engines the piston stroke is now less than the cylinder diameter; this has allowed an increase in engine speed to nearly 6,000 rpm for an average car, and to 8,000 rpm and more in sports cars. The present-day 1,000-cc engine yields a nominal output of 40—50 hp. Because of developments in drive design, overhead camshaft (OHC) valve gear—with its more accurate valve control—has now largely superseded the earlier side-valve (SV) and overhead-valve (OHV) designs. Multi-stage carburettors have also reached the limits of development, and are beginning to be replaced by fuel injection pumps. The role of the dynamo (dc generator) has been largely taken over by the smaller and more efficient alternator (ac generator). Ignition is provided by contactless thyristor or transistor systems with pulse control of electric discharges. The development of new materials and of heat-treatment processes allows the production of pistons, rings, connecting rods and

bearings of such a quality that an engine — with minimum maintenance — can cover 75,000—100,000 miles without a major overhaul.

A four-cylinder 1,300-cc engine averaging about 28 mpg, in one hour has to:
— open the distributor contacts 440,000 times;
— turn the camshaft 110,000 times;
— stop the pistons and set them in motion 440,000 times;
— circulate 8,800 pints of coolant by means of the water pump;
— force 264 pints of oil into the bearings by means of the oil pump;
— draw in 6,350 cu ft of air through its filter.
In motion, the wheels of the car would make 57,000 full revolutions.

Traditional petrol engines use an uneconomic reciprocating motion. Efforts to find an alternative are as old as the history of the engine itself, but only one solution to the quest for lighter and more effi-

261. A typical car chassis of 1930

262. A chassis-frame-cum-body of the present-day automobile

263. The Volkswagen Polo hatchback with three doors. An 895 cc engine gives 40 hp and a maximum speed of 82 mph

cient engines has been applied, at least in a limited way, in production. This is the Wankel engine with a rotating triangular piston developed by Felix Wankel. Its production was initiated in 1963 by the German NSU company. This piston turns in a chamber of a shape resembling the figure eight, and compression and expansion of the mixture takes place as in a conventional engine. Turning motion of the piston is transmitted to an eccentric shaft. In comparison with a conventional four-cylinder unit of the same power, the Wankel engine weighs about half as much. Its exterior dimensions are substantially smaller and it has only 60 per cent as many components and parts. Development of multi-rotor Wankel engines in Europe, USA and Japan was adversely affected and slowed down by the recent fuel crisis, for on average these engines have a consumption approximately 30 per cent more than that of reciprocating engines of the same power output.

The possibilities of the slow-revolution Stirling heat engine are under study as well. The advantage of this engine should be a more effective use of low octane fuel and much less air pollution from the exhaust gasses.

Front or rear drive?: The classical automobile concept of an engine at the front and rear wheel drive effected by a connecting propeller shaft appeared in the very first cars. The best-known exam-

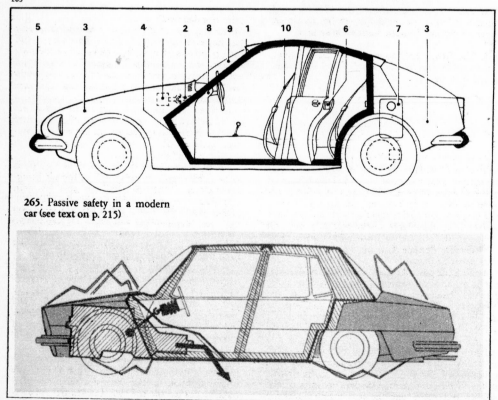

5   3   4   2   8   9   1   10   6   7   3

265. Passive safety in a modern car (see text on p. 215)

264. The Austin 1800, six-cylinder OHV engine, capacity 1,798 cc, power output 85 hp, maximum speed 96 mph, hydrolastic suspension system

266. The Rover 2200 four-cylinder OHC engine, capacity 2,204 cc, giving 100 hp and maximum speed of 99·4 mph

ple was Ford's Model T. This conception still prevails in most medium-sized and bigger cars, because it distributes the weight of the car between the front and rear axles. In exceptional cases, in order to ensure an even better-balanced weight distribution, the gearbox, sometimes together with the clutch, is moved from the engine to the rear axle. Such an arrangement can be found—among present-day cars—in the Porsche 924, the Volvo 343 and the Alfa Romeo Alfetta.

During the post-war years, mainly in smaller cars, the location of the engine at the rear became quite popular. Examples of this arrangement are the Volkswagen Beetle, Renault R8, Fiat 126 and the Simca 1000. In larger cars, the rear engine layout was applied in the Czechoslovak Tatra 603 and to the American Chevrolet Corvair—to give just two examples. The propeller shaft is no longer needed in this system and the drive, direct to the rear axle, is simplified. On the other hand the concentration of the weight towards the rear does not improve the ride characteristics, and the rear engine limits the boot space and does not allow the now popular third rear door to be used.

The location of the engine near the drive axle has, however, so many advantages, that the trend of the car drive system development led to the only rational solution, front-wheel drive. This conception was applied both before and after the Second World War in small cars with a two-stroke engine, in cars such as the Citroën and Auburn Cord. Nowadays, in order to reduce the length of the front part of the car as well as its height, the engine is sometimes positioned transversely across the car and is, moreover, inclined. This solution has been applied in many small and medium-sized cars.

Another layout used in some sports two-seaters is to have the engine in the middle of the car, bringing it closer to the rear axle. This does, however, limit passenger space. Examples are the Fiat X'/₉, Ferrari Dino, De Tomaso Panthera, Matra Simca Bagheera, Maserati, and most of the Lamborghini cars.

Development of the body: Before the Second World War, car bodies were usually mounted on a steel chassis. In the post-war period integral chassis-frame body types became prevalent. Pressed-steel sheet construction ensured the necessary rigidity while reducing weight substantially. The present-day body has the maximum space for driver and passengers, a roomy boot with easy access, all combined with easy production and maintenance.

During the last 15 years for sports and fast touring cars the so-called 'fastback' has gained popularity, mainly because of its sporty look. One of the first applications of this idea in a series-manufactured tourist car was the 1955 Citroën DS. An ever-

267

267. The Renault 16TS, front-wheel drive, OHC engine, 1,565 cc capacity giving 85 hp and a maximum speed of 99·4

268. The Fiat Polski 125 is an example of international cooperation of the Fiat Works. An adaptation of Fiat 124, it has four-cylinder OHV engine, capacity 1,295 cc, power output 60 hp, consumption 28 UK gal/hr.

widening knowledge of aerodynamics together with increasing requirements for multi-purpose bodies led to fastback bodies being used even for small family cars. With it the body can be wider at the rear, and rear visibility substantially better. At the back a transverse door allows good access to the luggage space often in one with the passenger compartment. Thus two-door cars became three-door ones and cars with four doors have been transformed into ones with five doors. This type of body is also called a 'hatchback'.

In cities the car has been increasingly restricted in use by lack of parking space. As a result, interest centred on cars with a large internal capacity but with external dimensions as small as possible. Inspired by these requirements, Alec Issigonis (now Sir), a designer with the British Motor Corporation (now BL Cars Ltd), introduced his totally unconventional Mini car in 1959, which marked a turning point in the history of small cars. He characterised his product with the following words: 'Just take four passengers, add the necessary luggage and the engine and the gear system, and arrange in such a way as to keep the ground plan as restricted as possible. Put the four wheels on the corners so that they are out of the way and at the same time guarantee the best possible stability and the necessary suspension. Wrap the whole thing with a body as

268

XXXVI The first series-manufactured electric moped, the *Solo-electra,* weighing 147 lb including two batteries, each of 66 lb. Max. speed 15 mph, 25-mile range per charge *(Solo-Kleinmotoren GmbH)*

XXXVII The prototype of a clean, noiseless and economic automobile steam engine by the Swedish Saab Co. Output 280 hp *(Saab-Scania)*

XXXVIII Peugeot's quadricycle of 1894 with a chain drive to the rear wheels and a tubular chassis. The wire-spoked wheels ran on ball bearings

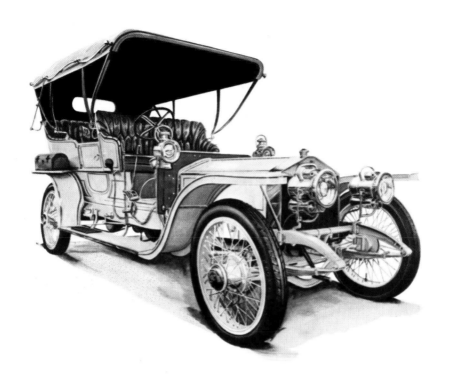

XXXIX The Rolls-Royce Silver Ghost of 1907 *(drawing by V. Zapadlík)*

XL De Luxe American Duesenberg, type J, of 1931, with a 260 hp engine

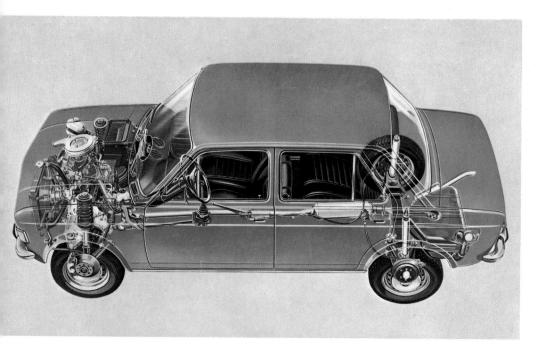

XLI An X-ray picture of Fiat 128 of 1969 with a transverse four-cylinder OHC engine. Capacity 1,116 cc, power output 55 hp, weight 1,697 lb, maximum speed 83 mph

XLII A 1975 Renault 17 TL. Engine capacity 1,565 cc, maximum power output 90 hp, maximum speed 105 mph

269. The Audi-NSU Ro80 has a Wankel engine. Maximum speed 110 mph, acceleration from 0 to 60 mph in 13·1 sec.

270. The twin-chamber Wankel engine used in the Audi-NSU Ro80. Capacity per rotor 497·5 cc (equivalent to 1,990 cc piston engine), power output 115 hp at 5,500 rpm, compression ratio 9 : 1

compact as possible.' The Mini became the first of a new series of popular cars that have since been continually developed and improved. Recent evolution has led from the Autobianchi, the small Fiat 127 and Fiat 128, the Peugeot 104, the Japanese Datsun Cherry, the French Simca 1100 and others to the new generation Volkswagens — the Polo and Scirocco — and even the rather larger Ford Fiesta really belongs to the same family. The success of the original Mini has been emphasised by the fact that even after 15 years of production it was taken over and further improved by the body-designing company of Bertone in the form of the Italian Innocenti Mini 90/120 (Plate XLIII).

Multi-purpose bodies have found favour for medium-sized cars, examples being the Renault 16 of 1964, and the Simca 1307/1308.

The fastback type is sometimes designed without a rear door, as in the Citroën GS, Alfasud, Austin Allegro, Leyland Princess, etc. The more traditional rear styling maintains its position mainly in luxury cars, but even here the new model Citroën CX, Renault 30T and others show that its position is not secure even there.

Development of the safe car: Designers are trying to provide their cars with properties reducing the risk of an accident to the minimum. This can be achieved mainly by: suitable weight distribution between the front and rear axles, reliable steering, suspension and damping, efficient and easily controlled brakes and sound tyre design. This set of requirements called active car safety can be augmented by easy manipulation of all controls, by a good driving view, good lighting of the road at night, by noise elimination, correct ventilation and heating and by a number of other measures.

It goes without saying that accidents cannot always be prevented as driver error is always possible.

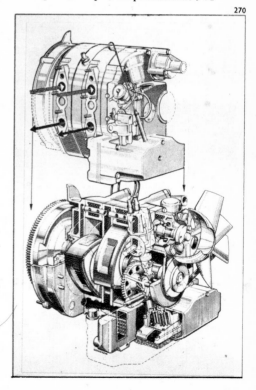

271

271. The Peugeot 504, OHV engine, capacity 1,796 cc, power output 80 hp, maximum speed 96·9 mph, Pininfarina body

272. The Citroën GS-X, engine capacity 1,015 cc, power output 55 hp, maximum speed 92 mph

273. The Fiat 127 with transverse four-cylinder OHV engine at the front, capacity 903 cc, power output 47 hp, maximum speed 87 mph

274. The Audi 80, OHV engine, capacity 1,496 cc, power output 80 hp maximum speed 93·2 mph

272

273

274

However, if they do occur, damage to the car's occupants should be minimised. Problems associated with this belong to the field of passive car safety, concentrating on making the interior of the car safe. As a start, all the edges of instrument panels and doors were rounded off and provided with a soft, incombustible coating. A number of safety steering wheels were developed. They were telescopic or used other systems to reduce injury to the driver's body. Safety belts have become routine equipment for drivers and front passengers at least. In some countries their use is mandatory.

Over recent years requirements in certain countries have become even stricter and designers have started to use the actual body of the car to protect the passengers. Its front and back sections form 'safety zones' capable of progressive deformation under impact. In case of a front or lateral impact they absorb the major part of the vehicle's kinetic energy and are effective provided that passengers are wearing seat belts. Passenger compartment construction must be rigid and solid enough to offer passengers the maximum protection and one safety programme carries out impact testing at speeds of up to 30 mph and also on the strength of the body when a car overturns. Special testing stations using the so-called destruction tests check that these conditions are maintained. The best-known of these tests is the barrier test when a car hits a concrete block at a speed of 30 mph.

There are ten items capable of further improvement for the passive safety of a modern car passenger (picture 265):

1. Passenger compartment rigidity
2. Telescopic or collapsible steering wheels
3. Front and back body deformation zones
4. A partition preventing the engine from penetrating into the cabin even on maximum impact

5. Safety bumpers
6. Safety locks preventing the doors from opening during impact
7. Fuel tanks protected from damage
8. Soft upholstery and rounded-off edges, especially those of the instrument panel and in the front part of the passenger compartment
9. Laminated safety glass for the windscreen
10. Safety belts.

American cars of today: In the USA 90 per cent of city transport and 70 per cent of the total transport to work is carried out in cars. There is one car per two inhabitants, but this ratio continues to increase. The three main American car companies — General Motors, Ford and Chrysler — are the biggest car manufacturers in the world. Three-fifths of all the cars in the world run in the USA. Seen through the eyes of a European, many American cars from the mid-1970s are uneconomic giant cruisers with an engine capacity of 4 to 6 litres, sometimes even more. The two-ton monsters average only 14 mpg. They are equipped with air-conditioning and automatic gearboxes. Windows are lowered, doors opened and seats tilted electrically. The American citizen often uses his car for drive-in lunches and dinners and to go to the drive-in cinema. With their broad windows American cars are ideal for touring. Models are modified every year, at least in details. For VIPs it is often a matter of prestige to own the latest model. Thanks to mass, fully-automated car production the American car is relatively cheap and good service garages can be found all over the country. However, competition from smaller European and Japanese cars and especially the oil crisis from the years 1972—75 had such a decisive influence that radical re-thinking was called for. The production of small cars, the 'compacts' and later on 'subcompacts', began. In 1976 the largest American car manufacturer, General Motors, initiated the produc-

275

275. The Mercedes 450SE, eight-cylinder OHC engine, capacity 4,520 cc, power output 225 hp, maximum speed 130·5 mph

276. The single-arm steering wheel of the Citroën CX2000 is as remarkable as its digital tachometer and other well-arranged controls

277. The Citroën CX2000, four-cylinder OHV engine, capacity 1,985 cc, power output 102 hp, maximum speed 108 mph, acceleration from 0 to 60 mph in 11·9 secs.

276

277

278. The Simca 130GLS, engine capacity 1,294 cc, power output 80 hp, maximum speed 96 mph, acceleration from 0 to 60 mph in 16·8 sec

279. The ten biggest car manufacturers in the world. (Figures in millions of units manufactured in 1974)

tion of a really small car, the Chevrolet Chevette, based on the conception of the Opel Kadett and Vauxhall Chevette. In the same period Ford relied only on the import of its smallest Fiesta from its European branch factory, while Chrysler prepared a version of the Simca 1308 for the American market.

279

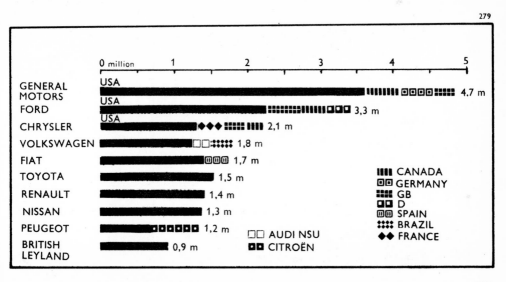

	0 million	1	2	3	4	5
GENERAL MOTORS	USA ████████████████████████████ IIIIIII ⊡⊡⊡⊡ :::::: 4.7 m
FORD	USA ████████████ :::::::::IIIIII⊡⊡⊡ 3.3 m
CHRYSLER	USA ███████◆◆◆ :::: IIII 2.1 m
VOLKSWAGEN	██████□□:::::: 1.8 m
FIAT	██████▥▥▥▥ 1.7 m
TOYOTA	█████ 1.5 m
RENAULT	█████ 1.4 m
NISSAN	████ 1.3 m
PEUGEOT	████⊡⊡⊡⊡⊡⊡ 1.2 m
BRITISH LEYLAND	███ 0.9 m

IIII CANADA
⊡⊡ GERMANY
:::: GB
⊡⊡ D
▥▥ SPAIN
:::: BRAZIL
◆◆ FRANCE

□□ AUDI NSU
⊡⊡ CITROËN

280
281

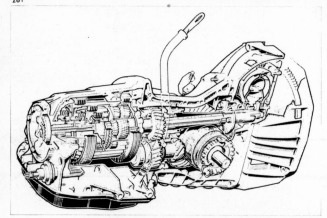

280. The Ford Capri II, sports four-seater produced with five sizes of engine, from a four-cylinder one of 1,298 cc, to a V six-cylinder of 2,994 cc

281. The automatic gearbox of the Renault 30TS

282. Renault 30TS, six-cylinder OHC engine, capacity 2,664 cc, power output 130 hp at 5,500 rpm, maximum speed 112 mph, acceleration from 0 to 60 mph in 9·2 sec

283. The engine compartment under the traditional Mercedes bonnet

282

284

284. Saab 99EMS, four-cylinder OHC engine, capacity 1,985 cc, power output 115 hp at 5,500 rpm (with Bosch mechanical fuel injection), maximum speed 106 mph, acceleration from 0 to 60 mph in 10·6 sec

285. The most expensive car in the world, the Rolls-Royce Camargue. V-8 engine, capacity 6,750 cc, power output 230 hp, maximum speed 114 mph

European cars today: There are several categories of these. Luxury cars are manufactured only in very small quantities, and consequently are very expensive. In 1976 the choice was between models from Rolls-Royce or Mercedes-Benz or companies such as Lamborghini producing luxury cars with sports-car performance.

A driver looking for high performance would consider, for instance, one of the Porsche models, the Ferrari, or one of the other more exotic high-performance cars mentioned later.

285

There are also a number of manufacturers of utility vehicles, notably BL Cars Ltd with its Land Rover and Range Rover models.

The largest investment in Europe and in Japan (which began building its car industry only after the Second World War and within 25 years managed to get ahead of Europe in car production) centres on the family car. In their struggle for sales many car factories have merged. In recent years the Citroën and Peugeot companies joined forces in France, NSU, Audi and VW in Germany, BMC and Leyland

286. A car for all types of terrain—the Range Rover—with four-wheel drive. V-8 engine, capacity 3,528 cc, power output 155 hp, maximum speed 99·4 mph

287. The Volvo 245DL, engine capacity 2,127 cc, power output 120 hp, maximum speed 99·4 mph

288

289

in England, the Dutch DAF with the Swedish Volvo company, etc. The original differences among smaller car makes, and even among medium-sized cars, continues to diminish as a result. Modular cars are being created, among them the new generation of VW, Mercedes-Benz, Simca, Renault, Fiat, etc. In one type a series of three to five engines with different capacities and power outputs can be fitted. Thus Simca has a basic engine type which is manufactured in capacities of 944 cc, 1,118 cc, 1,294 cc and 1,442 cc with the use of common production equipment. These engines can be installed in cars with front or rear drive. All of which results in holding down car price increases to some extent and easier servicing.

Most of the smallest family cars of whatever make are very similar in appearance. There tend to be variations only in the arrangement of the radiator grille, of the headlights and of the parking and tail lights.

The Car of the Year: This is an important competition. Since 1963 an international jury of specialised journalists has been electing yearly the best new car. Criteria are the greatest advances in safety, economy, advanced design and value in relation to the price. Production models bear the symbol of the competition with an indication of the year when they were chosen. At first a bevel gear served as a symbol; recently it has been replaced by six valves in the colours of the countries of the organising magazines.

CAR OF THE YEAR (1963—1977)

1963 Rover 2000

1964 Austin 1800

1965 Renault 16

1966 Fiat 124

1967 NSU Ro80

1968 Peugeot 504

1969 Fiat 128

1970 Citroën GS

1971 Fiat 127

1972 Audi 80

1973 Mercedes Benz 450

1974 Citroën CX

1975 Simca 1307/1308

1976 Rover 3500

1977 Porsche 928

288. Ford's Pick-up Ranger of 1975, carrying capacity 1·5 tons

289. An American hardtop sedan, the Oldsmobile Colonnade, with rectangular headlights and special safety bumpers

290. Chevrolet's Chevette economy design was imposed by the energy crisis. The hatchback coupe with a four-cylinder engine, has a capacity of 1,400 cc

291. This Ford layout of the steering wheel, instrument panel and arched lever for automatic gear change is called the 'Flight Cockpit'

292. The Chrysler New Yorker Brougham, eight-cylinder OHV engine, capacity 7,206 cc, power output 335 hp, maximum speed 118 mph

293. One of the most streamlined cars in the world—the Studio Cr 25. Doors are opened electrically by pushing a button

Beautiful car bodies

Bodies of modern sports cars are no longer a product of the thinking of engineers and technical designers only. Artist-designers are also employed. In their studios the general outline of the car is decided, and the interior of the car is designed to follow this. The most famous body designers of the present time come from Italy and the most outstanding among them are Giugiaro, Bertone, Michelotti, de Tomaso and Frua. One of the greatest of

Italian body designers was Pininfarina, who died in 1966. The second largest Italian body design studio still bears his name.

Pininfarina was the originator of the fastback used as early as 1946 in the Cisitalia car built on a Fiat 1100S chassis. The best known of Pininfarina's designs were for bodies of *GT* cars, made by Lancia, Alfa-Romeo and Ferrari. In Pininfarina's wind tunnel the most streamlined car in the world, the Studio Cr 25, was built on a Ferrari chassis. In this case the coefficient of longitudinal air flow re-

294. Bertone's Stratos is driven by a V-8 engine, with an output of 275 hp, cross-positioned in front of the rear axle. Maximum speed 149·1 mph

295. This Giugiaro-designed body of the Audi Asso Karmann has been conceived with mass production in mind

sistance was reduced to the value of 0.256. In practice this means that air current burbling never took place. The surface of the body as well as the bottom of the car was absolutely smooth, doors and windows had no projecting handles and were opened electromagnetically. The front bumper was conceived as a streamlined surface with wing spoilers, whose function was to keep the nose of the car firmly on the road for better control. In addition two lateral flaps assisted braking at very high speeds. The circumference of the car was protected by a strip of plastic rubber. The air-conditioned interior, designed according to strict safety criteria, had an instrument panel of soft material with digital indication of the power output, rpm and speed displayed by luminous figures. Just as a famous artist signs his paintings, the creations of famous body

designers bear their symbol: Pininfarina's works can be identified by the letter 'f' in a rectangle with a royal crown at the top.

Another successful body designer, Bertone, made his name with the Lancia-Stratos, and with the wedge-like body and large windows of the Lamborghini Bravo. Another of his designs, the Lamborghini Countach is shown in Plate XLVII. This has a V12 3,939 cc engine of 380 hp. In fifth gear and at 8,000 rpm this car can achieve a claimed speed of 197 mph. The girder frame is welded from special tubes and covered by aluminium and laminated panels. Bertone's three-litre Ferrari Dino 308 GT4 (Plate XLVD), designed for the USA and not quite so fast, has a four camshaft V-8 engine and an output of 260 hp. It reaches 150 mph.

Most of the 36 Italian designers and body studios

work only for specific car factories. For example, Fiore works for Ford and designs the big American 'cruisers'. His studio provided the shape for the new generation Ford Capri, for the Granada and the American Monarch.

G. Giugiaro founded the Ital Design studio. For his designs he uses as a rule technologies and techniques aimed at series production. For instance the VW Scirocco, Passat and Golf are now in mass-production.

Curiosities, racing and record cars

No other means of transport has had so many and varied shapes as the passenger car. Three or four wheels built in a frame and driven by an engine can support any kind of superstructure.

Some constructors put under the bonnets of vintage replicas eight to 12-cylinder engines with an output of two or three hundred hp. Others build replica bodies of the most expensive luxury cars of the past on mass-produced chassis parts. Eccentric expressions of individuality manifest themselves in inscriptions and strange colour schemes.

296. The Lincoln Continental Executive Presidential car of 1968

297. Prototype of an urban glass automobile from the Kangol Magnet company. Driven by electricity or by an internal-combustion engine

297

298

298. An amphibious run-about vehicle, the Attex. Weight 4,491 lb, power output 20 hp, maximum speed on the ground 34·8 mph, in the water 4 mph

299. A flying automobile from America, the 1976 Aerocar

299

XLIII The economical five-seater Leyland-Innocenti Mini 120. Engine capacity 1,275 cc, power output 65 hp, maximum speed 93 mph. Body is by Bertone

XLIV A 1975 American Ford Brougham with six seats, equipped with an eight-cylinder OHV engine, capacity 6,955 cc and power output of 390 hp. Weight 4,188 lb, maximum speed 136 mph

XLV The latest MPG model of the Ford Mustang II five-seater has an exceptionally low fuel consumption

XLVI The Ferrari Dino 308 GT4 with two to four seats, body by Bertone, engine a V8 with power output of 255 hp. Weight 2,534 lb, maximum speed 155 mph

XLVII A sports two-seater Lamborghini Countach LP 400, driven by a twelve-cylinder engine of 375 hp located in the middle of the car. It has a wedge-shaped body and the doors open upwards, operated by a hydropneumatic system. Maximum speed is 186 mph

XLVIII A Mercedes-Benz O 303 coach, power output 260 hp, dead weight 14 tons, maximum speed 87 mph, designed for 49 passengers

'Wild cars' are popular mainly in the USA and there are many Wild Car clubs and meetings. 'Dune-buggies' compete in short races or in thousand-mile treks through the wildest country such as can be found in Mexico. Copies of old cars with hotted-up engines, the so-called 'hot-rods', compete on race tracks. Also popular are the dramatic spring races of the 'dragsters'. These cars are built with a long frame with giant wheels at the rear and small, light-weight front wheels. The supercharged engines have a power output of up to 2,000 hp. Before the start the drivers heat the surface of the back tyres to 212°F by quick starting and braking and mechanics pour a solution of nitric acid over the tyres to increase their adhesion. By releasing the clutch at full engine revs the drivers, in asbestos overalls, are launched, rocket-like, and reach the finish about $1/4$ mile away in 5 to 6 seconds. Some cars at the finish reach 310 mph and have to brake by means of a parachute. Sometimes, the dragster overturns at the start, or falls to pieces under the tremendous strain of the extreme acceleration.

The car industry also has its own curiosities. The longest passenger car was the Bugatti Royale 41. The first of the six cars made was built in 1927 and was 22 ft long.

The widest commercially available passenger car is the Soviet de luxe ZIL 114. Its width is 7 ft.

The most expensive and the safest car is that used by the President of the United States, a 1968 Lincoln Continental Executive. It is 21 ft long, weighs $5^1/_2$ tons, 1 ton of its weight being the bulletproof glass. It is air-conditioned and is provided with transmitters and loudspeakers for Presidential speeches. Even if all the pneumatic tyres were punctured, the car could continue running at a speed of 50 mph on interior steel discs with a rubber lining. The output of the engine is 500 hp and the production costs were estimated at half a million dollars.

The most expensive series-manufactured car is the Rolls-Royce Camargue. Its May 1978 price was £ 47,367, equivalent to 23 Volkswagen Polos.

The most luxurious car was ordered by an Arab sheik from the English Panther West Winds company. The body, upholstered in mink, has a club interior including a bar with a refrigerator and a TV set. In the back there is a special place for the sheik's personal guard and a machine gun is mounted on the roof. A glass automobile for city traffic with alternative internal combustion or electric power system has been conceived by the British Kangol Magnet Ltd.

All Terrain Vehicles (ATV) have developed in the USA from small open 'dune-buggies', designed for pleasure riding on sandy beaches. The present-day vehicles of this type are usually manufactured with six low-pressure balloon tyres that are all driven, steerable and also replace normal suspension. The most popular ATVs—the Attex cars—have a body of laminated glass and engines of 7—25 hp. On level ground they can achieve a speed of nearly 40 mph, and in soft swampy terrain their speed is reduced approximately by half. In the water, where

300. The Formula 1 Ferrari 312 T which opened the way for Niki Lauda to win the 1975 world championship

301

301. The record-breaking *Green Monster*. The thrust of the jet engine corresponds to an output of 16,000 hp

302. Another record-breaker, the *Wingfoot Express* tricycle

they are propelled solely by the turning of the wheels, they reach a maximum speed of 4 mph.

Floating automobiles for sports purposes, for use by coast-guards and for lifeguard service were manufactured in Europe by the German Amphicar company. These four-seaters have a 1,147 cc, 38 hp engine at the rear, driving either the rear wheels (maximum speed 75 mph) or in the water propelling two screws (maximum speed 8 mph).

302

In spite of numerous tests the problem of a successful flying car has not yet been solved. If it is good in one role it is unsatisfactory in the other. However, an officially tested and approved flying car, the Aerocar, is offered in the USA in kit form for assembly, based on a modular system devised by its inventor, the engineer Taylor. The car is designed for one passenger, has a streamlined nose and a rear-mounted, air-cooled VW engine. For flying, wings and a laminated tail with rudders and a pusher airscrew are mounted in place. On the ground these are removed and the car tows them on a trailer. Flight range is 440 miles, at a cruising speed of 144 mph maximum.

Racing cars: New types of engines, tyres, brakes and other parts have always been tested on race tracks all over the world—in the early days in the competition for the Gordon Bennett or Vanderbilt Cups, and later on the Sicilian Targa Florio circuit on the oval Indianapolis track or during Grand Prix or Le Mans races. Acquired experience was then utilised in the series production of touring cars. Efforts to reach the highest possible speeds led to streamlined car bodies, and through racing research in body shapes Caracciola reached—in January 1939—the speed of 250 mph on the Dessau motorway.

To reduce the risk of accidents brought about by increasing speeds, in 1950 the Federation Internationale de l'Automobile issued the World Championship statute, restricting the engine capacity of racing cars. For Grand Prix racing (Formula 1), the capacity was limited to 1·5 litres supercharged or 4·5 litres unsupercharged, and has subsequently been (for unsupercharged engines) 2 litres (1952—53); 2·5 litres (1954—60); 1·5 litres (1961—65); and 3 litres from 1966. The latest 3 litre engines produce power outputs of over 500 hp. The shape of GP cars has been adapted to these new conditions. The drive system is located as low as possible between the driver's seat and the rear axle. Wheels have independent suspension and small and broad, treadless tyres for fine weather racing. Aerodynamic spoilers, built for the first time in 1966 for Jim Hall's American Chaparral, keep the wheels firmly on the ground. Formula 1 cars such as Lotus, Brabham, Ferrari, Wolf, Shadow, Ligier, Renault, McLaren, Surtees and Tyrrell reach speeds of about 190 mph.

The races in which these cars take part function as 'test benches' for the manufacturers of tyres, fuel and lubricants, bearings, brakes and so on; they provide valuable development pointers for engine and chassis designers. Much of the knowledge gained can be used on production cars.

Land speed records: In pursuit of world speed records these cars have always been designed to the limit of technological and theoretical possibilities of their time. Many of the early record attempts were made on Daytona Beach, USA, while on the dried-out Lake Eyre in Australia, in 1964 Donald Campbell, driving his *Bluebird II* equipped with a 4,200 hp Proteus jet engine, broke the world record by reaching a speed of 403·10 mph. Recent attempts took place on the Bonneville Salt Falts of Utah, USA. Every year in August the bottom of the dried-out salt lake provides an ideal 15-mile stretch. Driven by Art Arfons, the *Green Monster* was a famous American record-breaker. It was built from the 21-ft long fuselage of a jet plane, with a 16,000 hp jet engine. The car had four wheels with extremely thin pneumatic Firestone tyres. Braking was ensured by two parachutes. *Spirit of America*, belonging to the American Craig Breedlove, is in tricycle form and equipped with a jet engine. The highest ever speed until now was reached on October 23, 1970, by Gary Gabelich driving *The Blue Flame* at 631·36 mph (one direction only). His jet engine with hydrogen peroxide combustion developed an effective thrust of 12 tons, which, theoretically, should be enough for reaching a speed of 906 mph. (FIA regulations require that for a record to be recognised, an average must be taken of the speeds of runs in both directions.)

At present Arfons intends to break this record on his jet tricycle *Wingfoot Express*. His rival, who aims to reach a speed of 940 mph, will be Billy Meyer driving another jet tricycle, the *Aquaslide*, built in Japan. For that reason the last two lines of the record table have been left blank for the reader to fill in new speeds if and when the old record is broken.

The World's Land Speed Record

Year	Car	Driver	Speed (mph)
1899	Jenatzy (electric)	C. Jenatzy	65.79
1902	Serpollet (steam)	L. Serpollet	75.06
1902	Mors	M. Augieres	77.13
1904	Ford 999	H. Ford	91.37
1904	Mercedes	P. de Caters	97.25
1904	Gobron-Brillié	L. E. Rigolly	103.55
1905	Napier	A. Macdonald	104.65
1905	Darracq	V. Hémery	109.65
1910	Benz	B. Oldfield	131.72
1924	Delage	R. Thomas	143.31
1924	Fiat	E. Eldridge	146.01
1926	Sunbeam	H. O. D. Segrave	152.33
1926	Thomas Special	J. G. P. Thomas	171.02
1927	Napier-Campbell	M. Campbell	174.88
1927	Sunbeam	H. O. D. Segrave	203.79
1928	Napier-Campbell	M. Campbell	206.96
1928	White-Triplex	R. Keech	207.55
1929	Irving-Napier	H. O. D. Segrave	231.44
1932	Napier-Campbell	Sir Malcolm Campbell	253.97
1933	Campbell Special	Sir Malcolm Campbell	272.46
1935	Campbell Special	Sir Malcolm Campbell	301.13
1938	Thunderbolt	G. E. T. Eyston	357.50
1939	Railton	J. Cobb	369.70
1947	Railton	J. Cobb	394.20
1964	Bluebird II	D. Campbell	403.10
1964	Green Monster	A. Arfons	434.02
1964	Green Monster	A. Arfons	536.71
1965	Spirit of America Sonic I	C. Breedlove	555.48
1965	Green Monster	A. Arfons	576.55
1965	Spirit of America Sonic I	C. Breedlove	600.60
1970	The Blue Flame	G. Gabelich	630.38

Electric cars

From the very beginning the electric car had most of the qualities of an ideal vehicle. It was silent, easy to control and did not pollute the atmosphere. The major drawback was, and still is, its heavy and sensitive batteries, the source of the car's energy. The battery of an electric car plays the role of a fuel tank. Weight for weight the energy capacity of the battery is many times lower than that of petrol.

It is quite remarkable that in spite of all this it was a battery-electric car which was the first in the world to reach a speed of 60 mph. It was built by the Belgian Camille Jenatzy and called Jamais Contente (Never Satisfied), which characterised the thinking of its maker. From a flying start in a 1-km ($^5/_8$-mile) race in the park at Achères in 1899, Jenatzy, driving his Jamais Contente, beat the car of the Comte Chasseloup-Laubat, reaching a speed of 65·79 mph.

The most famous designer of electric cars at the end of the last century was the Frenchman Krieger. His cars, with front-wheel drive, served as taxis and were even used by several royal households. Each of the wheels had a separate drive. By means of a so-called combiner on the steering-wheel shaft it was possible to achieve speeds up to 25 mph, to activate an electric brake and to activate a reverse gear. In 1905 Krieger became famous by driving his electric car from Paris to Toulouse without charging or changing the batteries.

But in general the small range of electric cars, their great weight and the very fast development of the petrol engine brought about the stagnation of electric car development; finally their production was virtually stopped.

They survived only in America. As late as 1900 more electric cars were manufactured there than those with internal combustion engines. Most of them were driven by the well-proven General Electric motors. The last series-produced electric car was a $2^1/_2$-ton limousine, type 99, put out by the Detroit Electric Car Corporation in 1931. It had excellent riding properties and could reach a speed of up to 44 mph. By that time in Europe electric cars survived only as delivery vans and postal vans in cities where distances were short.

Nearly 80 years have passed since the first pioneer appearances of electric cars. Now once again big cities are starting to look for protection from noise and exhaust pollution and are hoping to find the solution in the electric drive. Lead batteries have been improved over the years. Major progress, however, has been realised in the field of electric motors, especially in their electronic control. Plastic materials and laminated glass have advanced the design of small elegant bodies.

In 1967 the American General Motors company began experiments with the Electrovair. In the boot of a luxury Chevrolet Corvair silver-zinc cells were mounted with five times the storage capacity of the old lead accumulator of the same weight. Power outputs were satisfactory, but the price of the silver-zinc cells was astronomical. Specialists in the field centre their hopes on the sodium-sulphur battery developed by Ford. With its storage capacity of 180 ampere-hours this battery, with ceramic electrodes, can replace three old-type lead-acid batteries.

Up to now the most efficient way of producing electrical energy—fuel cells—has been confined to spacecraft. By means of special microporous electrodes the fuel cells transform the chemical energy

303

304

305

306

303. Jenatzy's race electromobile, the *Jamais Contente,* with a cigar-shaped aluminium body

304. Krieger's electric taxi-cab in Paris in 1907

305. The Detroit Electric electric limousine from 1931

306. The American electromobile, Columbia Electric of 1904

307

of hydrocarbon fuels, e.g. of hydrazine, directly into electric energy. The transformation efficiency is 70 per cent. In one cycle the fuel cell can supply electric power sufficient for the electric car to cover a distance of up to 310 miles. The cooling of the cells, however, has not yet been reliably solved. The fuel cells get heated intensively by the reaction of the water and gases, which makes them impractical in a car. So, in their efforts to find a suitable energy source, designers have returned to the idea of a mixed or hybrid drive. This concept was applied by Ferdinand Porsche in his first electrically-driven automobiles. A small combustion engine, working at a constant load and hence great efficiency drives

308

307. This English electric van had to have its batteries charged once or twice during one working period

308. A modern sodium-sulphur cell (in the background) compared with conventional batteries

309. These light Stil tourist electromobiles help on sight-seeing tours along the banks of the Seine, reaching a speed of 16 mph

310. The Mixte electromobile with a mixed drive. The small, 6·75 hp, petrol engine is indicated by an arrow

a dynamo which continuously charges the batteries during travel.

An engine with a dynamo and batteries, linked with an electric motor, can form a closed driving unit.

Since the beginning of the 1970s an ever-increasing number of electric cars for city use—from sight-seeing tricycles to minibuses and delivery vans—have been appearing at various world car exhibitions. A layman may admire their ingenious bodies, but a specialist would be more interested in the electric motor used and in the manner of speed control. Prevalent are dc series electric motors. Revolutions are controlled by changing the voltage at

311. The direct-current electric motor of this city electromobile is connected by cables to an open thyristor unit

312. This two-seater Nissan electromobile covers a distance of 56 miles at a speed of 25 mph on one charge

the resistors or by connecting a varying number of battery cells. The latest electric cars are equipped with thyristors which, by a periodic interruption of the current supply to the engine, change the voltage.

Among the experimental electric cars built for two people and provided with another two small seats for children or shopping bags are the Ford Comuta, the Italian Zele-1000, the Czechoslovak Emu-1 made of laminated glass, or the more com-

312

fortable Japanese Nissan. Parameters of all these cars do not differ very much: weight about 1,325 lb, speed 25—30 mph, range 60 miles at the most per battery charge.

Briefly in series production were the English Enfield 8000 and the American City Car. The latter one is made of Cycolac plastic material, is provided with bumpers of polyurethane foam, and has radial pneumatic tyres and disc brakes. The power output of its electric motor is 4 hp and the batteries are charged overnight from the supply mains. Electric current for one week of operation, corresponding to a distance of about 155 miles, costs about £1.20.

Companies using electric delivery cars have their own charging stations or replacement stations where a set of discharged batteries is replaced by newly charged ones.

How will a present-day driver run his electric car when he becomes an experienced owner? In the garage housing his petrol car for long-distance travelling he will also have a small electric car, which, whenever it is out of operation, will be connected to the charging plug. After entering his car the driver will check the degree of battery charge on the instrument panel. Instead of the oil level and fuel level indicators he will find on the instrument panel a voltmeter and ammeter. For driving he will use only one pedal (accelerator-brake) and a switch for reverse drive. A special tachometer will indicate the number of miles covered and will issue a warning

313

313. Rear view of the Italian urban electromobile, Zele 1000. The layout of the two electric motors on the rear axles is interesting

314. The first series-manufactured British electromobile, the Enfield 8000, with an aluminium body. Maximum speed 40 mph, range 56 miles; charging takes 8 hours using a 13-amp battery charger

314

315

315. The experimental Mercedes-Benz LE-306 electromobile van can transport a 1 ton load to a distance of 50 miles

316

when the driver has either to return home or go to a charging station to replenish the batteries.

Many people think that electric cars will prevail for city transport and that petrol filling stations will be replaced by battery storage installations. Transport will be by small urban electric vehicles available to all on production of special identification cards. However, it is possible that electric cars will not be capable of replacing all the present cars and buses, as the demand for charging facilities might be greater than it was possible to provide economically.

316. The driver's seat in the electromobile built by Robert McKee of Illinois, USA. Maximum speed 56 mph

317. Twelve 6-V accumulators allow the McKee electromobile to cover a distance up to 137 miles on a clear road; in cities, however, the range drops to 62 miles

318

Buses

The history of the bus began in Britain where, in 1832, Hancock's Enterprise, with a steam boiler, opened a regular service in London. Steel sheathed wheels running along roads in very bad condition made the ride most uncomfortable and passengers soon returned to coaches or to the railway which, though in its infancy, was still more comfortable.

The first petrol engine bus had only eight seats. It was produced in 1895 by K. Benz in Germany and had rubber-coated wheels. Its task was to link the town of Siegen with neighbouring villages and communities. Further development of buses was carried out mainly by German manufacturers. In 1898 the first Daimler omnibus, with a separate driver's cabin, with a luggage compartment and with a body

designed to carry 12 passengers was put into service. In 1904 a bus service was provided between the towns of Braunschweig and Wendeburg by a bus constructed by Dr. Büssing, who began selling his products not only to the German market, but also to London bus operators.

Until 1904 omnibuses were provided with twin- or four-cylinder engines with power outputs of 7—14 hp. The rear axle was driven by chains, and the road-wheels with wooden rims had solid rubber tyres. Entry was made from the rear—just as in horse tramways—until Büssing started using side doors with steps. In 1907 K. Kaelble in Germany built a bus with the engine under the seats. In 1909 Büssing began using six-cylinder, 80-hp engines, and finally in 1912 chain transmission was replaced by a drive shaft. Wheels were then equipped with high-pressure pneumatic tyres. Double-decker buses were manufactured from the beginning of 1905. They were exported mainly to London. Nearly half the passengers travelled in seats on the bus roof—provided the weather was favourable. This was reached by a spiral staircase.

From 1924 the floors of the passenger compartments of buses became much lower, which was more convenient for passengers. Because of this arrangement the French Latil company began building buses with a front wheel drive. The increasing interest in bus travel induced the designers to enlarge the capacity of the buses. In Europe the Faun-Werke company and in the USA the Versare Corporation from Alabama were the first to build giant buses with electric power from a petrol engine connected to a dynamo which drove electric motors. Further development, however, favoured diesel engines and mechanical gearboxes. A lattice chassis structure inspired designers to present unconventional bodies, e.g. the tube-like bus of the Hansa-Lloyd company for Hamburg and Berlin was 30 per cent lighter than the buses with a conventional rectangular body. During the 1930s the shape of the bus acquired its present form. Large chassis-less bodies began to appear.

In small and city buses leather seats along the sides prevailed at first. In the American buses—the well-known Twin Coaches—transverse seats divided by a longitudinal gangway received priority,

and this seating arrangement quickly became universal.

In cities the network of double-deckers and low single-deckers was increasingly used. Sometimes for inter-city transport buses had a second passenger compartment attached as a trailer. During the 1930s tourist travel by luxury coaches became popular. In 1938 the Büssing-NAG company built a double-engine giant three-axle bus designed for motorway transport. The front engine had an output of 320 hp; the rear engine 270 hp. Before these buses became used generally, bus engines had to be adapted for wood gas fuel, since oil was needed for military use when the war started.

Development of present-day bus transport: In spite of the ever-increasing use of cars, modern buses still play a very important role in motorway and city street transport. While in Europe two-thirds of the total of half a million buses are used in city transport and only one-third in regular long-distance communications, in the USA this ratio is reversed. Luxury long-distance coaches, especially those of the Greyhound company who own more than 6,000, cross the country along the motorways, reaching speeds of up to 85 mph where permitted. Very often they have an individual lane reserved for their use. They are characterised by their exceptional safety. The probability of being killed in a bus is—according to statistics—three times lower than

319

320. The first Benz coach bus for 8 passengers on the first bus line in the world from Siegen to Deuz (1895)

321. The 1898 Daimler omnibus for 12 passengers

320
321

322. This omnibus by V.H. Büssing from the year 1904 has a side entrance

323. The M.A.N. mail bus of 1926 with a low-slung chassis

324

324. A de luxe M.A.N. coach from 1934 with a sliding roof and transverse leather seats

325. A long-distance Volvo coach of 1975

325

that of travelling by rail, and 24 times lower than when driving one's own car.

Bus driving mechanism: The bus engine — as a rule an 8- or 12-cylinder diesel engine — is usually located across the rear of the bus. Or a flat diesel engine is sometimes located just under the floor, as near as possible to the driven axle. Engine power outputs improve year by year. Smaller buses have 105—140 hp engines. Long-distance buses are provided with 200—240 hp engines (8 hp/ton), and express long-distance coaches and articulated buses have engines up to 400 hp (16 hp/ton). Consumption of fuel oil in these buses varies from 9—14 mpg.

A diesel engine of a modern bus is connected by a three-, four- or five-speed gearbox with a hydraulic converter. Starting is smooth and the driver shifts gears by depressing a button or by a pre-selector lever. In order to prevent disc brake overheating, a 'retarder' is installed in the gearbox. This is a controllable rotating hydraulic brake, the effect of which can be adjusted by the driver as necessary.

In the USA and USSR designers are developing combustion turbine engines of 260—400 hp, in order to achieve the highest and smoothest possible power in long-distance motorway coaches. City buses, on the other hand, are to be provided with cleaner and less noisy engines running on natural gas, propane-butane or hydrogen (these systems are at present being tested), with electric propulsion, or with a mechanical (flywheel) accumulator.

326

326. The transverse twelve-cylinder Scania engine at the rear of the Volvo coach. The power output is 220 hp

327. A short-distance electric bus in Long Beach, California

327

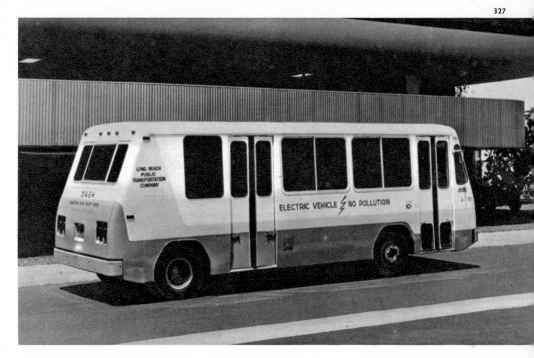

328

Electric buses are silent and do not pollute the atmosphere with exhaust gases, sometimes making the point by having inscriptions on their bodies, e.g., No Pollution. Due to its small storage capacity the present-day electric bus cannot cover a distance of more than 35—50 miles on one charge. Battery charging takes several hours, a problem which is solved in three ways. Since 1970 several lines in Munich and Düsseldorf are served by M.A.N. electric buses with a trailer carrying batteries. After two hours of operation the bus stops at a replacement station, where the discharged batteries are removed and replaced by newly charged ones.

In Hamburg, Wiesbaden, Baden-Baden and in the French town of Fontainebleau hybrid Mercedes-Benz buses are operated. Their three-ton batteries are charged—when the bus is running outside the city centre—by a diesel-driven dc generator, with an output of 60 hp, which extends the travel range of the buses to 188 miles. Lately a 'duobus' has been tested in Esslingen in West Germany, whose electric motors are fed while driving along the main avenues in the centre of the city from overhead mains which also charge the batteries. On routes on the outskirts of the city they are driven by the batteries.

Recently the comfort of the buses has been improved in a number of ways. Windows have been greatly enlarged and long-distance and tourist coaches are air-conditioned. The interior with carefully thought-out colour schemes, has well-upholstered aircraft type seats. Luggage is stored under the floor. There is often a washroom, a toilet and a kitchenette for coffee making, together with a refrigerator for cool drinks. The most sophisticated comfort is

328. A M.A.N. electrobus with a trailer for the batteries

329. Interior of a Mercedes-Benz O-303 de luxe coach

330. The lavatory and ante-room in the lower part of the coach

331. The kitchenette with coffee machine and refrigerator

offered in the biggest bus in the world, the German Neoplan Jumbocruiser N-138 (Plate XLIX), manufactured in West Germany. It is a 59-ft long double-decker, 8 ft wide and 13 ft high, which are the largest dimensions permitted by the authorities. The 430-hp engine, with an automatic gearbox coupled with an Allison retarder, gives a maximum speed of 90 mph. In the long-distance version for 102 passengers there is a bar, a kitchen and toilet facilities. The air-cushioned chassis has both the front and rear wheels steerable. The Jumbocruiser, even when running at a cruising speed of 70 mph, allows the passengers to move freely about the two decks. In fact the comfort provided equals that of a train or aircraft, with the difference, however, that the bus can go wherever passengers want to.

The bus of the future will very likely be driven by a turbo-electric system, and its speeds on specially provided motorway lanes will be of the order of 100—110 mph.

329

330

331

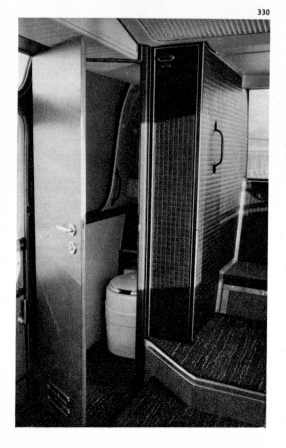

Lorries

332. A turbo-electric coach of the future

333. A five-ton Foden steam truck of 1920

As late as 1920 steam lorries with tall chimnies could still be seen among the petrol-driven passenger cars on European roads. With their solid rubber tyres on heavy cast-iron wheels, with their chains rattling, they looked rather archaic. Modified Sentinel and Foden steam lorries survived in Europe until 1940.

The Germans G. Daimler and K. Benz were instrumental in bringing about the birth of the petrol lorry. The first twin-cylinder engined lorry with an output of 10 hp and with a carrying capacity of 5 tons was manufactured by Daimler in 1896 for the British Motor Syndicate. Another similar vehicle was exhibited by Daimler and Maybach two years later in Paris, where it roused great interest. The first lorry built by K. Benz in 1901 was smaller than that of Daimler. It had a single-cylinder engine located at floor level and could carry a 1-ton load. During the first decade of this century the Benz and Daimler companies were building lorries with capacities from $1\frac{1}{2}$—6 tons, with engines of 7—16 hp. Although they were very slow (2—8 mph) they consumed twice as much fuel as the present-day delivery van capable of carrying the same load and reaching speeds of up to 50 mph.

The London department stores, market-halls and breweries especially showed an interest in lorries. There was great interest shown in the USA in lorries provided with Dunlop tyres. The first to use

them was the world-famous piano manufacturer W. Steinway. Daimler set up a sales centre in the USA with large service facilities, something unknown at that time.

In Europe interest in lorries increased mainly after they were equipped with diesel engines. The first vehicle of that kind was the Benz 5-ton lorry with a low body, an engine at the front and a cabin corresponding nearly to present-day design. It appeared for the first time on 10 September 1923, in Gaggenau, and had a chain-drive with rubber-tyred wheels. At that time in the USA the FWD company (Four Wheel Drive) was manufacturing reliable cross-country vehicles with the two axles driven by propeller shafts. The petrol engines of these were located under the floor—practically under the driver's seat. Thousands of these vehicles, capable of moving on roads, across fields and rough farm tracks, helped the western powers to win the First World War.

After 1918 Daimler and a number of other companies in Germany, France and Britain began manufacturing heavy lorries with a capacity of up to 20 tons, with diesel engines and very often with pneumatically-assisted brakes.

Büssing, Henschel and Faun in Germany tried various kinds of engines and transmissions, but they never found a better conception than that of the diesel engine with a mechanical gearbox. In 1920 trailers were attached to lorries for the first time. In 1928 the use of solid rubber tyres finally ceased. Before and after the Second World War the Germans used wood gas as fuel. It was produced by a special generator next to the driver's cabin and burned wooden blocks.

Present-day lorries: Lorries have a common basic concept: a welded frame, engine and a gearbox, body, driver's cabin and wheels. On the frame, various kinds of bodies, boxes and other superstructures can be mounted, adapted to the type of material to be transported. The relatively high revving 8—12 cylinder engines have outputs from 140 to 325 hp. In heavier lorries the rear axle is equipped with coupled wheels or they have a twin- or triple-axle layout. Leaf springs were first used, which were replaced by shortened spring suspensions. Nowadays pneumatic suspension with pressure control according to the load is widely used. Wilson's planet-wheel gearbox from the 1930s, enabling changes of gear without clutch release, has been developed to its present form of a semi-automatic gearbox, electrically controlled merely by depressing the selector push-button.

During the 1950s the design of drivers' cabins was advanced to the stage where nowadays they can be tilted to facilitate maintenance and give access to the engine. The cabins of long-distance lorries meet all the requirements of active and passive safety and are equipped nearly as well as the interior of passenger cars. The position of the seats can be adjusted freely and recently they have been provided with pneumatic cushioning. Behind the seats some long-distance lorry drivers have a bed.

The smallest types of goods vehicles are the delivery vans used in cities. Their capacity varies between 1½ and 3 tons, and they are usually petrol-driven. Access doors are located at a low level, so that the driver or his assistant can handle the load

334

334. G. Daimler (on the extreme right in the group) and Maybach (on his right) with their 5-ton truck in the course of a journey to Paris, 1898

335. The first lorry by K. Benz (1901)

335

336

336. The first diesel-engined lorry (1923). Capacity
7 tons

337. An eight-cylinder Scania diesel engine, capacity 14,000 cc and power output 350 hp

337

338

339

XLIX A 'jumbo' bus: the West German Neoplan N 138. The long-distance version takes 102 passengers, the town version 144 seated. Power output 420 hp

L This American GMC tourist coach for 42 passengers, with airconditioning and pneumatic suspension, is driven by an eight-cylinder diesel engine with an output of 265 hp

LI Interior of an American GMC tourist coach

340. A multi-purpose 10-ton truck used for a remote control experiment. It runs without a driver, following signals from a cable sunk in the road

easily. Medium types of lorries with capacities from 7 to 20 tons achieve as a rule speeds of 50—60 mph; their output per 1 ton of total weight (i.e. own weight plus the load) is about 5 hp.

The old-type open bodies with drop sides, and covered by a tarpaulin are being gradually replaced by specialised superstructures. In widespread use are saddle tow vehicles with a very short chassis and wheel base and with a support plate above the rear axle to which a semi-trailer is attached. Such a ve-

hicle can be used in conjunction with several types of trailer so that its utilisation is greatly increased. The driver does not lose time by waiting for loading or unloading; at the destination he just uncouples the semi-trailer, couples on an empty semi-trailer and returns with it to the place of loading. The performance of saddle lorries and others can be greatly increased by attaching semi-trailers and the possible combinations are illustrated in Fig. 343. The trailers are adapted to the character of the load. They are either of box type—for small goods, containers for larger items, refrigerating boxes—or of cylindrical type. These last are either tanks for transporting liquids or mobile silos for cement, flour, grain, etc.

Heavy-duty lorries have four-wheel drive. For instance, the well-known American FWD tow vehicles pull trailers with a load of 30—50 tons.

Dump lorries are built with capacities of 20, 40, 70, and 120 tons. The usual body covers the driver's cabin roof to protect it from falling stones when

341. A Hanomag-Henschel tractor and its semi-trailer, carrying a 20-ton container

342. A DAF tanker with an engine of 530 hp

342

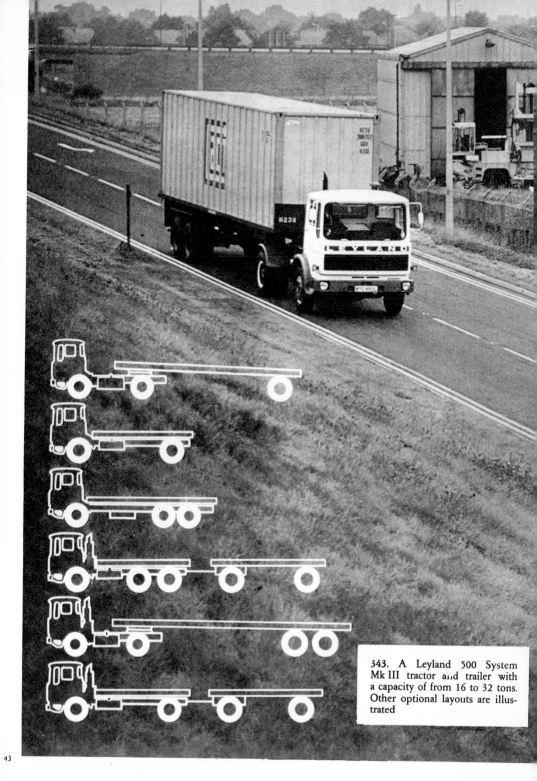

343. A Leyland 500 System Mk III tractor and trailer with a capacity of from 16 to 32 tons. Other optional layouts are illustrated

344

345

344. A heavy American FWD saddle truck with all-wheel drive, engine output of 400 hp and 16 gears

345. The biggest tip lorry in the world, the Terex Titan. Self-discharging, it has a capacity of 350 tons

346. A three-axle Tatra towing vehicle with an air-cooled diesel engine

loading by excavators. The vehicles are provided with giant pneumatic tyres, their diameter being sometimes up to 10·9 ft. Hydraulic tipping takes about half a minute. In the biggest of these lorries each wheel is driven by an electric motor. The power source is a generator driven either by diesel engines with an output of up to 800 hp, or by a turbine with an output of up to 2,000 hp. Due to their high axle load and to their dimensions these vehicles can be operated only off the public roads.

The world's biggest off-the-road vehicle is the Terex-Titan with diesel-electric drive and an output of 3,800 hp. It moves on ten wheels and can carry a load of 350 tons. The cabin, about 16 ft off the ground is reached by 15 steps. For the tyres of one Terex-Titan as much rubber is used as for the production of 600 normal pneumatic tyres.

Heavy-duty trailers are multi-wheel platforms with articulated-axle suspensions and high-performance brakes, which are hauled by tow vehicles, and which can carry loads up to 500 tons. The biggest of them are of modular design and in the longest combinations they have up to 120 pneumatic-tyred wheels. On the road such a trailer can only move at a speed of about 3 mph.

For the transport of exceptionally heavy loads—parts of ships, for instance—the West German Scheuerle company makes self-propelled platforms supported by hydraulically-controlled chassis units which are adjustable for height. The direction of travel of the chassis is electronically controlled from a cabin suspended at the front part of the platform. The record load transported on the biggest platform ever made was 800 tons. Since the platform can be raised hydraulically over a distance of 27 in, the heaviest loads he handled without a crane.

Some turbine lorries are equipped with twin-shaft turbines which, at a power output of up to 400 hp, have wheels only as large as the palm of the hand. A complete engine, including a large heat exchanger, weighs no more than 14 cwt. The first turbine lorry was the 1950 Kennworth-Boeing. A turbine tow vehicle, the Ford 707 carries a 50-ton load

347

347. Transport of a 300-ton transformer on a 48-wheel low-loading Goldhofer (West-German) trailer

348. A diesel-hydraulic truck of the Scheuerle company with hydraulically driven wheels and a carrying capacity of 300 tons

349. A Ford 707 turbine towing vehicle. The unloaded weight is 23 tons and the whole assembly is 75$^1/_2$ ft long

348

at a speed of 70 mph. It does not need a clutch and can start smoothly in any gear ratio. The driver, sitting in an ultra-modern cabin, has an excellent view and can control the vehicle by one pedal and steering wheel only. The turbine automobile can be easily identified by the large and powerful silencers which are to be seen quite clearly on the experimental M.A.N. European turbine semi-trailer set, which has a carrying capacity of 22 tons. The exhausts are directed upward. If the silencers were removed, the turbine would be heard within a radius of more than 6 miles.

At present, about 50 experimental turbine lorries and tow vehicles are running on the roads of the world. Ford, M.A.N., Chrysler, Chevrolet, Leyland, the Japanese Nissan and the Soviet Belaz organisati-

ons are all trying them out. Ceramic elements and new types of heat exchangers have prolonged the service life of turbines to thousands of working hours. It is estimated that turbines will become a common source of power for heavy-duty lorries as early as the 1980s.

350. The driver's cab in the Ford 707 turbine truck was designed like an aircraft cockpit

351. The M.A.N. turbine truck, capacity 22 tons, is driven by a compound turbine with a power output of 360 hp

352. A finisher compacting and levelling a concrete strip of road

351

Roads, bridges and tunnels

In the seventeenth century in France at the time of Louis XIV, the directors of the 'Ecole des Ponts et Chaussées', Pérronet and Trésaguet, began the construction of roads on a solid base consisting of pyramidal shaped boulders and stones, covered by pebbles and sand. In 1725 a roller was used for the first time to level the road surface. One hundred years later the roller became the most important machine in road construction and maintained this position for a very long time.

In Britain, John London MacAdam improved the surface of roads with a rolled mixture of gravel and damp sand. These roads were no longer dependent for their serviceability on fine weather; water could no longer erode their base layer and frost did not cause cracks. Solid rubber tyres, however, tended to break up the upper layer with their tread. In dry weather clouds of dust formed behind the vehicles, inspiring a Swiss physician, Dr. Guglielminetti, to try binding the sand and gravel with tar. Main roads coated in this way became dust-free. Many other techniques were tried out before the Americans began to mix gravel and sand with bitumen as a top layer over a stone or macadam base. The whole surface was then rolled.

In Europe, at the beginning of the First World War the first section of a road comparable with that of the present day was finished and a similar road, 33 ft wide and 40 miles long, was being built at the same time in the USA on Long Island. New York.

Present-day road building requires heavy machinery. Cuts and embankments are made by excavators, bulldozers. Cranes lay prefabricated concrete slabs. Special vibrating rollers compact the embankments. Before this embankment service-life was estimated to be 1 year per 1 metre (3·3 ft) of the height of the embankment. Dump lorries unload gravel, graders spread it and the finisher—after laying the stabilisation layers—spreads a concrete strip, 16—32 ft wide. Several miles a day can be laid. After hardening, the concrete strip is cut diagonally by a diamond disc saw to create expansion joints. In order to improve the properties of roads, which, nowadays, must resist axial thrusts of at least 10 tons, various innovations have been tried. For instance, in the Alpine passes crystal salt is added to the surface layer. The tyre friction releases the salt, preventing ice accretion and frost damage. Electric road-surface heating is at present being tested on bridges. Such a roadway, however, is five times more expensive than a normal one.

Motorways, freeways and expressways: After the First World War came the idea of building fast and safe roads for automobiles only. The construction of the first road of such a type—between Milan and Varese—was endorsed and approved by Senator Suricelli. As a result, a 50-mile motorway was built and called by the last word of the building company's name—Societa Anonima *Autostrada.* The German Reich motorways—the first of them connecting Frankfurt a/M. and Darmstadt in 1935—separated the lanes of vehicles running in opposite directions.

By the outbreak of the Second World War Ger-

352

many had many motorways in service and 1,500 miles under construction. At that time the USA had hundreds of miles of expressways in service, the most advanced of them—at Blue Ridge—with lay-bys, and the traffic lanes divided by steel guard rails. The expressways were built for speeds of 90 mph.

Europe is at present completing and connecting its motorway network on the principle no major city should have a road connecting it to a motorway longer than 25 miles. The original width of 78 ft has increased to 98 ft, in agreement with the European standard. Two two-lanes, each 25-ft wide are separated by a 13-ft central strip, and are provided with two 5-ft wide hard shoulders. The thickness of reinforced layers is at least 30 in. In mountain sections the two strips can be quite widely separated from each other, or built at different levels or, exceptionally, conceived as elevated roadways one above the other.

Due to traffic density, North American expressways increased to record widths of up to 14 lanes (e.g. the Dan Ryan Expressway); some of them are exclusively reserved for long-distance coaches only, a special lane being reserved for ambulances, the fire department and the police. Motorway crossings have usually a quatrefoil or triangular shape. Complex junctions are electrically lighted. If certain sections are overloaded, a light signal is given to select other sections.

Historic road bridges: As early as 3200 B.C. the ancient Sumerians knew how to build arched stone bridges. The oldest surviving stone bridge in the world is a single arch across the River Meles in Izmir, Turkey. The double arch Fabricius bridge over the Tiber river has survived from Roman times (62 B.C.). Among wooden road bridges the most perfect ones were the lattice girder bridges of the American R. Howe. His famous bridge, built in 1863 over the Potomac river, had a 330-ft span.

In some towns richly decorated, cast-iron bridges have survived. One example is the Paris Alexander III bridge, and the cast-iron bridge across the Severn river, built in England in 1779, is still in service. A steel arch can be more daringly conceived, the

roadway being either suspended from it or supported by it. Famous among arch bridges with a suspended roadway is the Australian Sydney Harbour Bridge, opened in 1932. The main span is 1,650 ft, and the bridge carries an eight-lane roadway, a double-track railway, a cycleway and a pathway, all 172 ft above the water level. Arch-supported bridges with slim struts are particularly suitable in places where the motorway or the road crosses deep river valleys. The span of some is as much as 1,600 ft.

The use of concrete and its pre-stressing allowed for the construction of daring and extremely long, though at the same time simple, bridges, requiring only very limited maintenance. Bridge builders have found ways to integrate a bridge with its environment. An example is the pre-stressed girder bridge 'Europe' crossing the River Sill in the Alps. About $1^1/_2$ million cars cross it annually. The building of modern bridges in urban agglomerations is complicated by the network of approaches and elevated ramps required as is illustrated in Fig. 360, which is an aerial view of one of the approaches to New York where, next to suspended structures, all types of stone, concrete and steel bridges can be found. Steel or concrete girder bridge construction can be accelerated by the method of overhung assembly (Plate LIV); which means a gradual extension outwards of fixed, temporarily supported or suspended structures.

The largest span between piers with the minimum of support from below can be seen in suspension bridges built mainly over estuaries of rivers. Progress in the design of very strong cables, capable of carrying the roadway and enclosed in a steel casing has enabled centre spans to be extended to remarkable lengths. Simultaneously the height of the towers for the cables supported on piers very often

353. Cross-section of a standard European motorway: 1 — concrete layer up to 12 in; 2 — antifreeze layer; 3 — permeable layer; 4 — drainage

353

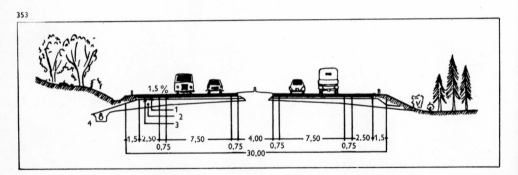

354

354. The Westhofener Kreuz motorway quatrefoil
at Dortmund, West Germany

355. Grade separation of two main arteries in Cologne, West Germany

356. The fourteen-lane Dan Ryad Express-Way in the USA

exceeds 650 ft. Since 1883, when the American Roebling bridged the East River of New York with a span of 1,595 ft, suspension bridge builders have been continually making new records:

1929	Ambassador, Detroit	1,850 ft
1931	George Washington Bridge, New York City	3,500 ft
1937	Golden Gate Bridge, San Francisco	4,200 ft
1964	Verrazano-Narrows, New York City	4,260 ft
1977	Humber Estuary, Lincolnshire (building)	4,626 ft

A suspension bridge across the Tokyo bay at Akashi Strait with a span of 5,840 ft is being designed; the longest span ever could be that of a bridge across the Messina Straits in Italy at 9,000 ft.

Not to be omitted—though its 3,254 ft span has been outdone by several other bridges—is the 1-mile, six-lane Atatürk suspension bridge which, in 1973, connected Europe with Asia over the Bosporus, thus fulfilling the old dream of King Xerxes. It is crossed every day by 20,000 vehicles.

The longest road bridge in the world is the concrete girder bridge across Lake Pontchartrain, New Orleans. It is 23·87 miles long and was assembled from 2,215 concrete segments manufactured on the site in a specially built factory.

A curiosity of construction technology is the floating Hood Canal Bridge not far from Seattle, USA, which was completed in 1963. Its total length is 9,373 ft, and the floating part made of a hollow concrete skeleton measures 7,131 ft. When ships pass, the floating part slides aside and then returns to its normal position.

A proposed glass bridge across the Thames in London is a technological curiosity. Besides the roadways it would have a parking area for 300 cars,

357

Road tunnels. If historians are not mistaken, about the year 2170 B.C. a 3,045-ft tunnel for horsemen and carts was built under the River Euphrates in Babylon. Slightly longer (3,168 ft) was the Pausilippo tunnel between Naples and Pozzuaoili built by the Romans in 36 B.C. However, it was only when the petrol car was making its first and rather rare appearance, that a 10,450-ft tunnel was built in the Alps at the Colle di Tenda between France and Italy. In Britain the first road traffic tunnel was constructed in the years 1925—1934 under the Mersey river. Its length was 11,253 ft. In 1927 in the USA, C.M. Holland was the first to build an underwater tunnel to relieve the traffic situation between New Jersey and New York, where the existing bridges were no longer capable of carrying the increased traffic. The tunnel was ventilated and was lined with tiles. In 1939 another parallel tunnel, the Lincoln tunnel, had to be built; it had two circular sections to separate the flow of traffic in either direction.

Tunnels under rivers, required by developing cities, can be constructed nowadays from the top, by submerging individual tunnel sections. This procedure was used not long ago, when the Elbe tunnel was completed in Hamburg. Eight prefabricated concrete sections, each 433-ft long, were sunk into a ditch across the river. The joints between them were sealed by frogmen. The six-lane motorway in each direction passing through the tunnel is 3,445 ft long, the tunnel approaches being three times longer. One hundred thousand cars pass through the tunnel daily at a speed of 55 mph.

Mountain road tunnels have been built frequently in the Alps. They cut journeys by many miles for hundreds of thousands of cars which otherwise would have to go over the Alpine passes, many of which are not easily navigated for the major part of the year. In 1975 a 32-mile motorway between Eben and Radstadt in Austria was completed. The motorway accommodates two tunnels: the 3 $1/_4$-mile Katschberg-autotunel and the 4-mile Tauern-autotunel. Powerful ventilation systems ensure air exchange, the permissible speed is 30 mph and drivers must use their headlights. The longest road tunnel in the world at present is the Mont Blanc Tunnel connecting France with Italy. The construction of the 7·2-mile tunnel took only six years, the actual rock boring only three years. In a year 600,000 cars pass through it. The traffic is TV-controlled. In 1980 the 10·1-mile St. Gotthard tunnel will be opened. The driving of the tunnel through the mountains lasted 2,133 days and was finished on 3 March 1976.

When driving through tunnels longer than

357. The unending zig-zags of the Gotthardstrasse with terraces as protection against avalanches

358. A bolted lattice-girder bridge by R. Howe over the Potomac river, dating from 1863

359. The cast-iron Alexander III bridge in Paris

358

359

360

9 miles some drivers suffer from mental stress called 'the spirit of the rocks'. It is, in fact, a kind of apathy caused by the monotonous environment, and could cause an accident.

Transcontinental motorways: These motorways are planned to facilitate and accelerate passenger and freight road transport. The Japanese began building a 3,750-mile Trans-Africa Motorway from Mombasa via Nairobi and Kampala to Stanleyville, and via Cameroun to the port of Lagos. This motorway will give access—among other things—to gigantic bauxite deposits in the centre of Africa.

Construction work is going on to complete the Trans-Asia Motorway leading from Istanbul to Singapore. It will connect all the major cities and ports of Turkey, Iran, Afghanistan, Pakistan, India, Nepal, Burma, Thailand and Malaysia. In 1980 it should reach the border of Burma.

Giant bulldozers are opening the way through the largest and most inaccessible jungle in the

360. Bridge approaches to New York represent nearly all types of construction used during the past 80 years

361. Cables suspended from the 689-ft high piers of the Verrazano Narrows bridge carry a two-level, 1,420-yd long roadway. About 50 million cars pass along the twelve lanes each year (p. 277)

LII A DAF truck with trailer

LIII The steel structure of the Askeröfjord bridge *(Werkfoto M.A.N.)*

LIV Assembly of the Danube box-girder steel bridge at Deggenau *(Werkfoto M.A.N.)*

362

world in the Amazon river basin for the 3,100-mile long Trans-Amazon Motorway which is to connect the Atlantic and Pacific Ocean coasts. On this unique construction, which has to stop every year for five months during the rainy season, workers must also contend with epidemics, wild animals and tribes of natives.

The most daring project of the future is to be a road connection between the USSR and USA along the roadway on the crown of a Bering Strait dam, about 40 miles long.

The role of the car in everyday life and road safety control

When, at the beginning of this century, the first cars turned up on the streets of Paris, Berlin, London, New York and other big cities, and when their owners were trying to get—with difficulty—the necessary fuel at various chemists and drugstores, nobody would have believed that within less than half a century cars would become an inseparable part of everyday life. At that time about 10,000 cars were in use in all the countries of the world, drivers were smiling at each other as they passed and exchanging friendly greetings. During the first decade, the number of cars increased dramatically and in 1920 the total number of cars all over the world was

362. Theoretical design for a glass bridge across the River Thames, near Westminster

363. Holland's tunnel for cars, connecting Manhattan and New Jersey, was opened for service in 1927

364. View of the 3·36-mile Katschberg car tunnel tube. Every 655 ft a phone and fire alarm system are installed, and the traffic is supervised by TV cameras

10 million. When the Second World War broke out there were about 45 million cars in the world, and in 1970 this figure had risen to 230 million. It is expected that by the year 1980 there will be about 400 million.

But even the fastest building of roads, motorways and parking lots lags behind the 'automobile explosion'. In cities the car lost much freedom of movement a long time ago. Queues jamming the motorways now get on drivers' nerves and bring traffic to a standstill. The atmosphere in big cities is polluted by exhaust gases, noise, dust and microscopic metal and rubber particles. The motorisation of the public

365

has changed the aspect of the landscape, transforming it into a dense network of elevated roads and fly-over crossings, destroying plants and much that was natural. Medical examinations showed a catastrophic drop in the physical condition of people in countries where the car is used for even the shortest distances and for entertainments such as drive-in cinemas. The reaction is to escape back to nature on Saturdays, Sundays and on holidays—but again by car. Caravans can transport people easily and quickly to places of beauty in the countryside, but due to the all-out tourist invasion such places are becoming increasingly rare.

There are, however, fields of human activity where the car is irreplaceable. In isolated communities or in unpeopled areas the car represents the only link with civilisation. Such areas and of course the cities themselves are supplied with commodities by delivery vans. Ambulance, fire department

365. A special traffic sign to show that drivers entering the Tauernautotunel should switch on their headlights

366. A Ford Transit Autohome

or police cars can act quickly to save human lives or property. But the social and economic evaluation of the car is rather gloomy. On the average, every tenth inhabitant of our planet is tied by his profession, directly or indirectly, to the production of cars or car operation. But the car, assembled from more than 10,000 parts, with an output of dozens or even hundreds of hp, occupying a surface area of at least 12 sq yds, serves one individual on average, for hardly one hour a day. A European driver covers annually about 6,000—10,000 miles, an American twice as much.

The permanent rent-a-car system has not developed in any striking way. Car ownership remains a symbol of wealth, prestige and social standing, but ever larger areas in towns have to be sacrificed to car parks and underground or multi-storey garages.

Road safety: Nearly a quarter of a million people die every year on the roads of the world. Scientists, state authorities, police and car designers are doing all they can to reduce this threat which causes higher losses than world wars.

Safety when using a car is influenced by three factors: the driver, the road and the car.

A lot of care is devoted to the education of the driver. Drivers who break road traffic regulations are facing increasingly heavier fines. Tests for drivers are becoming harder. But man's inaccurate assessment of a situation or some other form of human error can never be totally ruled out.

Roads are being improved. There are about four times fewer accidents on motorways than on any other type of road. But the rate of road construction very often does not keep pace with traffic density and makes it necessary sometimes to reduce speeds to a maximum of perhaps 50 mph.

The third factor affecting safety is the car. Designers are constantly reshaping and improving the car so that it meets the requirements of active and passive safety as nearly as possible.

One of the best-known passive safety tests is the so-called crash-test. A car with a dummy equipped with electric sensors, is launched against a concrete barrier at a speed of 30 mph.

It appeared that an unrestrained dummy in the case of a 20 mph crash hits its head against the windscreen with a force of about 780 lb, its chest is forced against the steering wheel with a thrust of one ton, and the knees hit the instrument panel with a force of about 90 lb. These forces, or the deceleration causing them can bring about dangerous, sometimes lethal injuries.

A number of countries have introduced safety belts by law, thereby reducing the risk of fatal injuries in impacts up to a speed of 40—50 mph. In order to remind the driver and passengers to fasten their belts, the ignition in some cars cannot be switched on until all belts are correctly fastened.

Another idea is the safety air cushion inflated at the moment of impact in front of the driver from a casing on the steering wheel. Within three hundredths of a second the cushion is filled with an incombustible gas; and presses the head and body of the driver back against the seat. It should offer protection even at direct impacts up to a speed of 60 mph, but with it there remains, however, a number of unsolved problems. Bursting of the cushion with a consequent pressure increase within the restricted space of a closed car could cause deafness. The expanding of the bag could injure people with spectacles or a pipe smoker. And it means an increase in the price of the car by about £ 60 per seat.

Development of these and other devices continues. For instance, the Alfa-Romeo company is developing a combination of safety belts and an air bag which is released at the moment of impact from a thickened part of the belt.

The protection of pedestrians also forms a part of passive safety. The Leyland company has developed

367

an experimental SRV car (Safety Research Vehicle) with a special frame which lifts a pedestrian and holds him on the bonnet.

Traffic control by signals as we know them today was first used in Detroit in 1919. Increasing traffic density on motorways and suburban roads nowadays requires the use of signals and information systems even outside cities.

An important aspect of road safety control is a speedy service making any necessary information available to drivers. In West Germany radio transmitters of the ARI-system are being tested, mainly serving lorry drivers. The radio is connected with a special decoder. No matter whether the receiver is switched on or off, as soon as important regional traffic situation news is transmitted, the decoder is activated and the driver is thus informed about traffic hold-ups, possible detours, etc. Elsewhere light or letter signals are used to give information about the danger of fog or black ice or to recommend a reduction in speed. Signals are positioned at the edges of roads or on gantries over motorways and are automatically switched on as soon as a dangerous situation occurs.

Other devices check the driver himself, like the system of warning of excessive speed, (when the driver can feel a 'stiffening' of the accelerator pedal).

367. A 1·5-ton van developed by the Fiat company in co-operation with Citroën

There are even some 'joke' warning systems, such as one invented in the USA. Here, as soon as the 75-mph speed limit is exceeded, a tape-recorder automatically starts to play the hymn 'Nearer, my God, to thee' with organ accompaniment. Or a push-button combination system checks if the driver's mind is not fuddled by alcohol.

Several new systems are being developed for connecting drivers directly to information centres. The electronic guide ALI, developed by the Blaupunkt company in West Germany, provides for the installation of 20,000 road boxes connected with induction loops under the road surface as it approaches crossings and branch roads. The boxes have a point-to-point communication with a central computer unit which passes on the latest information about traffic jams and weather conditions to cars equipped to receive it. These have a ferrite aerial, a small switch-box, and a simple display panel on

368

368. The Paternoster parking system of the Krupp company. The driver runs on to a platform and, on leaving the car, takes a key from the electronic control box. When he returns, he inserts the key into the lock and the Paternoster elevator will bring him his car

369. A steel multi-floor parking lot for 520 cars in Kiel fills the area between the railway station, bus station and the port

369

370

the instrument board. At the moment when the car runs over the induction loop, a point-to-point data transfer occurs within one two-hundred-millionth of a second. The display panel immediately indicates the turn to be taken at the next crossing, if the driver wants to take the shortest way to his place of destination. At the same time the central unit conveys to him the recommended speed and warns him of any danger of ice, fog or an approaching traffic jam.

The Japanese MAC system (Multifunctional Automobile Communication System) provides the driver with telephone communication with his home, place of work or with other vehicles. In addition, the driver's special number is fed into an apparatus in the instrument board by means of a coded card. When moving, the display can supply the driver with a possible 34 different instructions—e.g. about speed limits, traffic signs, partial road blocks and so on—including instructions about side turnings leading to his place of destination. The driver has an emergency push-button available enabling him to call the fire department, police or ambulance service.

Another aspect of road safety control is represented by induction systems in the roadway. Their function is similar to that of the railway auto-matic electric block. If, for instance, an undisciplined driver tries to overtake on a blind curve, signals are activated warning vehicles coming in the opposite direction. High-frequency cables can be installed in the road surface, guiding the car as if on a track. For this, cars have to be equipped with servomotor steering and dipole aerials. As soon as the car strays from the axis of the lane, a signal in the two arms of the dipole aerial instructs the servomotor to correct the error by slightly turning the front wheels of the car. The fronts of the cars are provided with anti-crash radars. A mini-computer in the car which receives a signal about a slower car approaching in the same lane will automatically cause the first car to brake or accelerate and overtake the vehicle in question.

The installation was tested for the first time in 1957 on the test track in Idaho Falls by the American RCA company. In Europe, systems of steering without driver's control are under tests as well. No country, however, has sufficient financial resources to cover the costs of such an automated safety system. Moreover, to be of any use such an installation would have to be mounted on every single vehicle. However, one could argue that even the most expensive electronic equipment is cheap in comparison with human suffering and material loss caused

372

by road accidents. One can but hope that electronically controlled car traffic will be put into operation at the beginning of the next century.

The car of the future

Car manufacturers agree almost unanimously that the car of the year 2000 will be a cheap, comfortable and safe vehicle, probably still with an internal combustion engine.

All the cars will look much more alike than to-day. The body will be designed to reduce air resistance as much as possible and thus save fuel at the higher speeds made possible by controlled motorway traffic. The body of the future may well look like a streamlined wedge. Shortages of raw materials may lead to having only the passenger compartment made of steel. The front and rear parts of the car will be of lighter metallic structure and make extensive use of plastic materials. Vehicles with a variable interior layout will be required. One American design incorporates a shopping cart as an

integral part of the luggage boot. The body interior will be upholstered; passengers on front and rear seats will be fastened in by safety belts which lock automatically as soon as the passenger takes his seat. Also headrests will extend automatically only when the passenger is seated or the car starts moving. The boot will be larger because there will be no need for spare wheels, thanks to new special pneumatic tyres consisting of a combination of rubber, synthetic fibres and plastic materials.

Nearly all manufacturers believe that the car of the future will be driven by a piston engine. Its capacity will be bigger than most in use now, probably of 2,000 — 3,000 ccs, and the fuel will be injected. Combustion will take place in two chambers — in one of them with lean mixture, and the other with a rich mixture. An electronic system will control the mixture ratio according to the engine load. It is quite possible that methanol will be used instead of petrol. In that way there would be no pollution of the atmosphere. The engine, with nearly horizontal cylinders, will very likely be mounted

372. An exceptional accident: the sudden collapse of a bridge over an irrigation canal cost 4 human lives and 11 people were injured

373. Just a fraction of a second of inattention—and this is the outcome

374. Crash-testing assures the passive safety of the car. The deformable front part absorbs the energy, while the cabin remains intact

373

374

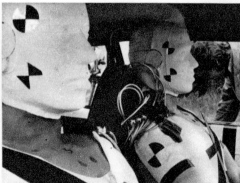

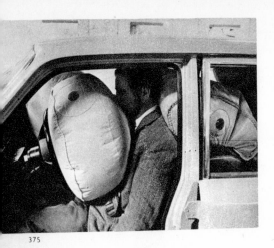

375

transversely in front of the front axle, and an automatic gearbox will be built into it. All the wheels will be independently suspended and hydro-pneumatically cushioned and the drive will be able to select the height of the body above the ground level within a relatively large range (low for motorways, high for rougher ground). Double-circuit disc brakes with a booster will be of varying power depending on the car load, and will be proof against locking. The engine performance will be optimised by a mini-computer ensuring the best working of the engine under varying conditions to obtain the highest power output with the lowest fuel consumption.

Cars will be manufactured on assembly lines and will not, as a rule, be repaired. The main parts will be designed in such a way as to make their service life identical to that of the car as a whole, giving on average a five-year life or 155,000 miles of running. During that period cars will be served by diagnostic centres checking or readjusting the automatic systems. Only in exceptional cases would engine items be replaced. At the end of its life the car would be scrapped.

Control of the car will be facilitated as much as possible by a computer controlling and taking over a number of functions from the driver. The computer would switch on the headlights, adapting their intensity to the visibility on the road, it would adjust the air-conditioning and change the light-filtering effect of the windscreen to protect the driver and the passengers from glare. The information indicator on the instrument panel, connected with

375. Two safety air cushions were activated at the moment of impact in this Volvo 142

376. This experimental SRV-Leyland safety car has a low bumper and a tubular frame which lifts automatically when hitting a pedestrian. The pedestrian falls on the bonnet in such a way as to prevent serious injury.

376

377. The ALI information system

A—target selector; B—function; C—display on the instrument panel (glätte-ice, nebel-fog, stau-traffic jam)

1—traffic situation; 2—central computer; 3—road transmitter; 4—double induction loop ensures connection with the car; 5—ferrite aerial on the car; 6—signal receiver in the car; 7—display; 8—target selector

A

B

C

378

378. A road with induction loops in the central lane and with a warning signalling system on a blind curve

379. A mobile press turns about 400 cars a day into scrap

379

the computer, would be in communication with the regional traffic control centre, virtually guiding the driver to the place of destination by the shortest and most advantageous way. By acoustic and visual signals it would warn the driver about all possible risks on the road. Moreover, the computer would inform the driver if anything is going wrong with the car and, for the purposes of the diagnostic centre, would store it in its miniature tape memory.

Even if automatic car control systems are not generally adopted, cars will at least be equipped with a microwave anti-crash radar, which will control gear shifting or braking depending on the speed of and distance from the car ahead.

Fuel filling may be automated as well. The driver will iust stop at a garage, take out his identification card and insert it into the sensor of the pump. The pump hose will be automatically sucked to the filler cap of the fuel tank, will open it, fill it with the required quantity of fuel and mark the quantity and price on the card.

In the near future a major change will very likely be represented by progress towards automatic car steering. The steering wheel will be the first part of the car to disappear. At present a universal control lever next to the driver's seat is being tested. Daring designers put forward the idea of cars controlled by thinking, or, more precisely, controlled by the driver's brain, which will be connected with the electronic steering system by means of a sensor the size of a wrist-watch.

380. In 1973 the experimental GEC Corvette with a Wankel rotary engine was regarded as a car of the future

380

381
382

381. This Chevrolet Impalla has no steering wheel. Direction is controlled by means of a short lever moved laterally, the speed or braking by moving it forwards or backwards

382. According to the American magazine *Motor Trend* the car of the future will have a beak-like front end. The rear-view mirror will be replaced by a TV circuit and the space for passengers will be provided with a bar and an automatic machine for coffee and ice-cream. The speed will be 150 mph and more

383. Thanks to the wedge-like body of the Runabout, it will be possible, after lifting the luggage boot cover, for a shopping trolley to be wheeled out of the car

384

384. Düsseldorf designer A. Schmidt thought up this hovercraft/car (with auxiliary wheels) as his car of the future

385. The driving position of the Ford car of the future, the Giron, is devoid of everything except a foot-rest. A programmed autopilot takes over the steering, replacing the driver

385

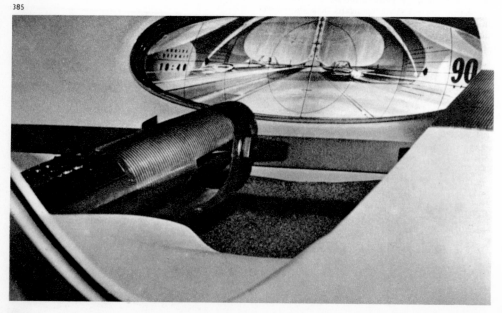

5. Water Transport

Development of the steamship and its successors

The first ship to cross the Atlantic propelled only by steam was the two-masted *Sirius* with 703 brt.*

She left from Queenstown (now Cobh), Ireland, and in order to reach Sandy Hook, New York, the crew had to burn even the wooden parts of the deck, having used all the coal reserves. The same day—on 4 April 1838—only a few hours later, the much larger paddle-wheel steamship, the *Great Western* (1,320 tons), arrived in New York. Her 15-day voyage from Bristol, three days faster than the *Sirius,* was also quite dramatic: fire broke out on her deck and while the crew was trying to extinguish it, the ship collided with a headland.

In spite of numerous improvements, the early paddle wheels were no longer satisfactory. They suffered in rough seas, often broke when the ship listed heavily, and their efficiency decreased when the draught of the ship was gradually lessened as the coal fuel was consumed.

The screw propeller, dating back to the time of Archimedes, did not suffer from these drawbacks. In the early days, individual inventors did not have money enough for expensive trials to decide the best shape for the propellers and to determine whether they were best located at the bow or at the stern of the ship. Consequently, they had no alternative but to experiment during actual voyages.

In 1829 the Austrian J. Ressel solved the problem for his particular ship, in particular the interrelationship of the propeller and the rudder. Unfortunately an explosion of the steam piping in the ship in Trieste ended the first and last cruise of his small steamship *Civetta.*

The French, on the other hand, regard their compatriot P. F. Sauvage as the inventor of the screw propeller, although in France and later on in the USA two counter-rotating wheels with screw blades, invented by the Swedish captain J. Ericsson were mainly used. Britain preferred the patent of F. P. Smith, who began testing long screw propellers with multiple spirals. During one of his experiments the long wooden screw propeller broke. The remaining part, however, propelled the ship even faster. Smith was surprised and as a result of this episode started designing a screw propeller with a single spiral. He used it in practice for the first time in 1839 in his ship *Archimedes* (230 tons).

The British solved the early rivalry between propeller and paddle ships in an original way. They organised a tug-of-war between two ships with steam engines of identical power. The screw propelled HMS *Rattler* soon began to tow the paddle-wheeled *Alecto* backwards at a considerable speed, and thus the screw propeller won the battle. However, even 40 years later, wooden paddle-wheel steamships could still be seen on the oceans of the world.

With the onset of the steam engine, timber as ship construction material was no longer really suitable. Ship-builders, however, could not find the courage to use iron only, because it suffered from corrosion, had a magnetic effect on the compass and, as a material, did not float. That is why the daring conception of the British mechanical engi-

---

* British registered ton = measure of volume representing 100 cubic feet. Registered tons express the capacity of all the ship's compartments that can be closed.

386

386. In 1838, the British steamship *Sirius* crossed the Atlantic at a speed of 7 knots with 94 passengers on board

387

neer I. K. Brunel, who in 1843 built a 280-ft-long iron steamship, the 270-ton *Great Britain*, was so outstanding at the time. She was the first steamship with an iron hull and a screw propeller. The hull was divided into six watertight compartments to

387. The *Great Britain* was propelled by a steam engine of 1,500 hp and reached a speed of 11 knots

388. The *Great Eastern* steamship, 680 ft long, with 47½ ft draught, could—according to calculations— carry 4,000 passengers and 6,000 tons of freight and coal

388

protect the ship against sinking. The screw propeller, with a 15-ft diameter, allowed a speed of up to 11 knots.

Supported by his country's interest in commercial and political expansion overseas, Brunel built a gigantic ship the *Great Eastern*, with a displacement of 18,915 tons. The ship was 680-ft long and was divided into ten watertight compartments. Her walls were of double-skin construction. A 4,890 hp steam engine propelled a screw with a 23-ft diameter. Another two steam engines drove side paddle wheels with a 55·7-ft diameter, but the cost of the construction of such a big ship with de luxe equipment for 4,000 passengers was never covered. Only 36 passengers took part in her first voyage to New York. After a number of accidents and failures the ship was put out of regular operation. For a certain time she served for cable laying, and before she was finally scrapped she was even used for coal storage.

At that time the era of major immigration to the USA had opened, bringing about an unexpected development of transatlantic traffic. A major role was played by Samuel Cunard who in 1840 founded the biggest British shipping company. Cunard introduced 14-day regular connections between the Old and New Worlds, advantageously combining passenger, cargo and mail transport. During the 1850s, 10,000 to 15,000 immigrants a month waited in Europe to get a place in a ship. As a result new ship companies were founded, ordering ever larger and more powerful ships. The German-American company HAPAG with its headquarters in Hamburg, and the Norddeutscher Lloyd founded in 1857 in Bremen, used at the beginning screw-pro-

389. The *Citta di Catania* (10,000 tons) is a typical example of thousands of passenger and mail ships which passed through the Suez Canal before the First World War

pelled steamships, of about 2,500 tons, carrying 500 passengers and built in Britain. Very soon, however, they had to increase the number as well as the capacity of the ships. Cartels and trusts were being established unifying tariffs and dividing among themselves old and new lines to North America, Russia, South America and finally even to Australia.

Steam engines were quickly improved. Compound steam engines from 1860 allowed the reduction of coal consumption from the original $4^1/_2$ lb/shp per hour to a mere 3 lb. After the introduction of triple steam expansion this coefficient dropped even below $1^1/_2$ lb/shp per hour.

New big double-screw steamships serving the lines of the Inman company cut down the voyage from Europe to America to under six days. That was in 1880 and the numerical relationship between sailing ships and steamships was being radically changed. In 1880 steamships represented only a third of the total world tonnage, but by 1900 16,000 steamships were registered with a total tonnage three times as large as that of the sailing ships. They were mainly passenger, cargo and mixed-type screw-propelled ships with a displacement of several thousand tons.

390

391

Sonnendeck. Grillroom. Passag.-Kammer I Cl. Sonnendeck.

Promenadendeck. Rauchsalon I Cl. Gesellschaftssalon. Promenadendeck.

Gang. Post-Bureau. Gang. Luxus-Cabine.

Speise-Salon I Classe.

Passag. II Cl. Küche f. Zwischendeck. Speise- u. Schlafraum f. Zwischendecker. Barbier.

Schlachterei. Gang. Fleisch. Proviant-Raum. Obst. Gang. Gepäck.

Kohlen. Ladung. Ladung. Ladung. Kohlen.

Kommando-Brücke.

390. On 17 September 1869, after ten years of construction, Ferdinand de Lesseps opened the 99-mile long, 72-ft wide and 26-ft deep Suez Canal. Before long the canal was widened to 197 ft and deepened to 43 ft

391. The locks of the Panama Canal can only accommodate ships with a maximum width of

105 ft, a length up to 984 ft and a draught up to 36 ft. The ships are towed by electric locomotives running along the edges of the locks and dams

392. Cross-section of the fast steamship *Deutschland*. It shows the quantity of food such a ship had to carry to feed the 2,500 passengers and more than 1,000 crew members

393

394. The four-screw *Mauretania*, with turbines of 70,000 hp, carried 560 1st-Class passengers, 474 2nd-Class passengers and 1,200 passengers in 3rd-Class accommodation

395. An eye-witness, the painter Willi Stöwer, depicts the fate of the *Titanic*. The lifeboats could hold only 1,178 people, and SOS distress signals were answered too late for many passengers and crew to be saved. At a distance of only 10 miles, the cargo ship *Californian* remained stationary, not recognising the Titanic's call for help

The Suez Canal construction played a decisive role in this expansion, since it reduced the distance between Europe and India by 3,125 miles and it would be used by steamships only, while sailing ships had to sail round Africa. The builder of the Suez Canal, French engineer, De Lesseps, tried also to build the Panama Canal. The attempt to connect the Atlantic and Pacific Oceans over the narrow Panama isthmus ended with the death of 22,000 workers and with financial scandals. Later technolo-

394

gically better-equipped American companies succeeded in driving through the 335-ft high Culebra
hills, in lowering the Gatun Lake water level and in
building six huge locks. On 15 August 1914, the
first ship passed along its 50-mile length, but for
the present-day huge cargo ships the two canals,
and especially the Panama locks, are too narrow.
The 41-ft deep Suez Canal has been deepened to
$47^1/_2$ ft and later on its depth will be increased to 62
ft.

At the end of the century British and German
shipowners began a prestige competition for the
Blue Riband of the Atlantic. It was to be awarded to
the ship which, taking any course, completed in the
shortest time a voyage across the North Atlantic
between the Bishop Rock lighthouse in the Scilly
Isles and the Sandy Hook headland at the entrance
to New York. At the beginning of this century its
holder was the fast German ship *Deutschland*
which, thanks to her 36,000-hp engines, arrived in
New York after five and a half days.

At that time passenger transport between Europe
and the USA was taken over by fast steamships with
a displacement of about 20,000 tons. Their hours of
departure from Hamburg, Bremerhaven and New
York, and their short stops in Cherbourg and

Southampton, were accurately scheduled to connect
with special express trains, whose carriages waited
next to the gangways on the quay. Comfort for the
first and second class passengers was constantly improved. The luxury German ship *Amerika* even had
electric lifts between the decks.

The capacity of the fast ships was also increasing
year by year. In ships above 30,000 tons the British
Cunard Line was the first to use the more up-to-
date and powerful steam turbine drive. Its inventor,
Sir Charles Parsons, thought up a daring scheme to
win general recognition. In 1897, with a small ship
propelled by an experimental turbine, the *Turbinia*,
he moved in among the fastest warships during the
naval manoeuvres at Spithead. He was chased, but
none of the ships could catch him. In 1909, the
31,000-ton *Mauretania*, equipped with turbines of
70,000 hp, cut down the transatlantic voyage to just
under five days and held the Blue Riband for another 22 years. The *Titanic* of 46,329 tons and carrying 2,584 passengers and 900 crew, was planned as
the fastest and the safest passenger ship of the
White Star Line company. On 15 April 1912, on
her maiden voyage from Southampton to New
York, the *Titanic* hit a floating iceberg which cut
the ship nearly to the middle of the hull. Insuffi-

396

cient lifeboats and other life-saving equipment caused the death of 1,502 persons.

Under the pressure of public opinion shocked by the tragedy, Boards of Inquiry were set up in Britain and America. Ship-building regulations became more strict. Competition among shipowners centred rather on increasing ship capacity than increasing speed. They became primarily interested in serving a greater number of passengers, even if some of the luxury lounges had to be given up.

Just before the outbreak of the First World War Germany built the turbine-propelled *Imperator* and two similar fast turbine ships with a tonnage exceeding 50,000 tons so that the number of passengers could be brought to 3,800. Each ship was operated by a 1,200 member crew. During the war most of these big ships and others served for military transport and many of them were sunk.

Blue Riband holders in the twentieth century

Year	Ship	Country	Tonnage	Time	Mean speed (knots)
1904	Kaiser Wilhelm II	Germany	19,361	5d 12h 44'	23·00
1907	Mauretania	Britain	31,938	4d 22h 29'	23·69
1929	Bremen	Germany	51,656	4d 17h 42'	27·92
1933	Rex	Italy	51,062	4d 13h 58'	28·92
1937	Normandie	France	83,423	3d 22h 7'	31·20
1938	Queen Mary	Britain	81,23	3d 20h 42'	31·69
1952	United States	USA	53,329	3d 10h 40'	35·59

396. The largest pre-war ship of the German HAPAG company—the *Imperator* of 52,000 tons

397. An aerial view of a group of fast ships in New York harbour (* *Normandie,* ** *Bremen)* is a reminder of the pre-war era of these Queens of the seas

The end of the 'Queens'

After the end of the First World War the immigration flow over the Atlantic lessened dramatically. On the other hand, ship technology progressed considerably. Boilers were fired by oil and large holds formerly used for coal became available for cargo and other uses. The number of stokers was reduced and their work was no longer so strenuous. Welded plates for hulls made the outer skin smooth and multi-storey superstructures gradually took on the aspect of modern architecture. All this facilitated a further increase in speed. The Blue Riband became a matter of national prestige.

At the end of 1928 two fast turbine ships left the Hamburg dockyards; the *Europa* and the *Bremen,* their displacement being over 50,000 tons. The *Bremen* was equipped with a newly shaped bulbous bow reducing water resistance. With this configuration in 1929 *Bremen* broke the old speed record of the *Mauretania.* The *Bremen* and *Europa* were splendid floating hotels for 2,225 passengers operat-

397

398

398. Launch of the French liner *France*

399. The Italian ten-deck *Leonardo da Vinci,* 33,000 tons, had 524 air-conditioned cabins, five swimming pools for adults and two pools for children

400. The *Queen Mary* (82,000 tons) with 160,000 hp turbines won the Blue Riband on 27 May 1938, after crossing the Atlantic in 3 days 20 hours and 42 minutes

ed by a crew of nearly one thousand. Even the cheap third-class cabins were provided with hot and cold water taps.

In 1937 the first ship longer than 1,000 ft won the Blue Riband. It was the French *Normandie* with a displacement of 83,423 tons. Turbines with a total output of 160,000 hp enabled her to cut the trans-atlantic voyage to under four days. Her average speed was 31·2 knots. Special emphasis was laid on anti-fire safety measures. The ship was protected by automatic fire alarms and by 46 firemen.

401

Meanwhile, the Cunard Line merged with the White Star Line and the two companies started building a fast ship which was about 3 ft longer than the *Normandie*. Launched personally by the Queen, the *Queen Mary* made her maiden voyage in 1936. Two years later she won the Blue Riband. During the war she served as a troopship and could accommodate 15,000 soldiers as well as her 1,000-member crew. Her sister ship, the *Queen Elizabeth* with a displacement of 83,673 tons, became the largest ship in the world. This 1,031-ft long ship with 14 decks for 2,300 passengers was propelled by steam turbines with a total output of 200,000 shp.

The long line of Blue Riband holders was completed by a substantially smaller fast American ship the *United States* after the Second World War.

The fate of the 'Queens'—of the giant floating hotels—was sealed by the rapid development and progress of aviation. Until 1956 the number of transatlantic ship passengers was slowly increasing, but the number of passengers who regarded their time as precious and travelled by air was growing in an unprecedented way. In 1957 the number of passengers by air and by sea was approximately

401. The *Queen Elizabeth 2 (QE-2)* is the largest present-day fast passenger ship. Turbines with a power output of 110,000 hp enable it to reach a speed of 28·5 knots. Her length is 963 ft, beam 105 ft and draught 36·5 ft

402. On 25 March 1975, when the *QE-2* was passing through the Panama Canal, there was only a few feet of clearance in the Miraflore locks

equal—about 1 million. Soon after big turbo-jet aircraft were introduced the air-ticket price in the tourist class was cut considerably, so that interest in travelling by sea dropped substantially. At the present time only one out of 20 passengers prefers ships which may be more comfortable but 20 times slower than planes. There are now no regular shipping times for trans-Atlantic passengers.

The giant *Normandie* was consumed by fire in 1942 during her overhaul in New York docks, the *Queen Mary* after her thousandth voyage ended her

403. On the *QE-2* navigation is controlled by a Ferranti Argos computer

404. A café-lounge on the *QE-2*

403

life as a coastal hotel and museum at Long Beach, California, in 1967, and the *Queen Elizabeth,* after retirement as a tourist attraction at Port Everglades, Florida, in 1968, was subsequently sold to a Hong Kong businessman after which she caught fire and was destroyed. Even the modern large turbine ships soon became out of date: in 1975 the French *France* (66,000 tons) and the Italian ships *Raffaelo* and *Michelangelo* were put out of operation. Another Italian ship, the *Leonardo da Vinci,* was transferred from regular service to cruises for recreation purposes and to three-month voyages round the world. In order to ensure maximum comfort cruise ships are provided with several swimming pools, TV,

cinemas, newspapers which are published during the voyage, etc.

Only one of the 'Queens' still survives: the *Queen Elizabeth 2.* She was built in 1967 for the Cunard Line by the British John Brown shipyard for £ 30 million. The interior was designed by a world-famous architect, Dennis Lennon. The ship has thirteen decks. On the sports deck there are various playgrounds, cinemas and a kindergarten. The second and the third decks have several cafes, bars, clubs and a chapel. On the fourth deck next to the Columbina restaurant for 500 diners there is a theatre and a library. Altogether the ship has 700 air-conditioned cabins for 2,025 passengers. The

404

LV The twin-screw motor passenger boat *Vistafjord* of 1973. Displacement 25,000 tons, two diesel engines of 12,000 hp each, maximum speed 20 knots

LVI The café and dance floor on the *Vistafjord*. 550 passengers are carried

LVII The Japanese container ship *Kurobe Maru* of 25,298 tons. Diesel engine with a 34,200 hp output and maximum speed of 26·3 knots *(Nippon Yusen Kaisha)*

LVIII The giant tanker *Globtik Tokyo* (483,664 tons) transports oil from the Persian Gulf to the central tanker port in Kiiro, Japan. *(Ishikawajima-Harima Ltd)*

LIX The first large LNG ship the *Gadila*, built by the French Chantiers de l'Atlantique shipyard at Saint-Nazaire.

LX This four-bladed ship propeller with adjustable blades is designed for motor cargo ships with an engine output up to 25,000 hp *(Escher Wyss)*

ship's structure is incombustible, insulated by asbestos and protected by fire alarms. The ship is controlled by a computer and can be turned by merely depressing a push-button on the captain's bridge. The crew and the passengers have a permanent telephone and teleprint communication with the mainland via satellites.

Other smaller, more economic diesel-propelled ships were adapted for pleasure cruises. Several companies recognised the advantages of the diesel driving system as early as 1925, when the Swedish luxury passenger ship *Gripsholm* (18,000 tons) started competing with the big transatlantic line ships. An example of a present-day passenger motor vessel is the Finnish *Vistafjord,* built in 1973 (Plate LV).

Sea cargo ships

Under 150 different flags about 65,000 cargo ships of over 100 tons displacement plough the world's oceans. According to Lloyds Register of Shipping their total tonnage is more than half a billion dwt*. It is ten times as much as the total tonnage of the world merchant fleets at the beginning of the First World War, when the traditional steamships were joined by the first diesel-propelled ship. This was the Danish *Selandia* (7,400 brt). The economy of

the diesel engine, the speed with which it can start into operation, its simple servicing—all this contributed to the popularity of the diesel driving system for smaller and medium-sized cargo ships, whose concept has otherwise not changed very much since the 1920s. Until the Second World War general cargo ships were in a majority. They were equipped with their own cranes and booms for loading. After the Second World War modified American Liberty ships became popular. More than 3,000 ships of this type were manufactured. The Liberty ships, propelled by one screw directly connected with a diesel engine with an output of 30,000 hp, reach speeds up to 15—20 knots.

In the early days cargo ships, the so called 'tramp steamers' sailed from port to port picking up goods according to the need of the ship owners. In more recent years these ships have tended to have an accurate, pre-determined timetable and serve regular routes. The departure and terminal ports are near industrial centres or in places with facilities for transfer to inland goods transport. Day and night ships of many different types and sizes transport fluid cargoes (mainly crude oil), grain, ores and many other things moving along the routes almost as if on motorways. From industrially developed countries they export machinery and goods manufactured from imported raw materials.

Very large ships specialising in certain types of cargo are appearing more and more frequently on these lines. Many things can be handled most con-

405. The screw-propelled steamship *Casaregis* (9,000 tons) is representative of cargo ships from the days shortly before the First World War

---

* Dead weight tons = the total weight that can be loaded. It is given either in metric tons (MT = 1,000 kg) or in British tons (LT = 1,016 kg).

405

406

406. Until after the Second World War small cargo motor ships, e.g. the *Castor* (12,000 tons), had a superstructure for the crew amidships

407. Main present-day cargo routes. The thickness of the lines increases with the tonnage carried. Coastal routes are shown by arches of uniform thickness

408. This drop-like bulbous bow reduces the water resistance, especially for broad ships

407

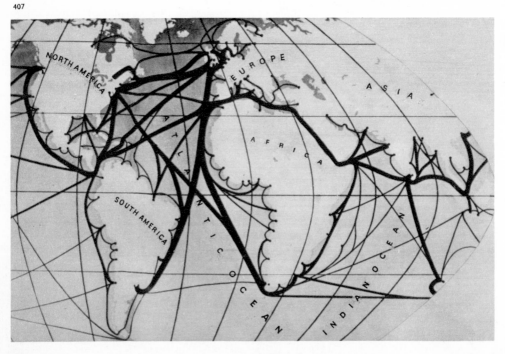

409. With a reserve of 5,000 tons of fuel, a ship equipped with a gas turbine (3) and sailing from Kuwait, will only reach the Gold Coast. With a steam turbine (2) and with the same quantity of fuel, the ship would reach the Canary Islands, while with a diesel engine (1) it would reach Hamburg

410. The *Kawasaki* steam ship turbine of 45,000 hp uses a double transmission system to the propeller shaft, reducing it to 90 rpm

411. Smaller cargo vessels load miscellaneous cargo into the hold using their own pillar cranes

409

410

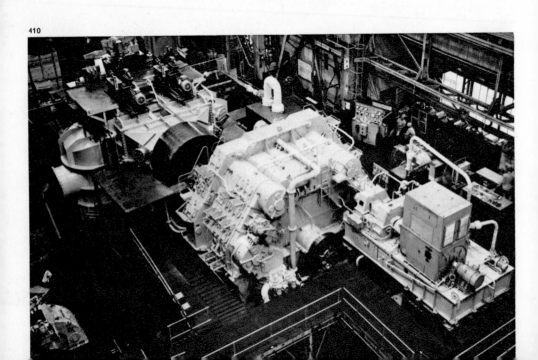

411

veniently in pre-packed containers carried by large and relatively fast ships.

The wish to increase the speed of cargo ships does not always tally with economic interests, since the consumption of driving energy increases at a faster rate than the increase in speed. For example, if a medium-size cargo ship with a speed of 15 knots is propelled by a diesel engine with a maximum output of 10,000 hp, if it is to reach a speed of 30 knots it will have to be provided with 120,000-hp engines. If the big tankers were to increase their speed to, say, 40 knots, they would become completely unprofitable. For a voyage from the Persian Gulf to the USA their engines would consume the equivalent of their entire cargo of oil.

Modifications to keel design and especially to the

bows helped to reduce the water resistance and thus to increase speed. The bulbous bow with its droplike shape reduces the resistance by 10—15 per cent in broad ships and by 5 per cent in narrow ships.

Present-day marine engines: The largest, lowspeed, diesel engines of cargo ships achieve outputs of nearly 50,000 shp, whereas the smaller, high-speed engines develop only a fraction of that output. For this reason large cargo ships increasingly use diesel engines or, even more advantageously, the steam turbine, which can reach outputs of up to 75,000 hp. Gas turbines are under test which drive an electric generator and the propeller is then driven in turn by an electric motor. These turbines have minimum dimensions, are comparatively light, and

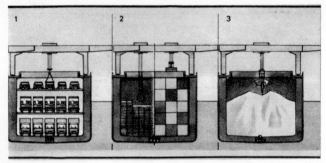

412

412. The space inside the hold of a universal cargo ship can be used in different ways. For car transport (1), for the transport of boards or containers (2), for loose cargoes (3)

413. The container ship *Joseph Lykes* belongs to the first generation of this type. Up to 592 containers can be placed on the upper deck, stowed between the cranes serving the hold

414. A large third generation container ship, the *Elbe Express*

415. A large car transport ship

have an output of up to 30,000 hp. They can be put into operation within three minutes, but consume, however, 50 per cent more fuel than a diesel engine.

Nuclear power for ships is only at its initial phase of development. The mixed passenger-cargo ship *Savannah,* made in the USA, has not been very successful; nor has the German nuclear cargo ship for ore transport, the *Otto Hahn.* The Japanese nuclear ship *Mutsu* had to be taken out of operation and is nowadays used as an oceanographic and technical laboratory.

413

Ships still continue to be driven mainly by either one or two propellers. The biggest screw propellers have a diameter of up to 29 ft and can absorb an output of 50,000 hp.

Tonnage and draught of ships: Increase in tonnage has its limits determined by the draught of the ship. Nowadays ports and canals restrict the maximum ship draught to 65 ft which corresponds to a tanker tonnage up to 250,000 tons. The biggest tankers built, with a tonnage over 400,000, can only use special terminals with a depth of at least 88 ft.

Future tankers with a possible 1 million ton displacement will require a minimal depth of 115 ft.

Cargo ships: The large space in these ships is divided by partitions into several holds, reached through sliding hatches. Cargo is lifted in or out by crane grabs or loader booms. In order to utilise a ship fully, big cargo ships are provided with tanks for the transport of liquids and with pumping equipment. They have several decks with variously designed hatches, so that individual holds may be loaded with different kinds of goods.

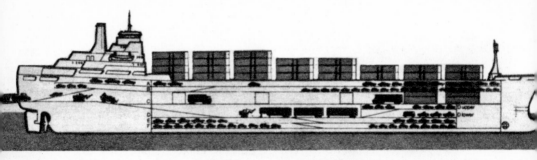

416

Since their introduction in 1960 container ships have undergone a rapid development and are now in their 'third generation'.

The 'first generation' (up to 1968) was really an adaptation of older types of ships and carried about 500—700 big containers on their upper decks. The most advance on the long routes between Europe and the USA and Australia produced the 'second generation', ships which were introduced after 1970 and accommodated 1,200—1,500 containers, stored partly in the holds. Their length exceeded 650 ft, and their average speed was 22—24 knots. Their control was automated to such an extent that only 40 crew members were needed. The 'third generation' of container ships appeared in 1973 on the East Asian lines. These ships, nearly 985 ft long, carry about 2,000 containers loaded in rows in the holds and on the upper deck. Their tonnage has

417

grown to 43,000 and their speed has increased to 26—28 knots.

Multi-deck 'roll-on/roll-off' container ships were developed to carry a mixed cargo of piece goods, heavy machinery, vehicles and containers. Such a ship approaches the landing stage with its stern, which opens with a draw-bridge mechanism to give access to its lower-deck space. Some ships have entry ramps in the side. These can be used by self-propelled loads like lorries, cars, etc., or fork-lift trucks, and special towing vehicles can transship piece goods through them. The interior layout of the ships is like a huge multi-storey garage. Decks are interconnected with inclined ramps or lifts. Special attention is paid to the securing of loads. To reduce the ship's pitching and rolling in rough seas, lateral

wing stabilisers of the Denny-Brown system are used. Operated by an electro-hydraulic system, these swivel as required, checking unwelcome movements of the ships in which they are installed.

A similar arrangement can be found in transporters. They have up to 14 decks for 4,000—6,000 cars or a lesser number of lorries and buses. **Barges** are convenient for transporting loads coming to ports along rivers and canals. The barges can be thought of as self-supporting, floating containers hauled by a tug and can be taken direct to a ship which does not have to enter a port and whose owner therefore does not have to pay harbour dues. At the stern of such a ship there is either a special bridge crane or a lifting platform. By means of this the barges can be lifted and placed on any of three or even more decks. When the barges are unloaded they are returned to the water. A tugboat marshals them and then hauls them to a new port.

SEABBE system ships can load—depending on their size—26-88 barges with dimensions of 125 × 36 × 17 ft. The greatest total weight of a loaded barge is 1,200 tons. After they have been taken aboard the ship special frames transfer them to their correct storage points. The loading of a complete cargo of barges takes no more than ten hours, while taking aboard the same amount of bulk load would occupy a week, even in a modern port.

416. The arrangement of the decks and ramps inside a roll-on/roll-off ship

417. The lowered stern of a roll-on/roll-off ship serves as a loading ramp

418. The large-ship SEABEE system can load up to 38 barges with a total load of 25,000 tons in about 13 hours

419

420

419. The *Atlantic Forest* (43,000 tons), length 860 feet, carries 73 barges

420. An overhead travelling bridge, carrying capacity 500 tons, loads barges into and on to the decks of the *Atlantic Forest*. Barge dimension: 60 × 30 × 14 ft

421. The bulk-carrier *Niizuru Maru* (165,000 tons), 1030-ft long and 148-ft wide, carries iron ore from Chile and Africa for the Japanese metallurgical industry

SEABBE ships are propelled by two medium-speed diesel engines with a total output of 36,000 hp. They are 740 ft long and reach speeds of 18 knots. By the use of suitable platforms a SEABBE ship can also be loaded by the roll-on/roll-off method. The platform serves as an entry ramp.

This cannot be done with the LASH (Lighter Aboard Ship) system, which loads smaller barges up to 400 tons by means of an overhead crane on a track running along the edges of the upper deck. Barges are always loaded in a transverse position. This type of ship can accommodate 75 barges.

Bulk carriers are large single-deck ships divided by partitions into several holds, where—by means of belt conveyors or grabs—loose materials are loaded, mainly ore, coal, phosphate or grain. At the end of the operation the hatchways are hydraulically closed by sliding covers. The biggest Japanese ship for ore transport is the bulk carrier *Niiauru Maru,* tonnage 165,000 dwt.

In the past, many bulk carriers transported, for example, ore from Scandinavian ports and returned empty. Giant tankers used to ship oil from the Persian Gulf and return only with water ballast, i.e. empty. This problem was solved by the development of big multi-purpose ships that could, for instance, take oil from the Middle East to Scandinavia and return with a cargo of ore.

Multi-purpose bulk carriers designed for ore, loose cargoes and oil transport are called OBO ships (international abbreviation for Ore-Bulk-Oil). They are relatively expensive because they have to be equipped with pumping, fire protection and cleaning mechanisms for the oil tanks. Next to pure tankers, they are the biggest ships in the world. For example, the Japanese *Tripharos,* with a tonnage of 165,000 dwt has under her ten sliding hatch covers a space for over 3,500,000 cu ft of ore; she can fill her longitudinal tanks with over 7,000,000 cu ft of

422

ore. With computer control the *Tripharos* needs only a 40 member crew.

Some multi-purpose ships combine transport of loose materials with container transport. The containers are placed on the upper deck above the holds for ore or other similar materials. This kind of multi-purpose ship is called OBC (Ore-Bulk-Container). Further development of these carriers involves a unique conception. Not only ore, but even coal and other loose materials can be mixed with water and pumped in a liquid state into the holds. At the place of destination they are pumped out again to a stock yard on the quay. Water content is removed by percolation.

Tankers: The world's first tanker, the *Glückauf*, was built at Newcastle-on-Tyne in 1886 and used to carry 3,000 tons of oil. Before the Suez Canal was closed in 1967 and before the oil crisis came in recent years, the tonnage of tankers increased only gradually. However, these two events encouraged the build-up of giant tankers for the long journey round Africa. The Japanese reacted most speedily. In 1959 they launched the first tanker with more than 100,000 dwt. She was called the *Universe Apollo*. Within a short period of time the tonnage of giant tankers approached half a million dwt. In tonnage, tankers outdid all other types of cargo ship.

Two of the largest present-day tankers are the Japanese *Globtik Tokyo* and *Nissei Maru* with 483,337 dwt. Their capacity corresponds to that of 8,000 railway tank wagons, i.e. 250 trains. Several tankers of this tonnage are 1,215 ft long, nearly 200 ft wide, their draught being 85 ft. The upper deck

422. The Japanese *Tripharos* (165,000 tons), is one of the largest multipurpose ships in the world. Maximum speed: 22 knots

423. The largest LPG tanker in the world, the *Palace Tokyo*, takes a cargo of liquefied gas. The ship is 767 ft long and 494 ft wide and propelled by a steam turbine of 24,000 hp

has a surface area as large as three football fields. An inspection bridge runs along the middle of the ship and the inspecting officer rides along it on a bicycle. The stern superstructure is as high as an 18-storey building. It is lived in by, and is the workplace for about 30—50 crew members. More are not needed since the ship is computer controlled. The cargo is evenly distributed in 10 to 14 giant tanks. High-performance pumps can evacuate it in less than a day. An empty tanker could not be controlled at sea and therefore it must carry water ballast. After each discharge of oil cargo the tankers are washed out. Polluted water must not be discharged near the coastline, but the number of undesirable oil slicks has been steadily growing, and for this reason tankers will be provided with water cleaning stations and with oil residue incinerating plants. In 1976 the *Batillus* tanker was built in France: she has a tonnage of 670,000 dwt, is 1,358 ft long and 216$^{1}/_{2}$ ft wide and her oil cargo is distributed in 40 tanks.

The American *Manhattan,* a combined tanker and icebreaker, has become a legendary ship, since she was the first to journey through the North-Western Passage, in a 30-day voyage, carrying a cargo of the newly discovered Alaska oil.

Liquid-gas tankers appeared for the first time in 1970 on the routes between Algeria and Europe. After liquefaction, the natural gas from oil fields must be kept aboard at a constant temperature of −50 °C (−58 °F). Ships of this type — LPG ships (Liquefied Petroleum Gas)—are provided for that reason with specially insulated cargo tanks.

As soon as marine technology had mastered natural gas transport problems, thought was given to carrying liquefied methane and other industrial gases that can be transported only at very low temperatures; −163 °C (−258 °F) in the case of methane. At such a temperature, however, even steel gets brittle, and should a tank be damaged and leak, its content would freeze everything on the ship and its surroundings. The first ship to be built in this category—called LNG (Liquefied Natural Gas)—was the French built *Gadila* (Plate LIX). In 1973, under the flag of the Shell company, she transported 2,650,000 cu ft of liquefied natural gas from Bruney to Osaka, which met the gas requirements of 100,000 Japanese households for one year. Between the aluminium surface of the tank interior and the ship structure are insulating layers consist-

ing of 12-in thick styropore braced with timber. The tanks themselves are not under pressure, and there is slight evaporation from them, the vapours being used to drive a gas engine propelling the LNG ship. Pumping of the liquid content in or out must be carried out with utmost caution and takes ten days. The ship-to-shore piping must be specially pre-cooled. At present about a hundred big LNG ships are under operation.

Ship trains: It is possible that certain ships, especially the tankers, have reached their maximum size. If their tonnage exceeds 500,000 these ships cannot pass safely through the English Channel or enter the Baltic Sea. But since an increase in capacity on long-distance routes is economically advantageous, experts believe that development will lead to the construction of SBT ships (Seagoing Barge Train). Large ships of different types—container, tanker, auto-transport, OBO ships and others—are coupled in one big set—or train—of ships with a total capacity of up to 1,000,000 dwt propelled by special short pusher units. Near the place of destination the set will be disconnected and big pusher barges with an output of 13,000−27,000 hp will take the individual ships to different unloading docks according to the type of cargo. Once unloaded the ships would be once again locked up to form a train more than a quarter of a mile long, and leave for their home port.

424. The specially modified tanker *Manhattan,* provided with 2-in armour plating and with 45,000 hp engines, took 30 days to break a new way through the ice of the North-West Passage, bringing the first oil from the Alaska region of Prudhoe Bay

425. A project for a modular ship with a total tonnage of 1,000,000 tons. It consists of ten individual ships of various types (tankers, container ships, car transporters, cargo ships) which are propelled as one unit by gas turbines, their total power output being 600,000 hp. When it approaches its destination, the whole set is disconnected and the individual ships are towed by tugs to the relevant unloading docks

425

Special purpose ships

Ships that serve simultaneously as laboratories, measuring stations or floating factories sail the seas and oceans all the time. In addition small fleets of fishing cutters, both large and small, trawl every day to supply food for mankind. Some ships lay cables, aid in the network of communication with satellites, or bear drilling rigs for submarine oil exploitation. Icebreakers help to keep sea routes in the regions of frozen seas open as long as possible. At places of high traffic density fire-fighting ships are ready for action at any moment against devastating fires on ships still under steam and in ports. Floating cranes help during construction work in harbours, and on man-made oil-drilling rigs, and mechanical excavators and suction dredgers clean and deepen navigation channels.

In straits between islands or across estuaries, ferry boats can be used instead of railway or road bridges and tunnels. With railway ferries, after their loading ramp has been swung down, tracks built into the decks linked with others on the dock side, can then push railway carriages directly onto the ship. The longest European railway ferry connects West Germany with Finland. A freight train with 50—60 wagons can be carried on its three-deck tracks. The ferry is 500 ft long and its engine output of 20,000 hp permits a speed of 18 knots when crossing the Baltic Sea. Passengers can pass the time in the boat's restaurants. In recent years ferries have been designed to transport trains and road vehicles. An example is the Japanese *Sun Flower*.

The fishing fleets of the world, which supply 70 million tons of fish a year to the world's markets, consist of 12,000 ships. The smallest are the cutters which assist in trawling. Lately plastic materials have been used in their building. For instance, the West German cutter *Juwel* (105 brt) is made entirely of laminated glass. It cannot rust, does not have to be painted frequently and its hull can easily be repaired. The larger fishing trawlers have a sloping ramp in the stern enabling winches to lift the net with its load of fish onto the deck with greater ease.

426. The railway ferry connecting France with Great Britain—the Le Havre terminal

426

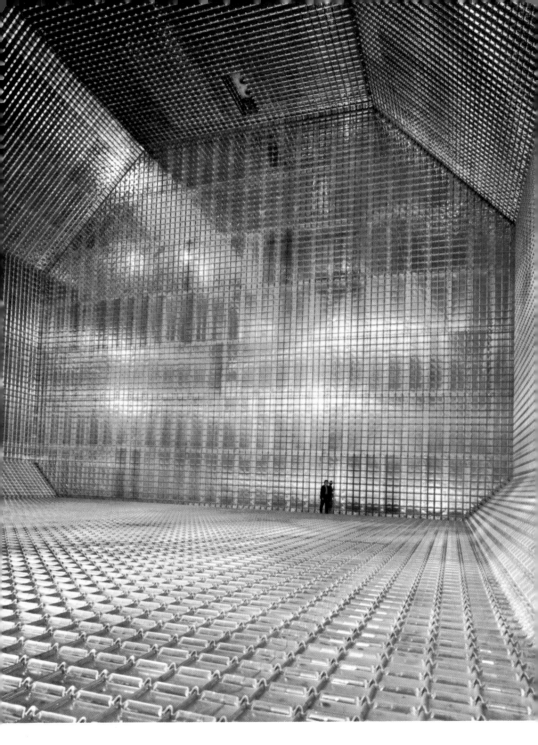

LXI View of the *Gadila* tank interior with a capacity of 600,348 cu ft of liquefied methane at a temperature −163° C (− 260° F) *(Chantiers de l'Atlantique)*

LXII Building tankers in the Japanese Chita shipyard of the Ishikawajima-Harima company

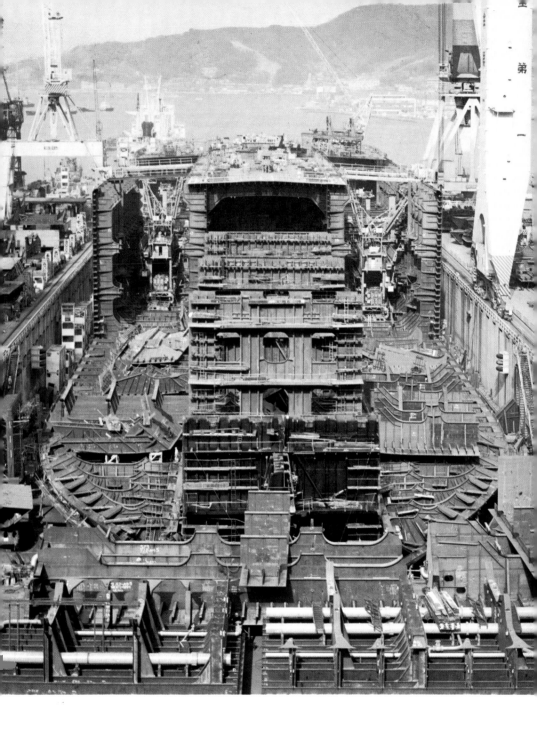

LXIII Assembly of a 400,000 ton tanker hull in the Kure shipyard *(Ishikawajima-Harima Ltd)*

LXIV The triple-screw polar ice breaker *Ermak*. Power output 36,000 shp, length 443 ft, width 85 ft, displacement 20,240 tons *(Wärtsilä-Helsinki)*

The largest fishing ships are the whaling factory ships with a slipway in the stern up which the whales, killed by the harpoons of the whale catchers, are hauled. Whale catching is nowadays restricted. The factory ships are used in strictly defined zones. There are about 450 ships of this kind, the biggest of them being the Soviet *Vostok*. On it, a crew of 300 men process the catch of 16 smaller whale catchers. The ship is provided with powerful refrigerating equipment and store rooms. These floating factories must be capable of operating in distant parts of oceans for 4 to 5 months at a time.

428

427. The Japanese ferry boat *Sun Flower* carries passengers, cars and trains

428. This European fishing boat, the *Juwel*, is made of synthetic material, is 85 ft long, and reaches a maximum speed of 14 knots (*Krupp*)

429

430

429. The *Vostok*, the largest ship of the Soviet fishing fleet

430. The *Yuri Gagarin* is one of six Soviet satellite communications ships. Among other things, she monitored the TV transmission of the Soyuz-Apollo docking operation

431. The four-propeller diesel-electric ice-breaker *Sisu* is 344 ft long, 79 ft wide, has a draught of 26 ft and reaches a maximum speed of 18 knots. She has a 120-member crew and is provided with a helicopter landing area

They communicate with the mainland by means of helicopters or planes.

Research and scientific ships have many functions. Oceanographic ships study the sea currents and the fauna and flora of the oceans. One of them is the former Japanese nuclear cargo ship *Mutsu* (Plate LXV). The crew numbers 80. The ship is propelled by a steam turbine with an output of 10,000 shp, and steam is supplied by generators heated by a nuclear reactor.

Meteorological ships and air and naval service radio-navigation ships are stationed at strategic points on the oceans to aid the weather services.

For satellite communication the USA and USSR use special ships equipped with parabolic aerials. A complex system enables the aerials to orient accurately at the satellites, even if the ship should be swinging round in the current.

Cable-laying ships connect continents with telecommunication cables. At a speed of 4 knots these ships uncoil insulated cables from their huge hulls and these slide into the water over large guide pulleys located on outriggers overhanging the bows. These cables are capable of transmitting up to 1,840 telephone calls at one time. The cable-laying ship *Mercury* can lay over 9,000 miles of cable in two months. At certain points engineers install amplifying stations in the cables, where they lie in the bottom of the sea.

In northern seas **icebreakers** open the way for ship convoys. In comparison with other ships the icebreakers are shorter and broader. The lower part of the bow is reinforced by armour plating up to the water line and a little above, but even the bow wave of the icebreakers is capable of breaking ice layers with a thickness up to 20 inches. If the ice pack is

432

432. A catamaran crane ship during the construction of an undersea oil reservoir

433. An old lighthouse at the mouth of the river Weser

434. Modern lighthouses are provided with helicopter landing areas

thicker, the spoon-shaped bow tends to ride up on the ice and to break it by the ship's own weight (Plate LXIV). Finnish icebreakers of the Sisu series are propelled by diesel engines. Both fore and aft they are equipped with two screw propellers. They can move forwards and backwards equally well and the backwash from the front screw propellers helps to release the ship if it is held by the bows in packs of ice. On the North Sea lines from Murmansk to Dalnij, the Soviet Union uses three nuclear icebreakers: *Lenin, Arktika, Sibir* (Siberia). The last two are equipped with two nuclear reactors enabling the electric motors to give an output of 75,000 hp. The uranium consumption per day does not exceed 4·5 grams. For that reason nuclear icebreakers can operate in arctic seas for a year without refuelling.

Floating cranes are used both for ship building and re-fitting in ports and shipyards. Or again catamaran crane ships of up to 2,200 tons can lay and assemble individual sections of submarine oil reservoirs. This innovation, which is becoming widely used, allows for the discharge of the cargoes of giant tankers far from ports. In docks and shipyards heavy-duty cranes are used. They are mounted on ferries hauled by tug boats or equipped with their own propulsion system. The biggest of them can carry 3,000-ton loads.

Sea transport safety

With the development of sea transport, the art of navigation advanced as well. For coastal navigation charts are especially needed. They give information on the depth of the water, indicate rocks and cliffs, bays and gulfs, sea currents and dangerous wrecks. Acoustic buoys, lightbuoys and nowadays even radio buoys indicate dangerous areas in the vicinity of main shipping lines. Chosen points on the coast have lighthouses installed whose signals, transmitted with differing intensities and at various set intervals, help to determine a ship's position in relation to the coast, even on dark nights and in fog. The traditional shape of the old lighthouses is giving way to strictly functional towers, even provided with landing platforms for helicopters.

On the high seas sailors for centuries used to orientate themselves with the aid of charts, a compass and a sextant. Nowadays a modern compass is based on the gyro principle, so that it is independent of the Earth's magnetic field deviations.

Between the two wars the echo-sounder was developed to determine the exact depth of the sea at a given point. From the time interval between ultrasonic signal transmissions and the reception of its echo from the bottom of the sea the instrument

433

434

435. A sextant enables a navigator to determine the position of a ship by indicating the angle between a celestial body and the horizon

436. On the basis of signals from navigation satellites, Redifon registers digitally the coordinates of a ship's position

437. Radar aerials are nowadays mounted on the superstructure of all larger sea-going and river ships

435

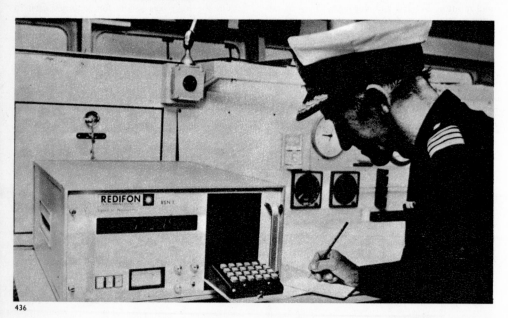

436

estimates the depth and records it continuously on a paper strip.

Methods of radio navigation were developed after the Second World War. Coastal lighthouses or light-ships transmit short-wave signals continuously on pre-determined frequencies. A rotary-beam frame aerial connected with a receiver on board the ship searches for these signals and, according to the direction from which they come and their strength, determines with high accuracy the position of the ship even in the worst weather.

All the North Sea is covered by DECCA, a modern radio-navigation system which allows ships to travel virtually guided by a radio beam. A similar system is LORAN, covering a part of the Indian Ocean.

To take advantage of this every ship must have a corresponding tele-communication installation. Its basic units are the main transmitter and receivers for frequencies from 125 to 27,000 kHz, a distress transmitter and receiver, portable walky-talkies for communication with the navigator and an automatic S-O-S signal transmitter on the 600-m waveband.

Every modern ship can be in radio communication with practically anywhere in the world. Twice an hour, at precisely determined time (between the 15th and 18th minute and between the 45th and the 48th minute) all the transmitters are switched off. This enables wireless operators tuning over the whole scale to hear even the faintest S-O-S signals or a distress *Mayday* call.

437

The majority of modern ships are equipped with an automated satellite navigation system. The aerial receives a signal from one ground control station transmitted over two different navigation satellites. A transmitter on board the ship transmits a signal via the same system to the ground station. From the time interval between the two, the ground station computer calculates the exact position of the ship and immediately gives it this information. Some small instruments, e.g. the Rediphone, can indicate on a digital display—immediately after depressing a push-button—co-ordinates of the ship's position with an accuracy within 0·6 miles.

Of primary importance for a captain, navigation officer or helmsman is radar, invented by Robert Watson-Watt in 1919 and developed during the Se-

cond World War. It acts as a radio-locator and uses a rotary-beam aerial, and provides a clear picture of any hazards there may be within a radius of several dozen of miles. The aerial of the PPI radar emits signals in centimeter wave lengths from a transmitter. From the time interval between the transmission and reception of the signal reflected back by a rock, another ship, by a coastline or special radar buoys, the electronic system of the receiver computes the distance and the angle of the position of the object and displays it in the form of fluorescent dots and configurations on a focusing screen. In that way, even at night and under adverse weather conditions, the screen of the radiolocator displays contours of the coast, the position and movements of other ships, etc. A radar screen is a very necessary

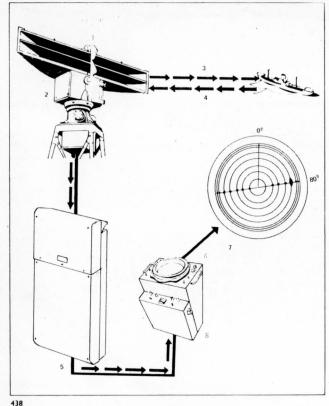

438. Schematic view of a ship's radar installation:
The aerial (1) of the radar transmits from the transmitter (2) signals (3) in centimetre wave lengths. From the time interval between the transmission and reception of the signal reflected (4) by a rock, another ship, etc., the electronic system of the receiver (5) computes the distance and the angle of the object's position and displays it in the form of fluorescent dots on a focusing screen (6, 7)

438
439

439. The background and the water remain dark on the radar screen. Radar signals in the form of light dots represent contours of a distant coast, nearby ships and other obstacles on the sea

440. The radar screen has a hood to facilitate data reading

441. This automatic Data Bridge system was installed for the first time in the Japanese tanker *Seiko Maru* (138,000 tons) and opened, in 1975, the era of super-automatic ships

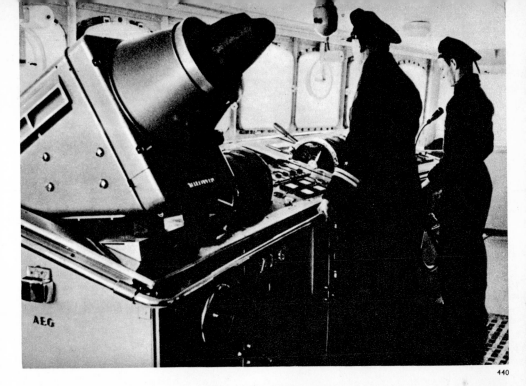

part of the equipment of any modern captain's bridge.

In spite of all these devices accidents still occur at sea every year. These may be caused by tornadoes and lesser storms, by ship fires, but most frequently by faulty navigation due to human error. Compara-tively recent cases of major sea disasters include that of the giant tanker, *Torrey Canyon,* which was wrecked in March 1967, when it ran on to the Sev-en Sisters reef in the Scilly Isles. In spite of imme-diate and large-scale measures, oil polluted the Bri-tish and French beaches for quite a long time. A true

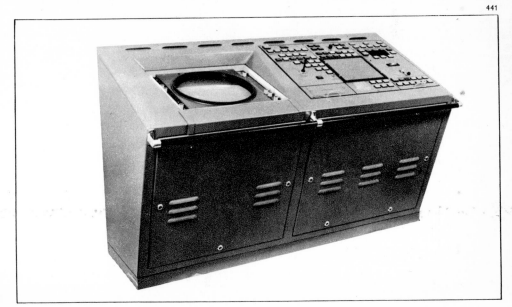

442

443

442. The French ship *Atlantic* in flames (1933)

443. The tanker *Torrey Canyon* broken in half after hitting a rock, finally had to be set on fire by aerial bombing (March, 1967)

444. A fast rescue boat in action

445. This lentil-shaped rescue raft is made of material which will resist the heat of burning oil and is also unsinkable

444

ecological catastrophe was caused by the tanker *Amoco Cadiz*, wrecked on 17. March 1978. About 200,000 tons of oil polluted the coast of Brittany.

In order to save lives and property, individual countries support well-organised rescue services along their coasts. Fast coastguard boats are on duty day and night in all weather conditions. They have high speeds and are highly manoeuvrable. The bigger ones carry auxiliary motor lifeboats and some even a helicopter on board. As possible replacements should they prove more successful than traditional lifeboats and life belts and life-jackets on ships, inventors are testing various devices to save the lives of people from sinking ships. A recent example is the bean-shaped life preserving raft which is proof against fire and capsizing and can accommodate 28 people.

Automation quickly found its place in the world

445

of ships. First to be automated were the ship engines. An engineer enters a modern engine room for inspection only once in 24 or 36 hours. For the rest of the time an engineer at a control panel in an air-conditioned room is responsible for the correct function of the engines. Fuel tanks are switched over, engines are lubricated, revolutions are controlled and other functions are monitored by electronic instruments.

In modern super-automated ships the computer has taken over not only the engine control, but also course determination. Working from data fed into it about the situation in a given zone the computer steers the ship to its destination in the most economical and safest way, practically without intervention from the captain or navigator. On the bridge of such ships a central control panel is installed connected with the board computer. The navigation programme and destination are fed in. The computer receives further information about the ship's position from navigation satellites and about the wind direction and speed, or approaching storms from meteorological satellites. Radar provides data about the positions of nearby ships and any other obstacles. Taking a route thus determined by the computer the ship can avoid the centre of a storm or other hazards. In cargo ships the computer checks the stability of the ship and, as the level of fuel diminishes, issues instructions to redistribute the weight of the cargo to compensate. With such systems crews even in the largest ships can be reduced to 30—40 men.

Ports

With the coming of steamships and with rapidly increasing overseas commerce, the idyllic era of small and often primitive ports being used to supply sailing ships and to handle cargo loading and unloading came to an end. The waters of natural

harbours in sea bays and gulfs had to be deepened for the bigger vessels. If the ports were built far up from the mouths of big rivers in the centres of industrial and commercial cities, the river beds had to be deepened so that larger ships could sail up them. Many completely new ports were built for the increased trade and to accommodate the increasing number of shipping lines. In these ports basins for loading and unloading are separated and are adapted for the handling of different kinds of cargo. Since individual conditions vary so much, no two ports are the same.

If a port is subject to a considerable difference between high and low tide—which makes loading and unloading more difficult—such a port is called a *tidal basin* (e.g. Hamburg or Rotterdam). If a port or part of it is separated from the sea or river by locks, it is called a *dock port* (e.g. London, Amsterdam, Bremerhaven, etc.).

Traditionally, a ship was anchored alongside a quay and might be joined by coastal or river boats. Cranes transported the cargo from the ship either to one of the smaller boats or directly onto the quay. In loading, the order was, of course, reversed. But after the Second World War docks became seriously over-crowded. Direct transfer of the cargo from ships to railway waggons helped. Piece goods were transported on standard frames called pallets. Ports increased in size, covering hundreds of square miles. Even now, ships have sometimes to wait at the entrance to a port several days before they can be brought in by a tug.

446. An 18th-century wharf with a wooden rotating crane

447. Trans-shipment of goods from ships directly to river boats has led to overcrowding of ports

447

Increase in the size of merchant ships, development of tankers and bulk carriers as well as that of container ships, required specialised ports very often located in deep waters as often as possible right on the coast. Old ports remained at the mouths of rivers, but new specialised ones were built for various types of cargo.

Grain trans-shipment ports (e.g. Antwerp, Buenos Aires and others) are characterised by tower silos filled by means of suction piping, the hoses of which are introduced into the holds of the ship.

Ore or coal trans-shipment ports or ports for other kinds of loose materials are equipped with huge grab cranes or bucket unloaders whose arms — after the hatches on the upper decks had been removed — reach down into the holds. Container ter-

448. Trans-shipment of cargo on pallets from a wharf along which ran a railway track was typical of most ports fifteen or twenty years ago

449. A 260-ft-high grain silo in the port of Antwerp

450. The coal and ore trans-shipment point of the Europort in Rotterdam

minals are where the most radical developments have taken place. Heavy-duty overhead cranes load and unload the containers. They put them either directly onto railway wagons or onto the trailers of container lorries, or else onto fork-lift trucks which transport them to large storage areas and stack them in rows several layers high. The newly-built container terminal at Bremerhaven has a manipulation and storage surface area of 1,196,000 sq yds. Nine big overhead container transhippers serve the whole area.

If such a big surface area is not available in the vicinity of a port, some countries build man-made islands in the water outside the port.

For safety and hygienic reasons ports for tankers are separated from the rest of the port zone. They have a typical skyline characterised by the glossy cylinder reservoirs for oil, petrol, asphalt, etc. Ships usually stop at jetties penetrating far into the sea. At their extremity articulated or flexible piping is connected to outlets from the ship's tanks which are emptied or filled by high-performance pumps. The output of these pumps is 6—10,000 tons of oil per hour. Since the draught of big tankers is more than 65 ft, in some ports underwater piping leads from tanks on the shore to deep water pumping buoys. The tanker anchors at the buoy and connects its piping with the filler neck on the buoy.

450

451

451. Aerial view of the container port in Bremerhaven harbour

LXV The experimental Japanese atomic cargo ship, the *Mutsu*. Steam turbine output 10,000 hp *(Ishikawa-jima-Harima Ltd)*

LXVI The bow of the cable ship *C.S. Mercury,* 8,972 tons, diesel-electric drive, power output 7,528 hp, with extended inclined cantilever mounting pulleys for cable laying *(Cable and Wireless)*

452. The modern railway ferry port of Puttgarten,
West Germany, which can accommodate simultaneous arrivals and departures of two passenger train
ferry boats and of one freight train ferry

453

A modern port must offer all the necessary services, from supplying the ship with fuel, water and food to minor repairs. The crew must have facilities for relaxation and entertainment, a health care service and so on.

In a busy port in order to avoid possible chaos in ship loading and unloading and in the closely linked railway, road or river transport, all the activities are controlled by a dispatching centre. Transshipment points are connected by radio with duty officers in the individual ships. Important transshipment points are continuously monitored by TV cameras. The dispatching centre can also organise repair work for damaged ships, supervise such things as fire fighting, etc.

Modern ships are growing faster and, consequently, shipowners urgently require the so-called 'fast ports'. A ship should proceed as quickly as possible to a basin where up-to-date machinery can unload it and load it in the shortest possible time. The number of roll-on/roll-off ships and ports explicitly designed for them is growing, and they can handle a number of ships at one time. Experts believe that fast ports in the near future will look like the hexagonal buildings of airport terminals. The hexagon will mean that ships will not be obliged to undertake complicated manoeuvring in order to reach the unloading position. Each side — about 820 ft long — will serve one ship and loading and unloading operations will be checked and controlled by computer.

Passenger facilities represent nowadays only a minor part of present-day ports. They require only a terminal building and embarkment quays. In ferry-boat ports, embarkation areas are separated from entry ramps for railway carriages. Cars, lorries or buses have individual approach ramps.

River transport

The main advantage of river transport can be easily expressed in mathematical terms: at a speed of 3 knots (3·5 mph), the power necessary to transport a 1-ton load is only one quarter of that which a locomotive has to develop to transport the same weight. A lorry needs 15 times as much power, the last two being calculated for a speed of 36·8 mph (32 knots).

The Romans and many other nations knew the advantages of river transport. As early as the thirteenth century the lower Rhine, Mosel and Loire rivers were teeming with boats and rafts. In the Danube basin merchants used to reach their markets by river, and the towns of Regensburg and Passau became important inland ports. Until the eighteenth century, river transport was impeded by unnavigable sections; goods had to be trans-shipped to wagons and the unnavigable sections bypassed.

Enlightened European countries very quickly recognised the necessity of the canalisation of rivers. Bottoms were deepened and cleaned, river beds levelled and dangerous sections made safe and clearly designated. Differences in altitude were overcome by locks. One of the first locks was built in the fourteenth century in the Stecknitz canal, connecting Lübeck with Hamburg.

By 1778 about 800 miles of canals were in operation in Europe. They were used mainly by open boats of approximately 25 tons, towed by horses or, in exceptional cases, provided with a sail where conditions were suitable. Ships with a tonnage of 150 tons upwards used the big rivers—on the Rhine there were often ships of 500 tons.

In the eighteenth century the Americans started to build canals to connect the rivers coming from the area of the Great Lakes (Erie, Ontario, Huron and Michigan). They created a first-class transportation network which contributed to the development of industry and agriculture in the north of the USA. After ten years of construction the 348-mile Erie Canal between Lake Erie, just north of Buffalo, and Waterford, near Troy, was opened in 1825. An ingenious system of locks helped the canal to overcome a 755-ft difference in altitude between each end. When in 1856 this canal was connected with several other inter-lake canals, and when finally the 2,625-ft Wabash-Erie channel was opened as an extension of the Erie Canal, about 4,000 ships and boats moved continuously along this waterway.

About the year 1816 the first paddle-wheel steamships appeared in the USA on the Hudson and Mississippi rivers, and in Europe on the Rhine, Seine and Elbe. But their number did not increase as might have been expected, because by the 1850s the railway had already become a powerful competitor.

About the year 1870 a short-lived development occurred. A heavy link chain was laid experimentally in some river beds, on the Elbe, for instance, from Hamburg to the Czech town of Ústí on Elbe. Steamships wound the chain over a specially installed drum which was driven by a steam engine.

453. A river sailing ship passes through a lock on the Danube-Mainz canal in the 18th century

454. The opening of the Erie canal in North America, 1825

454

353

By this means the ships were drawn forward the chain being released into the water at the stern. The traction power was greatly increased, but the chains very often broke and wore through quickly. For that reason designers returned to the principle of paddle-wheel steamers.

In 1900 a large-scale reconstruction of all the central European canals was initiated to allow the passage of ships of 500 tons upwards (on the Oder river) and 1,500 tons upward (on the Rhine). During the reconstruction works steam excavators were used extensively.

In 1922 the first diesel engine tug appeared on the Rhine. This event marked the beginning of modern river transport. The tugs tow mainly welded metal barges which average 1,000-tons, are approximately 262 ft long, 34 ft wide, the deepest draught being $6^1/_2$ ft.

Barges hauled by a tug have a number of drawbacks. The tug has to overcome the water resistance

456

455. A paddle wheel passenger steamship, the *Roland*, on the Weser river in 1890

456. A motor cargo boat on the Europacanal

457. Pusher boat set *Lyon* on the French Rhône river

458. Pusher boat set *Westphal* consisting of floating containers, each of 42 tons. The containers can be individually detached and loaded on railway wagons

457

of each boat separately; and the wash caused by the propeller of the tug made this resistance even more pronounced. Manipulating barge trains is time-consuming, especially at their entry to locks. During down-stream navigation a convoy of barges can be halted only by turning upstream once more.

Motor cargo boats do not suffer from these drawbacks. In Germany the barges have been transformed into motor boats by adding a so-called Z-drive. These have a vertical drive shaft turning a horizontal propeller shaft, and are mounted at the stern in a swivelling unit having a configuration of

458

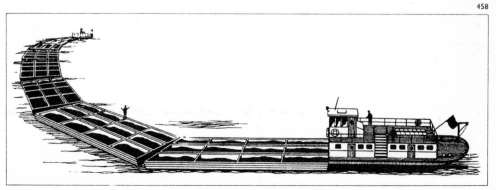

459

the letter Z. Far more efficient, however, was the 'pusher transport' applied much earlier than in Europe on the North American rivers. The sequence of boats is reversed: a short rectangular pusher boat with two or four propellers pushes a set of rectangular boats. These are coupled by cables or special couplings to function as one very long ship. Pusher transport—as far as energy consumption is concerned—is twice as efficient. The boat's speed of turn-round increases as well. They are loaded or unloaded individually while the pusher boat moves on to other fully-laden boats. The average speed of a set of pushed boats is about 5$^1/_2$ knots. On large North American rivers twin-screw pusher boats with 10,000 hp engines operate. The whole assembly can

460

459. The twin-propeller push boat *Rheinstahl II* is equipped with two diesel engines of 1,000 hp

460. Three ways of overcoming a waterway gradient: 1 — a lock; 2 — a ship lift; 3 — pressure of the water wedge

461. The canal at Askeröfjord runs on a viaduct across a road cutting

462. This ship lift at Lüneburg lifts ships in two basins. Each is 328-ft long, 39-ft wide and 11$^1/_2$-ft deep. The total weight of each basin, including the ship, is 5,700 tons

463

quite frequently be about half a mile long. They can transport a load of up to 40,000 tons, i.e. the equivalent of a load carried by a large transatlantic ship.

River transport intensified to such an extent that ships had to be equipped with radar; navigation on rivers and in locks is radio controlled and scanned by televison. The mouth of the West German Jade River at Wilhelmshaven was the first to be under automatic radar control. Captains of river boats receive radio information about the most convenient route.

Specialised ships, mainly river tankers, container ships and boats for many other cargoes appeared gradually on rivers, and the introduction of container boats in sets should be mentioned. At their destination they are lifted from the water one by one, and a crane places them on railway bogies. In North American channels about 20,000 boats, of which 4,000 are pusher boats, are under operation nowadays.

The waterways of the USA and of Europe are constantly being modernised and integrated within an economically planned navigation network. In Europe the Yugoslav-Rumanian dam in the Iron Gates helped to develop navigation of the Danube. In 1982 the Rhine-Danube, or 'Europa', canal over

464

463. The river boat *Britannia* on the Rhine

464. A passenger boat with a swimming pool cruises on the Rhine

465. The sight-seeing hydrofoil *Sea World,* with 28 passengers, near the Californian San Diego coast. It reaches a speed of 56 mph

the River Main will be opened. Later on it should be connected with the Elbe and Oder over Czechoslovakian territory. This network is built for boats of 1,000—1,350 tons.

When overcoming altitude differences of over 65 ft, locks are slow to operate, so ship lifts are built instead, with diagonally or vertically lifted basins using the so-called water wedge principle. This system was applied to overcome a 42·6 ft altitude difference on the French Canal du Midi at Toulouse. The ship enters the lower part of the basin which has a concrete bottom sloping gradually upwards. Locomotives provided with pneumatic bogies and moving along the edges of the canal are connected with tilting and sealing stop-logs. When moving forwards they push the water and the ship with it up-hill.

The biggest ship lift in operation is on the Elbe Lateral Canal at Lüneburg. The ship enters one of the two basins and within 3 minutes is lifted, still in the water, to the upper level. It overcomes an altitude difference of 105 ft. Instead of using 17 locks an inclined ship lift was built at Arzviller on the Rhine-Marne canal. Supported by 236 railway wheels the basin moves up and down tracks on an inclined plane, overcoming an altitude difference of 204 ft.

Since the era of the first paddle-wheel steamships, pleasure trips on rivers have been very popular. From the decks of modern ships, fitted out with every comfort, passengers can relax and admire the everchanging scenery. The upper deck is often provided with a swimming pool. In the Soviet Union hydrobuses are used in cities built on large rivers. They are a very cheap means of local transport.

Hydrofoils

For nearly a hundred years, designers have been looking for ways to increase the speed of ships without having to use excessive power. Water resistance is 800 times higher than that of air, and a speed increase over 27 knots means an exceptional use of driving energy. As far as hull shapes are concerned it seemed that all the physical and technological possibilities had been exhausted. The only solution was a radical change in ship design. Boats with flat bottoms, using the planning technique, lift the bow above the water level, so that only the stern with the screw propeller remains submerged. Racing boats reach a speed of 55 knots and record breakers propelled by jet engines can reach a speed of 270 knots. Their size, however, is restricted, because they do not have sufficient stability in choppy seas.

Hydrofoils with stub wings or foils fixed beneath the hull on streamlined struts seem likely to increase their present-day cruising speed of 55 knots to 135 knots in the future. At the moment the use of a propeller limits the speed to 55—75 knots.

The patent for a vessel with foils was first registered in 1892 by the Frenchman Lambert. Later, a small boat designed by the Italian Enrico Forlanini became a world sensation in 1906. It reached a speed of 70 knots on the Lake Maggiore, and at that speed the hull of the boat was lifted about 3 ft above the water.

Finding the correct shape for foils for boats was difficult. An aircraft wing, which works on the same principle, moves continuously in the same environment. Boat foils, on the other hand, if there are

waves, are alternately submerged in the water or cutting the air. At present several thousands of fast hydrofoils are in operation in the world. Some of them carry out regular public transport on lakes, rivers, and are used for crossing wide bays. But on the high seas these boats were only used for the first time in 1975.

The most frequently used hydrofoils have slim, V-shaped steel foils at the bow and often at the stern as well. They were invented by the German mechanical engineers Tietjens and Schertel. After the Second World War the Swiss company Supra-

mar AG manufactured them. Many countries are nowadays building these boats under license from this company.

The Soviet Union is building these hydrofoils as well, but with a modified shape to the foils which come in different sizes for different requirements according to the design of R. Alexeyev. The *Raketa* (Rocket) design cuts down travelling time from days to several hours only, not only on the rivers in the USSR, but also on the Danube, Rhine, in the Messina Strait or on the Thames in London. It is propelled by a diesel engine with a normal service out-

467

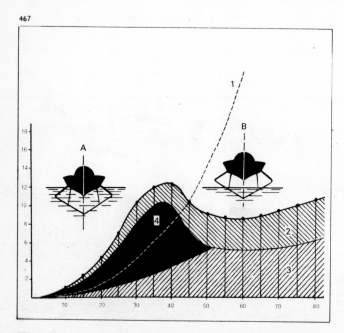

466. The Soviet hydrofoil, the *Rocket,* achieves an average speed of 40 mph. Length 89 ft; width 16 ft

467. Changes of resistance factors during acceleration of an 80-ton hydrofoil boat, (see text)

468. Hitachi-Supramar boats, manufactured in Japan under licence, are designed for 126 passengers and propelled by two diesel engines with a total power output of 2,000 hp. At full speed the hull bottom is lifted $4^{1}/_{2}$ ft above the water surface

468

put of 850 hp, and with 50 passengers reaches an average cruising speed of $32^{1}/_{2}$ knots

In a stationary position the hydrofoil's hydrodynamically-shaped hull floats on the water surface and the foils on the end of their struts are deep under water. When the boat begins to move, however, the hull's resistance (1), Fig. 467, starts to increase sharply from a speed of about 16 knots. The same applies to the resistance of the struts and foils (27). At the same time the lift of the short foils increases as well. At a speed of 22 knots it overcomes the weight of the boat, lifting its hull above the surface. The resistance of the hull to the water no longer plays any role and only the resistance of the foils and of the screw propeller remains.

V-shaped foils ensure excellent stability of the boat. If the lift on one side lessens, the boat is slightly inclined in that direction. Thus the length of the submerged part of the foil gets longer, the lift on this side increases and the hydrofoil balances again. Boats of this type are particularly suitable for river transport as they create very little wash, which can be a nuisance to water-side construction works. Moreover, hydrofoils do not need any special water

depth except when at rest. On the sea they easily overcome waves up to 6 ft high, but unlike river boats they have to be provided with longer hydrofoil struts to prevent the larger waves from overturning the boat.

Most hydrofoils are at present operating on routes connecting important recreation resorts on the beaches of Europe, the USA, USSR and Japan.

For coastal transport the Supramar and the Soviet *Kometa* (Comet) hydrofoils are very popular. One hundred and two passengers can be seated in aircraft-type seats in the $115^{1}/_{2}$-ft *Kometa*. The driving system consists of two diesel engines with a normal service output of 900 shp each. During a 12,500-mile demonstration cruise in 1971 the *Kometa* visited 34 European ports.

The size of hydrofoils continues to increase so that many of them can now be used for open sea navigation. For that purpose the USSR supplies boats of the Typhoon type whose slender foils are always fully submerged. Their trailing edges are fitted with electronically controlled flaps. The hull is made of a high-strength aluminium magnesium alloy. The boat is propelled by two gas turbines with

469

a total output of 3,500 shp and by two auxiliary diesel engines with a Z-transmission in case of foil or turbine failure. The Typhoon is designed for 105 passengers, while another type — the Sputnik — can accommodate 300.

In 1975 the Americans introduced on lines connecting the individual islands of the Hawaii group four double-deck Boeing-Jetfoil hydrofoils for 250 passengers. Instead of screw propellers the Jetfoils are equipped with a hydro-reactive propelling system. Centrifugal pumps, driven by two Allison gas turbines with a total output or 6,705 shp pump water up through the struts supporting the foils and push it out at high pressure through two nozzles at 17,600 gallons per hour. Two-metre water jets with a diameter of about 12 in hit the water at a distance of 33 ft behind the boat, driving it forward at a speed of up to 55 knots. The hull is lifted about 16 ft above the water surface. On the basis of data supplied by an accelerometer and by several echo-sounders measuring the distance of the bow and of the stern from the water surface, an on-board computer controls the driving force and the position of the flaps on the submerged foils. In its cargo version the Jetfoil should carry a 25-ton load.

The first hydrofoil to cross the Atlantic was the American *Denison* propelled by a gas turbine. Dur-

469. The Soviet hydrofoil *Kometa* is designed for 102 passengers

470. The Boeing Jetfoil 929-100 reaches a speed of 34 mph one minute after the start, and is lifted 16 ft above the water surface

ing her 1962 experimental cruise, the world speed record was broken when she reached 87 knots. It seems that the highest speed for hydrofoils could be 135 knots at the most. Already at lower speed problems occur at the lower edges of the foils. Owing to low pressure there, millions of bubbles are released from the water. These disperse immediately, but innumerable small implosions adversely affect the material of the foils. Experts believe, however, that by the year 1990 1,000-ton hydrofoils will appear, capable of transporting about 3,000 passengers on three decks at a speed of 108 knots.

471. The driver's cabin of the Denison boat does not differ very much from a big aircraft cockpit

472. The Denison jet boat on its record transatlantic cruise in August 1962

473. A small Britten-Norman hovercraft for 6 passengers

Hovercraft

When in 1959 the British mechanical engineer Christopher Cockerell crossed the English Channel in his small hovercraft, this event was regarded as signalling a new means of transport which might replace not only ships, but cars and planes as well.

This has certainly not happened yet, but at present several hundred hovercraft serve regularly as fast ferry boats—especially in the English Channel. In 1975, on 24 regular services, hovercraft transported 30 per cent of all the passengers travelling between Britain and France, and 25 per cent of their cars. Other smaller hovercraft enabled scientists to pene-

472

trate the Brazilian swamps and engineers use them on construction sites laying the Alaska pipe-line, even in the severest cold. In ground transport the hovercraft were not as successfull as expected because they could not so easily be controlled and, moreover, raised clouds of dust. On water, however, the situation is different, as the hovercraft can travel three to four times faster than classical boats and ships. For that reason the majority of hovercraft are used for water transport, though they are also used for short distance travel on dry land.

The design of the hovercraft is quite simple. A roughly rectangular aluminium box forms the hull on which is mounted the superstructure for the passengers and their luggage. Propeller fans drive air between the ship's bottom and the surface of the water. A comparatively small pressure creates an air cushion which lifts the hovercraft. In order to reduce air escaping all round, the edge of the box is sealed between the ship and the water by a single or double rubber skirt which becomes inflated and stiffened under the action of the air pressure.

In smaller hovercraft serving private owners and on occasion used by scientific expeditions into unknown territory as an amphibious means of transport, the propelling force is air released when valves in the rubber skirt are opened.

In larger hovercraft that are used for water transport services, three types of driving systems are applied:

1. A diesel engine or gas turbine drives both the fans and air propellers to drive the boat.

2. An engine or a turbine drives a propeller in the water.

3. An engine drives a pump and a water jet generates a reactive driving force (hydro-reactive driving system).

Hovercraft development is headed by Britain, where the British Hovercraft Corporation produces two types of hovercraft.

The Winchester-type SR.N 6 is 48 ft 5 in long and can comfortably accommodate 38 passengers. It is powered by one Rolls-Royce Marine Gnome gas turbine with an output of 900 shp, behind which the steering rudders are located. Even more successful is the 190-ton Mountbatten-type SR.N 4. Four Rolls-Royce Marine Proteus free-turbines, turbo-shaft engines, located in pairs at the rear of the craft, have an individual output of 3,400 shp when cruising. Inside the superstructure a car deck occupies the large central area of the craft with large stern doors and a bow ramp, providing room for 30 cars. Separate side doors give access to the passenger cabins flanking the car deck. Outer cabins have large windows extending the full length of the craft. The SR.N 4 can accommodate 254 passengers.

The terminal buildings on the Channel coasts are sited near the shore and approach roads. The hovercraft waits for the passengers and cargo on a large concrete apron in front of the buildings. When all the cars have entered and all the passengers are seated, the turbines are started. The hovercraft is lifted gradually to a height of $6\frac{1}{2}$ ft. The rubber skirt is inflated and stiffened by the air pres-

473

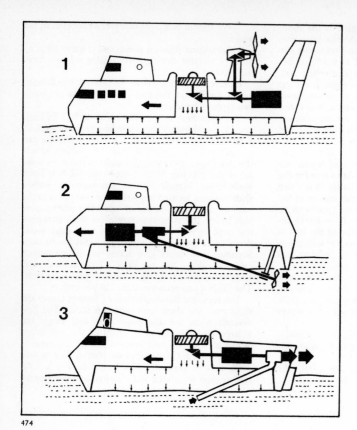

474. Basic types of hovercraft propulsion systems: 1 — turbo-prop; 2 — propeller; 3 — hydro-jet

474

sure. After adjustment of the air propellers the craft begins moving down the ramp and slips onto the water. As its speed increases, the craft is covered by a cloud of spray and in less than 40 minutes it reaches the other side of the Channel. The hovercraft can operate in waves up to 12 ft in height.

The Soviet and American hovercraft have a turbo-prop driving system as well. In order to increase their efficiency, air propellers are arranged in a ring configuration. The French hovercraft have a ground plan approaching the shape of a circle and their air cushion is divided by the skirt into a number of circular closed rings. The Naviplane N-500T type (Plate LXIX) is designed for 200 passengers and 60 cars or 400 passengers and 40 cars. Its propelling system consists of three 3,200-shp gas turbines located at the stern between the rear rudders. In 1977, the world's biggest hovercraft was put into operation on a regular line between Boulogne and Dover.

Screw propeller hovercraft can, of course, move only on water, but the power needed to drive them is relatively low and, very important, they do not generate as much noise as the turbo-prop units, so that they are much more suitable for densely-populated areas. The British company Hovermarine Transport Limited is currently building HM.2 Mk II and HM.2 Mk III hovercraft to carry 62—65 passengers. The HM.2 Mk II has two diesel engines with a total output of only 600 shp, reaching speeds of up to 35 knots, but their fuel consumption is only a quarter of that of the turbo-prop hovercraft SR.N 6.

High-speed hovercraft with hydro-reactive drive are still at the development stage. The hydro-reactive driving system will be most convenient for bigger hovercraft with speeds over 110 knots, where the number of air propellers would reach an unrealistic number of perhaps 20 to 30 and where a screw propeller cannot be used. The first civil hovercraft with a hydro-reactive drive was built for naval service by the American company, Bell Aerospace. This hovercraft is not amphibious. Its skirt has solid longitudinal walls and the flexible skirt is only at the front and at the rear.

LXVII The biggest floating crane in the world, the Japanese *Musashi,* of 3,000 tons *(Ishikawajima-Harima Ltd).*

LXVIII Departure of the hovercraft *SR.N 4* which is about to cross the Channel

LXIX A model of the biggest French hovercraft, the Naviplane N 500 *(S.E.D.A.M. Paris)*

Cargo hovercraft are suitable only for special needs. For a 1-ton cargo the power output must be about 40 shp, while a fast container ship needs for the same load only 2 shp. In most common use are the American Voyageur platform hovercraft, with a carrying capacity of 25 tons, i.e. of two containers ISO-C. At the stern they are propelled by two turbo-prop engines with a total power of 3,000 shp. A large number of these hovercraft are used as fast ferry boats in the Hong Kong bay.

475. The British Winchester (SR.N6) hovercraft for 38 passengers, and of 900 hp

476. The British Mountbatten (SR.N4) hovercraft for 250 passengers, 13,400 hp

477. The experimental U.S. Navy hovercraft, with two turbo-prop units and with water propellers, achieves a speed of 80·7 mph

478. Cars leaving the British SR.N4 hovercraft by its rear ramp

479. Small cargo hovercraft

479

480. The 600 hp Hovermarine (HM-2) can carry 60 passengers

481. The Bell 2KSES (US Navy), with reaction propulsion and four water jets, reached speeds above 124 mph

481

6. Air Transport

Airships

In one of his novels Jules Verne featured a vessel called *Albatros* which took the form of a ship maintained in the air by a large number of counter-rotating propellers rotating on vertical shafts driven by electric motors. At the time when this novel was first published, a number of inventors were designing airships as long dirigible balloons driven by an air propeller. By 1850, a search was going on for the best type of engine. The French engineer, Henry Giffard, used the lightest steam engine that could be built at that time, with an output of about 3 hp. During its first flight from the Paris Hippodrome on 24 September 1852, his airship reached a speed of 5 mph. Better results were not obtained at the time, even with a substantially larger airship. The experience of the first aeronauts showed that only a gas or combustion engine could offer a light and effective driving system. Such an engine was used in 1872 by the Austrian Paul Haenlein to drive an air propeller. In 1884 two French army officers, C. Renard and A. C. Krebs, used a 10-hp electric motor, fed from a battery of accumulators, to power their airship *La France*. The 170-ft, cigar-shaped airship carried an oblong frame slung in a net, along which a heavy ball slid, enabling the crew to control the pitch of the airship. On 9 August 1884, they succeeded in flying above the streets of Paris—even into the wind—and in maintaining a flight path in the shape of the figure eight which brought them back safely to Chalais-Meudon on the outskirts of the city.

The foremost pioneer of airships built on the non-rigid, balloon principle, and having a suspended nacelle for the crew and engine was the Brazilian, Alberto Santos Dumont. During the years 1898—1908 he built 14 different airships in which he used to fly over the suburbs of Paris. In 1901 he flew from the Aero Club in Saint Cloud, round the Eiffel tower and back to Saint Cloud in just under 30 minutes, not only winning a substantial cash prize but demonstrating his considerable courage and skill.

In the following years, dirigible airships were provided with a rigid base of steel tubing to make them safer and to give them rigidity. Gas was distributed in several chambers with air-filled ballonnets placed in between. Fans controlled air pressure and

482. The first airship by Henry Giffard (1852), with a three-bladed airscrew driven by a steam engine

482

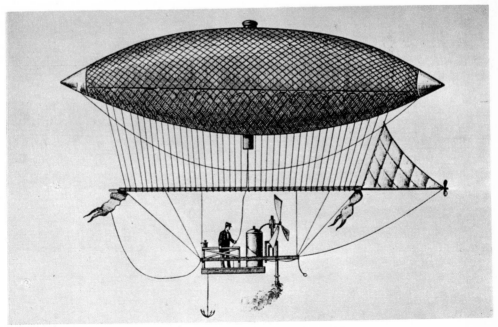

373

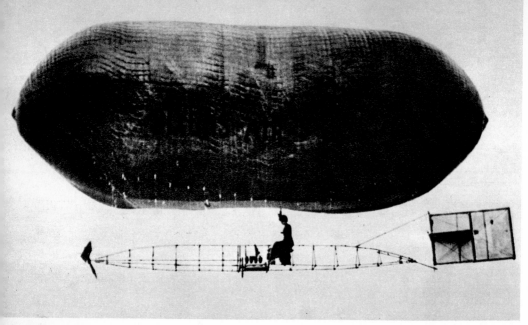

483

483. The American, Mrs. Dixon, propelled her non-rigid airship by bicycle pedals (1909)

484. The German Parseval airship of 1909 with a Daimler engine and two pusher airscrews

484

485. A sudden gust of wind during landing destroyed this 330-ft long airship in a matter of seconds. By a miracle it did not explode

486. The airship LZ-127 *Graf Zeppelin* before its first flight to the USA on 11 October 1928

the passage of gas from one chamber to another. By changing the gas volume at the nose and at the tail the airship's fore and aft level could be balanced.

Non-rigid airships were quite dangerous. If the gas pressure in the skin or the air pressure in the ballonnets, if they were used, dropped, the whole structure collapsed. Nevertheless, many designers preferred this principle for its simplicity. Before the First World War rapid development led from using airships in sports events, in which a number of women-aeronauts were involved, to use by the military.

French sugar manufacturers Paul and Pierre Lebaudy, with the help of their chief engineer Henri Julliot, were the first to build a semi-rigid airship with a capacity of 90,000 cubic feet. It was driven by a Daimler 35-hp engine, and on its first flight reached a speed of 25 mph. They tried to fly over the Channel, but crashed when landing on the English coast. From 1906 Major von Parseval was the leading designer in Germany of non-rigid airships; the first of them, with a capacity of 88,000 cubic feet, reached a speed of 25 mph. But neither he nor

dozens of other designers could prevent frequent crashes. Even the famous *Norge* met with the same fate. It was flown by Colonel Umberto Nobile together with the explorer Amundsen, with a crew of 15 men. On 14 May 1926, after a flight of 71 hours, they reached the North Pole and their epic flight of 3,000 miles ended finally in Teller, Alaska. An attempt to repeat this flight with the airship *Italia* in 1928 ended in disaster.

Rigid airships were expected to overcome the weaknesses of the balloon-type non-rigid design, but they were only really practicable after the introduction of aluminium and duralumin into the structure. The first airship of such a type was built in Berlin in 1897, by David Schwarz. The 156-ft long airship with an aluminium framework was cigar-shaped and was filled with pure hydrogen and propelled by a twin-cylinder Daimler engine with an output of 12 hp. Further development proved that the best all-round performance in airships could be obtained at gas capacities over 530,000 cubic feet. Engines in nacelles were fixed directly to the rigid structure, enabling the propeller's traction

487. The American airship *Acron* used helium in place of the less safe hydrogen

488. Disaster as flames engulf LZ-129 *Hindenburg* when landing at Lakehurst at 6·21 pm on 6 May 1937

to give forward movement during take-off as well as in the air. Pioneers in this field were the German Count Ferdinand von Zeppelin and Dr. Johann Schütte. The first 'Zeppelin', the LZ1, was 420 ft long. Its aluminium structure had an impregnated skin. Gas was distributed in 17 chambers with safety and control valves. The LZ1 took off for the first time on 2 July 1900, from the surface of Lake Constance. It was fitted out with two Daimler engines, each with an output of 16 hp, and reached a speed of 20 mph. Altogether 150 'Zeppelins' of increasing size and power output were manufactured in the assembly shed at the lake. A number of them were destroyed during the First World War.

In 1919 the British built two big hydrogen airships R-33 and R-34. Between 2 and 13 July, in spite of adverse weather conditions, the R-34 flew the round trip across the Atlantic Ocean, under the command of Major G. H. Scott. During one flight 4,840 gallons of petrol were consumed. In the same year German Zeppelins opened a regular flight service between Berlin and Friedrichshafen using LZ-120 Bodensee airships. Between 8 and 29 August 1929, the Germans flew round the world in the LZ-127 *Graf Zeppelin* airship. The *Graf Zeppelin* was 775-ft long and weighed 60 tons. Under the command of Hugo Eckener she covered a 21,000-mile distance on a route from Lakehurst, New Jersey — Friedrichshafen — Tokyo — Los Angeles — Lakehurst, flying at an average cruising speed of 70 mph. She was powered by five engines with a total output of 2,000 hp. In 1931 the Zeppelins opened a regular service on the route Frankfurt — Rio de Janeiro — New York accommodating 100 passengers. The flight was very comfortable and took only four days.

However, the number of catastrophes increased

as well. These air giants were sensitive to gusting winds during flight, especially when landing, and were subject to static electricity discharges which could cause explosions. Two large British airships, R-38 and R-101, crashed, as did the largest American airship the *Akron,* though filled with the safer helium, which nevertheless exploded and plunged into the Atlantic in flames. The series of accidents culminated with the disaster to LZ-129 *Hindenburg* during her 21st flight from Europe to the USA on 6 May 1937. Owing very likely to an electrostatic discharge, the airship exploded when being anchored to a mast at Lakehurst airfield. Sam Shere caught the falling and burning debris in a remarkable photograph (Fig. 488). Thirty-five persons lost their lives. From that day most countries lost interest in this means of transport.

Renaissance of airships? The need to carry heavy loads is inspiring some American and Soviet designers to once again investigate the cargo-carrying possibilities of airships.

Structures made from light metals and synthetic materials, nylon covers, considerable reductions in the price of helium, the possibility of using high-performance turbo-prop units and, thanks to satellite weather forecasts, computer control enabling the airships to avoid storms, inspired several designs of airships up to 1,200 feet long capable of carrying up to 500 tons of cargo at a speed of 100 mph. Even nuclear drive is being considered. Soviet scientists would like to fill airships with heated natural gas from Ural fields and transport it in that way to the USA, Japan and Europe. At the place of destination the gas would be pushed out by steam fed into the ballonnets. A double nylon cover would improve thermal insulation.

489. The *Avion III,* with a wing span of 52¹/₂ ft, was designed by C. Ader and propelled by two steam engines with a total output of 40 hp

History of powered flight

In 1890 the Frenchman Clement Adler was the first to try powered flight. His *Eola* with her wooden, fabric-coated wings looked like a bat. Four-bladed bamboo propellers were driven by a steam engine heated by alcohol with an output of 20 hp. Over the ground she flew about 164 feet. Adler also tried a similar but larger plane *Avion III.* The Russian A. F. Mozhaysky also designed a steam plane, as did the Englishman Hiram Stevens Maxim though neither were very successful. In Maxim's machine two steam engines with an output of 180 hp used 20-ft diameter propellers. On its first flight the multi-wing plane started moving along its launching track, lifted a little, bucked and then overturned.

Soon after that the Wright brothers in the USA fixed an internal combustion engine in their flying machine. They had a lot of difficulty with propeller location, with weight distribution and in deciding the right number of wings. At about the same time French aeronauts Ferber, Blériot and Archdeacon had their engineless gliders towed into the air by cables fixed to automobiles, while the Voisin brothers had their plane towed above the Seine by a motor boat.

The first and historic powered flight took place at Kitty Hawk on 17 December 1903. An engine with an output of 12 hp drove the machine's two pusher airscrews behind the trailing edges of biplane wings. Orville Wright took his place behind the controls, Wilbur released the plane from its launching ramp and five nearly frozen spectators saw the machine lift about 2 ft above ground level and cover a distance of about 40 yards. During the next trial the distance covered was about 20 yards longer and finally the plane covered a distance of about half a mile. Two years later the Wright brothers were capable of controlling their plane so well that they covered a distance of 25 miles.

In September 1906 the untiring aeronaut Alberto Santos Dumont, who had given up his interest in airships, received a prize of 25,000 francs for covering a distance of 55 yards in his monoplane. At the end of 1906 his *14-bis* took off, reaching an altitude of 20 feet and covering nearly 274 yards. On the

Issy-les-Moulineaux meadow near Paris the number of flying experiments increased constantly and new records were broken thanks to various technical innovations: four-bladed airscrews, new and sometimes weird wiry configurations and the use of light bicycle wheels. The meadow was also the site of Blériot's early failure with a plane fitted with paper-covered wings. More successful were the Voisin brothers with their biplane, gradually extending their flight range to 110 yards.

In 1908 Henri Farman, an Anglo-French sportsman, flying Voisin's plane, won a prize of 50,000 francs put up for the first man in Europe to fly a closed one kilometre circuit.

On 25 July 1909, Louis Blériot crossed the Channel in 37 minutes flying from France to England in his monoplane equipped with an Anzani engine giving an output of 25 hp.

Planes needed lighter and more powerful engines than automobiles. Air-cooled Gnome engines with

490. Trying out Maxim's steam plane at Baldwyns Park in 1894. The total weight, including 3 passengers, was 8,156 lb

an output of 55 hp and water-cooled eight-cylinder Antoinette engines, of 100 hp, contributed considerably to the development of aviation. First, though modest achievements stimulated the spirit of competition. At the early international races and competitions Farman biplanes were mainly used. Pilots sat on a simple uncovered seat, their feet resting against a wooden bar. Later lever (joystick) control of the elevator and of the ailerons (hinged wing flaps) was introduced. Rudders were controlled by foot levers or rudder bars. A lattice-girder fuselage was covered by sewn canvas or linen.

In August 1909, on the occasion of the Great

491

Aviation Week, 38 planes gathered at Reims. The winner of the long-distance flight race was Henri Farman who covered 112 miles in 3¼ hours. With two passengers on board, he managed to fly for 10 minutes. The American Glenn Curtiss, flying his *Golden Flyer* biplane with a V-8 engine producing 55 hp, claimed the overall speed record reaching 43·38 mph on a 20-mile circuit. Curtiss claimed that he could achieve such a high speed thanks to the wind, which he thought destroyed the 'vacuum'

formed behind a flying plane, slowing down its movement. This explanation reveals a rather poor knowledge of the theory of flying by these very courageous men.

During the following years pilots mastered their low-powered machines to such an extent that they even dared to carry out acrobatics. In 1911 the American, Lincoln Beachey, flew under the Niagara Falls bridge; at about the same time Claud Grahame-White performed risky acrobatics over the

492

493

streets of Washington. In 1913 the Frenchman A. Pégoud demonstrated the first loop.

On 28 March 1910, a Marseilles citizen Henry Fabre took off in the first hydroplane. In September of the same year the Peruvian Geo Chavéz flew in his Blériot over the Alps from Brigue in Switzerland to Domodossola in Italy. However, before landing, a wing broke off and the courageous pilot was killed.

Other brave pilots wanted to prove that planes were capable of long-distance flight. The American F. Rodgers, flying the small Wright biplane *Baby*, crossed North America in 82 days in several legs.

At the beginning of the First World War there were about 3,000 planes in Europe. Their engines did not usually exceed about 100 hp, and their maximum speed was about 60 mph. These machines could climb to an altitude of about 3 miles, and maximum flight time with full tanks was between 4 and 5 hours. An exceptional speed of 120 mph

494

491. One of the first flights of the Wright brothers in 1903. The wing span was 40 ft, weight 750 lb, and output of the air-cooled four-cylinder engine was 12 hp

492. Santos Dumont in his first plane, which had box-like wings of 39-ft span (1906)

493. Bleriot's monoplane, *La Manche* (1909), wing span 27 ft, weight 750 lb, reached a speed of 40 mph

494. A picture of Glenn Curtis, Gordon Bennet Cup winner, on his *Golden Flyer* (1909)

495

496
497

495. Lincoln Beachey flying under the bridge at the Niagara Falls on 28 June 1911

496. Henry Fabre preparing to take off in his hydroplane on 28 March 1910

497. The high-wing *Spirit of St. Louis* weighed 5,290 lb, including fuel, at the take-off for its flight over the Atlantic. The wing span was 47 ft and the engine a radial Wright Whirlwind of 210 hp

was achieved in 1913 by the Frenchman Prévost flying a Deperdussin monoplane which was especially streamlined. He used an engine with an output of 180 hp. The appearance of planes changed considerably in the course of the following decade. Outstanding European physicists studied the most efficient shape for the wings. Some manufacturers replaced fabric-covered fuselages of wooden or metal tube structures using plywood to cover them instead. In 1915 the German professor Hugo Junkers built the first all-metal plane. Before the war the Russians had started to manufacture large multi-engine planes. The Sikorsky biplane *Ilya Murometz* of 1913 had four engines mounted on its wings, which had a span of 92 feet. It broke several records for carrying capacity, flight range and altitude reached.

The First World War brought about a rapid development of the aircraft industry. However, major progress in aviation technology, was achieved only later, when scientists began detailed studies and experiments in the field of the theory of air flow and the dynamics of flight. They applied their results especially to powered planes.

Until 1919 there had been no successful nonstop transatlantic crossing by air. On 21 June of that year Capt. John Alcock and Lt. Arthur White-

498. Claude Graham White flying his biplane close above a Washington street on 14 October 1910

ten-Brown, former RAF flyers, set out from Newfoundland in a converted Vickers Vimy bomber and made the crossing in 15 hours 57 minutes before crash-landing in a bog in County Galway, Ireland. A great reception was prepared for them in London. They received £10,000 from *The Daily Mail* and were both knighted for their achievement. Another early hero of the air was the young American Charles A. Lindbergh who flew across the Atlantic from New York to Paris and landed on 21 May 1927 after a 33¹/₂-hour flight. He was received with honours usually reserved for statesmen only. His single-engine plane the *Spirit of St. Louis* was fitted with a 210 hp radial engine. In the opposite direction, East to West, it was the German Herman Köhl flying a Junkers W-30 who first succeeded in flying over the Atlantic one year later. In 1928 Charles Kingford Smith and C.T.P. Ulm, in their monoplane *Southern Cross*, made the first trans-Pacific flight from the USA to Australia, and in 1931 Pangborn and Herndon flew in a Bellanca monoplane non-stop from the USA to Japan. The efforts to connect continents by air culminated with the flight of a three-member crew headed by the legendary Chkalov; in 1937 they flew in a Russian ANT-25 monoplane from Moscow over the North Pole to Vancouver, landing 63 hours later with their aircraft badly iced up. By that time some of the existing airline companies already had 15 years of experience with passenger transport on much shorter and comparatively easy routes.

Civil aviation in the period before the jet

In February 1919, Britain and France inaugurated regular London—Paris military courier services, and in August 1919 the first scheduled commercial airlines were flown between London and Paris by DH4A aircraft of Air Transport and Travel.

Aviation became a matter of big business. Every week a new airline company was born. It was necessary to assess the differing interests of all these and to divide up rationally routes between individual European cities. For that purpose the International Air Traffic Association—to which the present IATA owes its origin—was established in 1919.

In the 1920s British Imperial Airways began using Handley Page biplanes. The lines served mainly for mail transport. After mail had been loaded luggage came second and then came the turn of the passengers; about 15 of them could be seated in the plywood covered fuselage. The engines were started by manual airscrew turning. With two engines of 440 hp each, fixed to the wing struts, the Handley Page reached a speed of about 100 mph. Because of very low wing-loading the landing speed was only 45 mph so that even an emergency landing was relatively safe. Constantly improved biplanes were manufactured into the 1930s, until research proved that the future belonged to streamlined monoplanes.

In 1925 the Dutch Fokkers became widely used in Europe. These were high-wing monoplanes with a fuselage consisting of steel and aluminium tubes and with a cantilever wing of wood. The three-engine Fokker F-VII was designed for eight passengers, a pilot and a wireless operator. It had a maximum speed of 100 mph and a flight range of 500 miles. Using these planes Pan American Airways opened their service between Florida and Havana, Cuba, in 1927.

Technological development of civil aircraft in the years 1920—1939: Cantilever low-wing, high-wing or mid-wing monoplanes took a long time to prove their advantages over biplanes. To achieve

499

499. An early flight of Imperial Airways from London in 1924

500. A French twin-engine biplane the Farman Goliath of 1920

501. The interior of the wooden, plywood-covered Farman Goliath on the Paris — Brussels line in 1920

502

503

504

502. The Junkers all-metal F-13 for 4 passengers and 2 crew members. Flying weight 4,078 lb, output 190 hp, maximum speed 105 mph

503. A single-engined high-wing Fokker of mixed structure (wood, steel and fabric). Wing span 65·6 ft, power output from 402 hp to 697 hp, speed 121 to 130 mph

504. The three-engined French Brequet 393 of 1932 with radial engines

505. The Junkers G38 flying wing of 1930. Power output 4 × 800 hp, maximum speed 114 mph

economy in running planes are built to have the highest possible lift-drag (resistance) ratio. If they fly fast the problem arises of how to brake efficiently in the air before landing, in order to reduce to a reasonable distance the landing run. This requirement was met by mounting flaps on or into the leading and trailing edges of the wings. These altered the flow over the wing surfaces and generated the necessary lift even at low landing speeds. Retractable undercarriages contributed to the reduction of air resistance. In 1928 radial engines were given ring-cowlings, which brought about unexpectedly good results. Research results of the American NACA Committee proved that turbulence in the air flow was largely removed and that cylinder cooling was improved. Moreover, under certain conditions the air leaving the rear of the cowling generated a certain additional propulsion effect. The first plane with a NACA long-chord cowling, called the Vega, was manufactured by the relatively unknown Californian Lockheed company and was early in the field of fast streamlined transport planes. The aircraft reached a maximum speed of 135 mph and a later version 195 mph. A monocoque plywood fuselage with a smooth surface was used for the first time in the Vega.

The power-weight ratio of engines was constantly increased; the engine performance was further improved by variable-pitch airscrews designed by the British engineer, Dr. Hele-Shaw. By adjusting the incidence angle of the airscrew blades during the flight it was possible to increase the flight speed by 10 per cent for the same engine output, and the ceiling by 20 per cent. Take-off distance could be reduced as well. During further development the reversible airscrew offered the possibility of use for braking on the ground, shortening the landing dis-

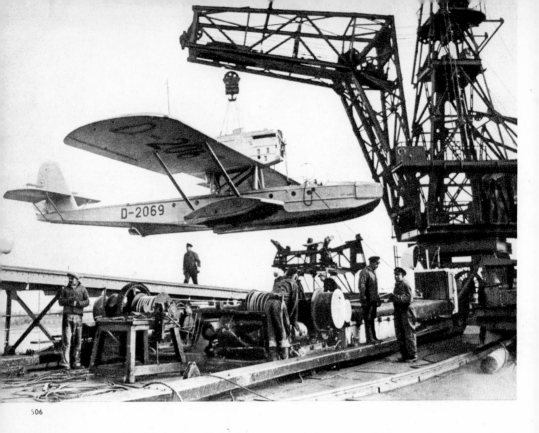

tance. When designing its He 70 mail plane, the German Heinkel company profited from American experience with fast planes. Its thin-profiled steel structure was covered with pressed laminated plywood. The machine, with a flying weight of 5,070 lb and equipped with a Mercedes engine of 630 hp, reached a maximum speed of 221 mph and was used to transport five passengers.

Professor Hugo Junkers set the guidelines for all-metal plane development, which, in the end, proved to be the only feasible solution when speeds got really high. The Junkers J-1, which took off on 12 December 1915, can be regarded as the first all-metal plane with a shell structure and a cantilever wing without the external struts.

In European civil aviation the most widely used

507

506. A Dornier-Wal flying boat lifted by crane on to the launcher on the steamer *Westfalen* (1935)

507. The Junkers Ju 52 with three engines, power output 3 × 670 hp, cruising speed 161 mph, flight range 776 mph

508. The dining saloon of the all-metal Ju-G 31

509. The Boeing B-314 Yankee Clipper

508

type was the Junkers F-13 with an engine producing 190 hp. This type, in fact, represented the starting point for the later Junkers G-24 with three engines, and also for the G-38 of 1926. During the 1930s Junkers tried to gain a leading position with his big flying-wing plane, the G-38. It used to fly with 30 passengers on the Berlin—London route. Passenger cabins were partly located in the root of a large, thick, 144-ft-long wing. With its flying weight of 23 tons and driven by four 800-hp engines, the flying-wing G-38 achieved a speed of 115 mph. Of all the Junkers transport planes the most successful was the Ju-52 of 1933, designed for 15—17 passengers. With three engines in ring cowlings it reached a speed of 160 mph. Several variations of the type had diesel engines.

In the early days, only flying-boats were used for transatlantic flights. Many efforts to build giant aircraft of this type failed. The nine-wing Caproni flying-boat built in 1919, which was to transport up

509

to 100 passengers, could not even take off. In 1928 the German Dornier Company built a similar monster, the Do X for 70—80 passengers. The 52-ton machine with all the necessary comforts—smoking room, sleeping compartments and a bar—could fly, thanks to its 12 engines of 600 hp each, but proved to be very clumsy and uneconomic. When the Do X completed its maiden flight on 25 July 1929, it was undoubtedly the largest plane in the world. On 21 October it made a flight with a total of 169 persons on board.

In 1939 Dornier-Wal flying-boats for carrying mail were put into service on the route from Berlin to Buenos Aires. In order to refuel en route, however, the flying-boats had to land beside depot ships, the *Westfalen* and *Schwabenland*, waiting for them at sea. The planes were refueled and hoisted by crane onto a catapult launching system for take-

off. Transport of mail along this route took three days.

Planes of the Dutch airlines KLM flew from Amsterdam to Batavia, Air France routes led from Paris to Dakar, Buenos Aires and Saigon. Pan American Airways, on their overseas routes to New Zealand, Australia and Hong Kong, used the giant Clipper aircraft manufactured by the Sikorski, Boeing, Douglas and Martin companies in co-operation. Other non-sea routes were directed to the north from Seattle to Alaska; some of the aircraft, like the three-engine Ford Tri-motors and other single-engined Fords were provided with skis for landing on snow.

Only big planes with three or more engines could fly over the Atlantic without intermediate landings and ensure direct communication by air between the USA and Europe. In 1938 the German

Focke-Wulf FW 200 Condor succeeded in this direct flight. The aircraft with 26 passengers and a four-member crew took off from Berlin and reached New York after a 24-hour flight. It was not until 17 June 1939, that Pan-American Airways began their regular flights from New York to Lisbon over the Atlantic.

In 1934 the Douglas company in Santa Monica, USA, began manufacturing an exceptionally successful twin-engined plane the DC-2 for 14 passengers. With two Wright Cyclone radial engines of 710 hp each, it reached a speed of 213 mph; using one engine only it could climb to an altitude of 12,000 ft. In 1937, based on this type, the most successful all-metal cantilever monoplane of all times, the DC-3 — the well-know Dakota — was manufactured. The skin of the fuselage and wings was of riveted duraluminum sheet. The undercarriage retracted into the engine nacelles in such a way that the lower parts of the wheels projected 10 inches downwards, which facilitated landing if the under-carriage itself failed to come down. For the Dakota the engine power output was increased to 2 × 920 hp, the flight range was extended to 1,700 miles. This excellent aircraft, safe and with a good reserve of power, carried 24 passengers and then, in its tourist version, 32 passengers. All the world was buying Dakotas; by the end of the Second World War altogether 11,000 of these planes had been manufactured and as late as 1974 nearly 2,500 of them were still flying. In 1938 Douglas started producing a four-engine DC-4 with an output of 4 × 1,340 hp and a range of 2,200 miles for long-distance flights.

This aircraft and after it the Boeing Stratocruiser were flying at altitudes which required the use of pressurised cabins. Further increase in engine power (up to 28 cylinders in four-row radials), the reduction of the weight/power ratio below 1 lb/hp, higher flight path altitudes — all this enabled later aircraft such as the DC-7 and Lockheed Constellation (1950), Super-Constellation (1951) and Super Star Constellation (1957) with a total engine output of 14,000 hp, to achieve a cruising speed of 300 — 340 mph. Their flight range was extended to 6,250 miles. Through to the 1960s these planes were used on all the world air routes, and some of them are still in service today. At length, however, they were superseded by even faster and more efficient turbine aircraft. Single or twin-engine planes still using piston engines continued in use for private or business purposes.

Turbojet aircraft

The first patent for a turbojet engine was granted in 1930 to the British engineer Frank Whittle. An engine on these lines powered the Gloster research aircraft when it made Britain's first jet flight in May

510. The Douglas DC-3 of 1936. Wing span 95 ft, flying weight 11 tons, power output 2 × 920 hp, maximum speed 221 mph

511. The Lockheed Super Constellation of 1957. Wing span 148 ft, take-off weight 70 tons, 66 — 102 passengers

512. A modern private or business plane, the Cessna 207 Skywagon

512

1941 at Cranwell. The Americans took the British documentation as their starting point and tested their own jet engine system in 1942, using a Lockheed Shooting Star aircraft. The plane crossed the United States at an average speed of about 600 mph. In Germany experiments were initiated by Ernst Heinkel, aided by Dr. Pabst von Ohain, in 1936, and on 27 August 1939, Heinkel's test pilot Warsitz made the first jet flight when he flew twice round the factory airfield in Warnow in the turbine He-178, which had an engine developed by von Ohain.

The jet engine signified a great advance in aviation. For the same weight it can yield a power output two and a half times as great as that of the piston engine. Its efficiency is highest at speeds approaching the speed of sound; it can function well even at very high altitudes.

The principle of the jet engine is very simple. Air sucked in through the front of the engine is com-pressed by a compressor. In the combustion chambers the compressed air is mixed with fuel sprayed in from nozzles. This mixture is ignited and expansion of the heated gases which come out from the tail pipe generates the thrust. In its passage it operates the compressor, fuel pumps, the electric current generator, etc.

Turboprop aircraft: These are a half-way stage to the pure jet aeroplane. Reduction gearing reduces the very high speed of the turbine shaft to drive a conventional propeller, and the use of turboprop units did not greatly change the shape or conception of planes. Their performance, however, increased in comparison with piston engine planes to such an extent, that at altitudes between $2^1/_2 - 3^3/_4$ miles they could fly economically at speeds from $375 - 500$ mph.

The high performance of the turboprop engines encouraged designers to think again about giant

513

514
515

513. The Saunders Roe SR 45 flying boat with ten turbine engines giving a total power output of 35,000 hp (top). The Brabazon II b (bottom)

514. The British Hawker-Siddeley 748 MF turbo-prop passenger and freight aircraft for 40—62 passengers or 5 tons of freight

515. The tail of the Fokker F 28 jet plane (1974) showing the airbrakes and the two side-mounted jet engines. The fully open position of the landing flaps on the wing can be seen

516. The undercarriage of a DC-10 undergoing test. In this picture the multi-disc brakes can be seen

517. The Comet IV B jet aircraft

flying-boats which had always tended to be under-powered. Turboprop Bristol Proteus engines with an output of 3,200 hp were installed in the Saunders Roe SR/45 *Princess* flying-boat. The ten-engine *Princess* was designed for 105 passengers and had a take-off weight of 135 tons. Serious mechanical trouble developed during tests, however, which would have necessitated extensive modifications involving much time and expense. Production was finally cancelled, the future of such aircraft still undecided.

Other developments of turboprop aircraft were

much more successful. The world's first turboprop airliner was the Vickers Viscount and in 1953 the first passenger services by turboprop were inaugurated. The Viscount was powered by four Rolls-Royce engines, had a speed of 350—400 mph and a flight range of 1,200 miles. Vickers later replaced the Viscount with the Vanguard which had a larger seating capacity—up to 100 passengers—and a flight range of 2,500 miles. However, by the time these were in service airlines were preferring to use jet aircraft on their routes.

Principally for this reason other turboprop air-

517

518. The instrument panel in the cockpit of the L-1011 Tristar jet: 1 — engine boost; 2 — flight course indicator; 3 — autopilot control; 4 — navigation switch; 5 — flight altitude selection; 6 — engine function indicator; 7 — warning signals; 8, 9 — automatic landing system; 10 — aircraft balance indicator; 11 — main control column

519. The Vickers VC-10 landing

518

craft such as the Bristol Britannia, the Lockheed Electra and the Soviet Ilyushin Il-18, did not achieve wide popularity although most of them remained in airline service into the late 1970s.

The biggest of the turboprop airliners is the Soviet Tupolev Tu-114, introduced in 1961 by the Soviet Aeroflot company. This low-wing monoplane, with a span of 168 ft and with a flying weight of 145 tons is driven by four turboprop units with counter-rotating propellers with a total output of 48,000 hp. It carries 120 passengers for intercontinental flights and is still used on Aeroflot's long-distance routes

such as Moscow—Khabarovsk, Moscow—Delhi, Moscow—Havana. For short stages there is a 220-passenger version.

Turboprop units have continued to be viable in smaller planes, e.g. in the Soviet twin-engine Antonov An-10 and An-24 and in medium-size passenger and freight planes such as the Hawker-Siddeley 748 MF and the Dutch Fokker Friendship.

The turboprop engine is reliable and has the advantage of low fuel consumption.

Development of jet engines: After the Second World War the size and power of jet engines in-

519

creased rapidly as did the size and the number of turbine rotors and of compressors in the engines. Nowadays two-stage compressors are usually used and each stage is connected by its own coaxial shaft with the rotor of the turbine.

By-pass turbojet engines, introduced just after the Second World War by Metropolitan-Vickers, substantially increased the total efficiency. The same shaft that drives the multi-stage compressor drives, after an rpm reduction, a large-diameter fan wheel.

Behind the fan the air is distributed so that only a proportion of it passes through the compressors to play its part in fuel combustion and the turbine drive. The rest, i.e. the cold flow, passes round the circumference of the engine cooling it and going some way towards reducing the noise level. At the outlet the two flows merge, considerably increasing the thrust of the engine.

In turbofan by-pass jet engines for giant airliners, the combustion gases reach a temperature of

520. The Trident II

521. The American Boeing 737 for shorter routes. Cruising speed 560 mph, fuel consumption 704 UK gal/hr, capacity 10·4 tons

522. The Soviet Ilyushin Il-62 long-distance aircraft

523. The American Boeing 727 with three engines

1,280° C (2,336° F) generating a thrust of up to 25 tons. Units for supersonic aircraft develop a thrust of 35 tons (2·2 lb of thrust corresponds to an output of approximately 4 hp.). The service life has risen to 10,000 and more flight hours.

Jet airliners: Jet engines, which made possible high speeds, have influenced the design of planes to a large extent. Most are designed for speeds just below 625 mph and for this wings and tails have taken on an arrow-like swept-back shape. The wings

themselves are slender, their profiles thin. The fuselage surfaces must be perfectly smooth. These parameters suit conditions of high speed flying at altitudes above 26,000 ft. To provide the aircraft with sufficient lift during take-off and landing, wings are fitted with a system of flaps at the trailing and sometimes the leading edges. During landing flaps are fully extended which increases the wing curvature and helps to smooth out the air flow over it. In their early stages jet engines used to be built directly into the wing; in most subsequent multi-engine planes they are suspended individually in nacelles beneath the wings, but in some successful twin- and triple-engined aircraft they are located at the tail. Engines are fitted with noise suppressors though it is difficult to achieve anything worthwhile without serious loss of power. During the last decade they have been provided with a means of reversing the thrust which reverses the jet in such a way as to function as a brake during landing. Before that a few airliners used braking parachutes launched from the tail.

Undercarriages of jet aircraft are exceptionally low, since airscrew dimensions no longer need to be taken into consideration when allowing for ground clearance. Wheels with special tyres designed for exceptional loads have multi-disc brakes. In heavier machines undercarriages with four or more wheels are used. Cabins are pressurised; at high altitudes a pressure is maintained corresponding to an altitude of 6,500 ft. The cockpit can accommodate the pilot, the co-pilot and the navigator; in large airliners a flight engineer is present to keep a check on the functioning of the engines and other mechanisms, usually seated at a separate panel of pressure gauges and other dials. For safety, all instruments are duplicated.

On 2 May 1952, BOAC (British Overseas Aircraft Corporation) inaugurated the first jet passenger service in the world with a De Havilland Comet 1 flying the London — Johannesburg route. The same year, the aircraft was assigned the London — Ceylon (Sri Lanka) and London — Singapore routes, cutting flying time almost in half. The low-wing plane had four jet engines in the wing roots. Unfortunately a series of accidents followed due to structural deficiencies in the design and the type was withdrawn from service after two years. In 1956 the Soviet twin-engine Tupolev Tu-104 began its first flights. With 70 and later on 100 passengers, it reached a cruising speed of 500 mph, at an altitude of 6 — 7 miles, and a maximum speed of 625 mph.

In 1955 France entered the era of jet airliners with her Caravelle for 80 passengers which was the first to have engines at the rear, these being two Rolls-Royce jets, each with a thrust of 10,500 lb (4·68 tons). After further research into the problems which had been encountered before in the Comet 1, Britain introduced the four-engined Comet 4 Series on her air routes. The USA made a start with the Douglas DC-8 with four Rolls-Royce engines. The airliner in its tourist version accommodated 130 passengers and its flight range was 4,000 miles. But the four-engine Boeing 707 aircraft have really proved the most popular the world over.

These, together with a number of other types manufactured up to about 1960, are regarded as the first generation jets. The engine weight represented about 9 per cent of the total and the useful load was never higher than 11 per cent. This ratio has been substantially improved in planes of the second and third generations.

The second generation of jet aircraft, manufactured in the years 1962—72 is equipped with more

525

powerful and economical engines, usually of the by-pass turbojet type, with thrust reversers. They have been designed specifically to suit various established routes. Distinction is made between planes for ultra-short distances of less than 200 miles, for short distances of 200—1,000 miles, for medium distances of 1,000—2,500 miles and finally for long distances over 2,500 miles. Western European

524. A Hawker-Siddeley business jet

525. A General Electric turbo-fan engine. Fan diameter just over 8 ft

countries had to overcome a crisis in the years 1960—63, when the increased availability of seats in large capacity aircraft suddenly considerably exceeded the number of would-be air travellers, but the introduction of the more economical second generation planes and the reduction of tariffs once again stimulated interest. International agreements on the standardisation of equipment and maintenance procedures helped in the economic operation of these aircraft, since any type of plane could find the necessary service facilities in all the world's major airports.

For short distances twin and triple-engined planes for 70—90 passengers are usually used. The United States have been manufacturing a twin-engine Douglas DC-9 and a twin-engine Boeing 737, Britain the BAC One Eleven with two engines and the Trident with a third engine mounted under the tailplane. In this category the Soviet Union produced the Tu-124 and Tu-134 and more recently the Tu-154, which carried up to 164 passengers. After a modification of the fuselage length and a reduction in the number of seats, some of these planes can be used on medium distance routes. The most popular type is the Boeing 727 with three engines and a door under the tail for passenger entry, as well as conventional entrances in the fuselage sides.

For long distances, special versions of these aircraft and others such as the American Convair 880, the Vickers VC-10 and Super VC-10 and the Soviet

526. One of the cabins of the Lockheed Tristar aircraft. The lockers between the centre rows of seats are for coats and hand luggage

Il-62 with a capacity for 160—190 passengers are widely used.

Small jets for private purposes have also been an outcome of the transition from airscrew drive to the jet system. In Europe especially, the twin-engine business jet HS-125 of the Hawker-Siddeley company and the three-engined French Falcon 30 are popular.

Third generation of large jet airliners: It is expected that in 1980 about 800 million passengers per annum will be transported by air. If they were to travel by first generation planes, the airliners of the world would have to make 25 million take-offs. This being quite beyond the capacities of world airports and of air traffic control systems, the only solution is to increase the passenger accommodation of jet airliners to 400—500 passengers. These giant aircraft, already coming into being, are for medium and long-distance routes. For short distances

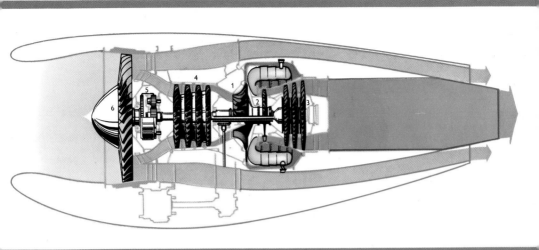

LXX Cross-section of a turbo-fan engine: 1—compressor; 2—first turbine stage; 3—second turbine stage; 4—compressor; 5—reducer; 6—fan

LXXI A Boeing 707 with four Pratt and Whitney engines. Wing span 146 ft, length 152 ft, range 5,095—5,716 miles

LXXII The Boeing 747SP in the foreground has four Pratt and Whitney engines. Wing span 195 ft, length 321 ft, range 4,473—5,026 miles

527

they will be provided with only the most basic
equipment; this type of plane is called an airbus.
Existing fuselage lenghts have really reached a maximum so the circular section of the fuselages has
been increased from something like 12·5-ft diameter to 22 ft. In such a fuselage, the passengers in the
tourist class are sitting in rows of eight or nine
people. These large aircraft require far powerful engines. Giant turbofans are generally used, whose diameter at the inlet is up to 8 ft and the engines'
thrust weight ratio has been improved four times in
comparison with the first generation to approximately 20:1. The engine weight represents only 4 per
cent of the total plane weight (as compared with 9
per cent in the first generation) and the useful load
is nowadays 33 per cent of the total aircraft weight.

The Boeing 747—the Jumbo—ordered by
BOAC was put into operation on 15 March 1970.
At present about 500 aircraft of this type are in
service on all the world routes. The Jumbo has 18
wheels in its undercarriage and is as high as a five-
storey house. Four turbofan engines are suspended
in nacelles under wings. They each develop a thrust
of between 43,500 and 47,00 lb. The take-off weight
is 308 tons, and the flight range 5,800 miles. The
luggage of up to 470 passengers is placed in 26
containers under the floor. The interior is divided
into a number of compartments. There can be
either a bar or a first-class dining room. The American firm McDonnell-Douglas invested 1·2 milli-

ard dollars to develop the slightly smaller DC-10
aircraft (Plate LXXIII) for 345 economy-class passengers, the flight range being 4,400 miles. The
plane has three engines with a total thrust of
155,000 lb. A similar arrangement is that of another
airbus, the Lockheed L-1011 TriStar, where 345
passengers can sit looking through windows
equipped with polarisation glass against direct glare.

In comparison with these de luxe giant airliners
the European airbus, the A-300B (Plate LXXIV) is
more modest as far as its equipment is concerned.
It is the outcome of co-operation among several
west-European countries headed by France and
West Germany. The aircraft has two engines and its
take-off weight amounts to 132 tons. According to
the seating arrangement used, it can accommodate
261 or 306 passengers. The most up-to-date General Electric turbofans make the airbus operation
extremely economic: per passenger and 60 flight
miles only 7·4 pints of fuel are consumed, i.e. half
the consumption of a passenger car.

In 1977 the Soviet Union put into service the

Ilyushin Il-68 airbus, a low-winged aircraft with four by-pass turbojet engines. The most heavily loaded parts of the airframe are made of steel alloy and titanium. In three compartments there are seats for 350 passengers. The aircraft has three main and three emergency exits. A staircase from the lower floor leads to the main entrance.

The introduction of giant airliners had made all airport activities far more complicated. Only a few major airports can, for instance, handle a departure or arrival of passengers from three jumbo-jets simultaneously. It is expected that by about the year 1990 these types of aircraft will be transporting

1,000,000,000 passengers in a year. By that time the number of civil aviation employees (including manufacturers, organisational staff and ground services) will have reached 13 million.

Giant freight planes

From the very beginning of regular air transport planes used to carry mail. For heavier freight transport, however, planes were too expensive and were used only in exceptional cases, e.g. in Australia where they were used to carry cattle between distant towns. Fresh fish used to be sent by air from Iceland to Europe.

The large-scale development of freight transport took place only after the dividing of Berlin into two cities in the summer of 1948. West Berlin with 1·5 million inhabitants was supplied for a certain time

528. The hinged nose of the Boeing 747 F cargo plane raised for freight loading

528

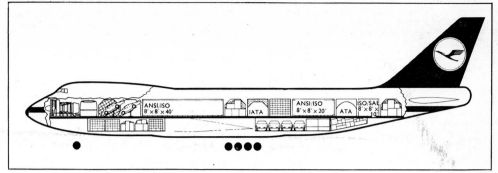

only by air, when aircraft had to supply it, not only with food, but also fuel such as coal and oil.

Experience was joined, but the interest in freight transport was still not strong enough to stimulate the production of special freighters. The types of planes used were those in which it was possible to remove unoccupied passenger seats and to fill the space with freight. It was not until 1968 that interest in fast and economically advantageous air transport of goods quickened, such as the carrying of transistor radio receivers from Japan to the USA and Europe, and of perishable foodstuffs, etc. In 1968 8 milliard ton-kilometers were flown and in 1975 it was three and a half times as much. By 1980 the figure should be exceeded eight times.

Because of increasing demand for freight planes some big airliners were re-designed to meet the

529. Load distribution in the 230-ft long fuselage of the Boeing 737F freight plane with different types of containers shown

530. Loading containers through side doors from a mobile lifting platform

need. Stackers and fork lift trucks could load pallets or cargo containers direct into the aircraft from the side, using approach ramps located under the tail or by means of a large opening in the nose, which could be swung aside on hinges. The increased capacities of freight compartments allowed for tariff reduction and, consequently, stimulated freight

531. By means of push-buttons the loading operator controls the roller drive of the transport system on the fuselage floor. In the background are two ISO-C containers

532. The largest Soviet turbo-prop freight aircraft, the Anteus An-22 has a take-off weight of 250 tons. It needs a runway only 1,200 yd long. The main under-carriage, retracting into side fairings, has 12 wheels

533. The American Super Guppy aircraft, with hinged nose cone, is designed for large volume freight transport, e.g. missiles and big aircraft parts

531

532

transport by air. The American Boeing 707 in its freight version can hold about 45 tons of cargo. Transportation costs can be cut by another third if the freight is carried in a Boeing Jumbo B-747-F (freight version) and if it is loaded on pallets, in international containers or in special air containers.

This carrier can take up to 90 tons of cargo, the flight range being 4,400 miles. By depressing a push-button in the pilot's cockpit or on a mobile control panel near the nose-wheel, the nose itself is tilted electrically within $1^1/_2$ minutes, giving access for the loading. Electrically-driven pulleys which bring the load aboard are built into the floor of the plane and the aircraft can be loaded in less than 45 minutes.

Special light air containers with chamfered corners can be taken aboard the aircraft, either from lift platforms or through lateral doors, and in some cases the passenger luggage compartment is used. The Boeing Jumbo B-747-F is equipped with an automatic weighing and balancing system. This receives signals from sensors on the undercarriage and calculates—by means of a board computer—the position of the centre of gravity and the total weight and its distribution. If permissible values are exceeded, it gives a warning signal.

In the Soviet Union the turboprop Antonov An-22 is used to transport heavy freight. Loading and unloading of cargoes of up to 80 tons is carried out by a ramp under the raised tail section. Four turboprop units with a total output of 60,000 hp enable the plane to fly at a speed of 460 mph.

The biggest plane for freight transport is the modified American military troop carrier, the giant Lockheed C-5A Galaxy with the designation L-500. The capacity of the freight compartment, accessible both from the front and from the rear by a tilting platform is 1,288 cu yd. The machine can carry 120 tons of cargo (i.e. 100 cars). It has a take-off weight of 350 tons, a flight range of 3,000 miles and its cruising speed is 530 mph. If modified, it could accommodate about 900 tourist-class passengers.

An even larger freighter—a flying container ship—is being designed. Its creator is a German professor, Claudius Dornier.

It is planned as a high-wing flying-boat, 340 ft long, with ten engines, which could take aboard 400 tons of cargo in a specially designed port—e.g. 50 ISO-C containers. Compared with the B-747-F, the costs would be cut by a half and the aircraft could compete even with fast container ships.

533

Supersonic aircraft

Civil supersonic aircraft were developed with the objective of substantially cutting flight times for long-distance routes. The first pilot to fly faster than the speed of sound was the American Charles Yeager—on 14 October 1947. Even at a little over Mach 1* parts of a plane become extremely hot. At Mach 2·5 the rigidity of aluminium alloys is reduced and hardened window glass may break. At Mach 5, aluminium alloys melt and steel softens.

If an airliner is to fly at supersonic speeds, its resistance has to be one third that of other planes.

535

534. The largest freight aircraft in the world, the Lockheed L-500

535. Dornier's flying container ship has a wing span of 334 ft and a flight range of 3,728 miles

536. The projected American supersonic aircraft, the Boeing 2707-300 was to have had a 30° angle sweep-back to its arrow-like wings during supersonic flight (above), and when landing this angle would change to 72° (bottom)

This can be achieved by reducing the thickness of the wings, paying especial attention to the smoothness of all surfaces, and by a very slender fuselage. The sudden great difference in the lift values during the passage from subsonic to supersonic speeds and vice versa was satisfactorily solved by using variable delta wings. Some delta wing supersonic aircraft use elevons for steering rather than a rudder. These are steering flaps at the trailing edges of the wings. They combine the function of ailerons and of elevators, so that they can control the longitudinal and lateral direction of the plane.

Because of the experience of American specialists when developing big supersonic bombers it was expected that supersonic civil transport by air would be first introduced in the United States. But the Americans suffered a set-back when the giant supersonic aircraft XB-70-2 Valkyrie crashed, though in 1966 it reached a speed of Mach 3·08. Later on rivalry developed between the Boeing and Lockheed companies concerning the concept of a supersonic civil airliner. Their competing aircraft were designed for Mach 2·7 and were 60 ft long. With four high-performance engines they were to have a flight range of 4,000 miles. The Lockheed model with a double delta wing failed in wind tunnel tests. The Boeing company—mainly for weight reasons—had to give up the principle of wings with variable sweep. Economic problems, public feeling against the sonic bang, and engine noise and its pollution of the atmosphere all accelerated the deci-

sion of the government to stop its financial subsidy of the projects. Development of the Boeing 2707—300 prototypes ceased in 1970.

The initiative was taken over by France and Britain. The two countries developed a joint project, the Concorde, smaller and slightly slower than the American designs. Unofficial competition developed between Concorde and the Soviet supersonic Tu-144 aircraft prepared by a team headed by A. N. Tupolev and his son.

The prototypes of Concorde 001 from France and of Concorde 002 from Britain left the assembly lines in the summer of 1968. The 150-ton aircraft, driven by four Rolls-Royce Snecma Olympus jet engines, were manufactured using the light alloy Hiduminium-RR58 for the majority of the structure.

The 130-ton prototype of the Soviet Tu-144 for 140 passengers reached supersonic speed at an altitude of 9·3 miles on 15 June 1969. The British Concorde prototype achieved supersonic speed only a year later.

A serious design problem is the change of balance and stability during flight. Concorde solves this by pumping fuel from one tank to another, the

* Mach number: This expresses the ratio of the aircraft speed at a given altitude to the speed of sound. (The speed of sound at ground level is roughly 767 mph.)

537

Tu-144 by a special wing shape. The development of Concorde was relatively straightforward and it is now in regular passenger service. The Tu-144 had to be largely redesigned following the prototype's dramatic crash at the Paris Air Show in 1973.

Before being able to meet the strict safety regulations set by the ICAO (International Civil Aviation Organisation) and by IATA (International Air Transport Association) even the successful Concorde had to be modified several times. The Soviet supersonic Tu-144 took off for its first regular proving flight on the Moscow—Alma Ata route in January 1976, carrying cargo only, one week before the Concorde entered full passenger service. On 21

538

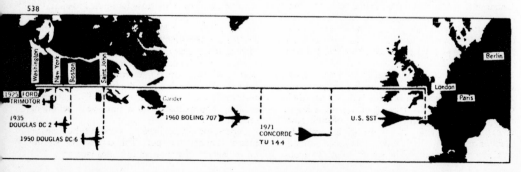

537. A front view of the Soviet supersonic Tu-144 aircraft. Capacity 150 passengers, cruising speed Mach 2·5, take-off weight 130 tons, flight range 4,039 miles, take-off run 4,000 yd

538. How far we used to get, how far we get nowadays, and where we shall get in the future after a two-hour flight

539. The Orbiter rocket plane for 100 passengers is 121-ft long, the span of the delta wing is 75$^1/_2$ ft, and it has three liquid hydrogen/oxygen propulsion units. The tow for the carrier rocket can be seen in the background

539

January 1976, the French Concorde took off from Roissy completing the 6,000-mile flight to Rio de Janeiro in 6 hours 45 minutes. At the same time the British Concorde 002 (Plate LXXV) took off from Heathrow Airport for its destination, Bahrein on the Persian Gulf.

Specific features of supersonic flights: Because of their powerful engines supersonic aircraft only need a relatively short distance for take-off and their climb is exceptionally steep. During the take-off their engines work at only 80 per cent of their power to reduce the noise to a permissible level. The plane is allowed to reach supersonic speeds only at an altitude of 7$^1/_2$ miles. The transition to supersonic speed involves an increase in the fuel used. In the course of this operation Concorde consumes 2,800 gallons of fuel per hour compared with its usual average consumption of 1,800 gallons per hour. The flight is computer-controlled. During the landing operation the slender nose of the aircraft is inclined downwards mechanically to ensure a better view for the pilot. The service life of the first civil supersonic airliners is estimated at 5,000 hours flying, corresponding approximately to a three-year period of service.

Supersonic aircraft have yet again cut the time for intercontinental transport. This can be best shown on a diagram of transatlantic routes (see page 410)

which illustrates the distance covered by a passenger in 2 hours when flying by several generations of transport aircraft. Today, New York and Moscow are divided only by a three-hour flight. Interesting paradoxes occur. If a supersonic airliner flies in the direction the Earth rotates, it lands—according to local time—a few hours earlier than the hour of its take-off.

Development of HST aircraft (Hypersonic Transport) is being studied especially by the Lockheed company. These aircraft, which should be put into operation by the end of the 1980s, should reach speeds corresponding to Mach 6 at an altitude of 18·75 miles and Mach 8 at an altitude of 23 miles. The fuselage with backswept wings will look like a rocket and titanium and nickel steels will be used. The cruising speed of the aircraft with 250 passengers on board should be 6,875 mph.

Rocket planes or shuttles are being prepared for orbital piloted flights. Rocket-shaped planes for 100 passengers will be lifted off from the earth by a carrier rocket with a solid propellant. A liquid propellant rocket engine will take over and enable them to reach the determined orbit. Return to Earth will be by gliding flight. In 1979 the American rocket plane or shuttle *Orbiter* is to carry out its first expe-

rimental flight. About 70,000 American specialists are working on its development. By 1985 about 60 shuttles should take off in a year. When fulfilling research tasks they are planned to work in orbit at an altitude of 100—600 miles for 30 days.

World airports

At the beginning of civil aviation about 50 acres of level meadow were quite sufficient for take-offs and landings. A single storey terminal building with a primitive transmitter station on the edge of the field served the passengers. Planes were kept in small hangars. Only a few flights a day were operated.

Just before the Second World War major airports were equipped with 540-yd or 870-yd concrete runways and sometimes two intersecting runways. The angle of intersection depended on prevailing winds and other local conditions. A pilot could select the appropriate runway to avoid the effects of side winds.

Airfields used to be built as close to towns as possible, which proved to be an unwise decision when civil aviation developed beyond all expectations. Cities spread to the very edges of airports,

540. Frankfurt airport, with two satellite embarkation points, has parking areas for 72 planes, including 18 Jumbo jets

541. Passenger conveyor belts at Amsterdam's Schiphol airport which is the lowest in altitude of any of the world's airports

542. Mobile telescopic entry corridors

543. Frankfurt airport building is connected by a system of corridors to an underground station. Another corridor leads to a parking lot for 6,000 cars

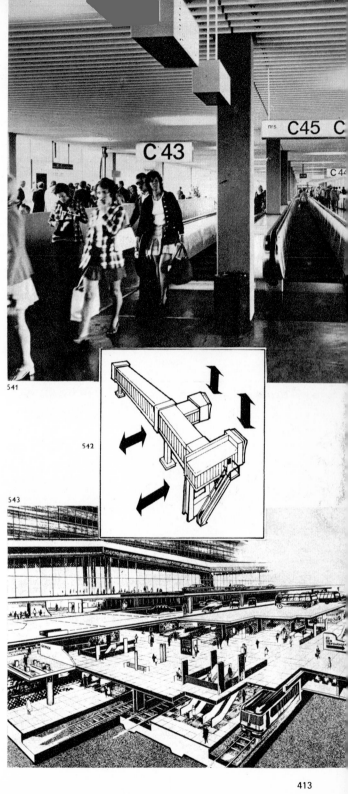

541

542

543

544

restricting their expansion. When the period of jet aircraft came, cities became victims of excessive noise.

Nowadays there are about 30,000 civil aviation airports. The major airports have as many employees as large factories. Kennedy Airport in the USA employs more than 50,000 technicians, engineers and other workers, while Orly Airport in Paris has 25,000 employees.

A present-day international airport requires an area five hundred times larger than those of half a century ago. It has to be connected with neighbouring cities not by one, but by several roads or motorways, fast rail transport, helicopter services or by underground lines. Big international airports are in fact the first impression many visitors have of a country, and for that reason a great deal of money

544. Passengers can get to satellite embarkation points through seven tunnels leading from the circular main building of the new Charles De Gaulle airport near Paris

545. The Florida Tampa International Airport covers an area of 3,212 acres. To the four existing satellites another three will be added, extending the number of aircraft parking areas to 74

546

547

is used to provide them with the necessary equipment, attractive architecture and efficient services.

Even quite large airports built during the last decade usually had only one terminal building for the reception of prospective passengers who came to it by rail, bus or in their own cars. Recently, however, the rapid increase in air transport has necessitated several terminals for different destinations, together with exceptionally large parking areas, sometimes even for 10,000 cars or more. In the appropriate airport terminal, the passenger hands over his air ticket and luggage, passes through customs and personal checks (for arms) and enters a waiting-hall. The waiting areas of the terminal have duty-free shops and restaurants. Information installations, sometimes by close-circuit TV, tell the passengers when and where to board their planes. In big airports where a long walk might be involved, conveyors and escalators are installed. Boarding gates are sometimes connected directly with aircraft by means of telescopic covered bridges. Elsewhere, e.g. at the large Canadian Mirabel Airport in Montreal, passengers are transported by a special bus for 150 passengers to the aircraft waiting at a distant parking area. On arrival, the cabin of the bus is elevated

to the level of the aircraft doors and passengers can board easily. Transport for arriving passengers is provided and controlled as well and in order to prevent confusion, the arrival and departure halls are separated.

A modern airport has about 20—75 parking areas for aircraft. The original system of corridors with parallel piers for boarding ceased to be satisfactory at large airports and caused delays. Consequently large independent boarding centres, the so-called *satellites,* began to be built. Usually these are hexagonal in shape. Each satellite can serve five planes simultaneously, and are connected with the terminal buildings by underground tunnels, by buses or automatically-controlled transport bridges. Airports whose capacity is planned to be substantially increased in future years are usually built on the linear system. Here a row of independent terminals, each with its own function, serves either internal or international routes, or else different airlines.

When giant airliners began to be built in ever-increasing numbers, airport authorities had to face a new, very complex problem. For really economic operation a Jumbo jet should not wait more than 45 minutes at an airport before it takes off again. If,

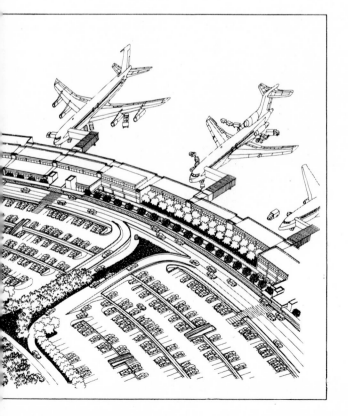

546. Satellite boarding points of Tampa International Airport are connected with the main building by tracks, along which run small coaches for 100 passengers

547. The American Dallas Fort Worth airport has six semi-circular buildings along both sides of the approach motorway. The drawing shows details. By the year 2001 fourteen semi-circular terminals will have been built, covering a total length of 4 miles

548

however, perhaps five Jumbo jets—arrivals or departures—arrive within a short time, their 2,000 passengers could never be handled in the required period. In addition the technical services and maintenance crews are faced with other problems. In 45 minutes, 470 ashtrays in each of the five planes have to be cleaned out and the cabins tidied, luggage has to be unloaded and loaded, refuelling must be carried out, kitchens re-stocked with food and so on. Various measures are being tried out, such as speeding up the procedures at customs.

Major world airports at present serving about 10 million passengers a year, expect that this number will increase from three to five times within the next decade. In Europe the densest traffic is at London's Heathrow airport—25 million passengers annually—next comes Orly airport in Paris with 14 million passengers and the extended Frankfurt air-

549

548. A special rubber conveyer belt delivers luggage to passengers

549. The passengers say what they want, the operator depresses the necessary keys and the Uniscope automatic booking system, in a matter of seconds, shows which seats are vacant on the suitable aircraft. The Uniscope then books the required flight and issues a ticket

LXXIII .The Douglas DC 10/30, with three General Electric engines. Wing span 16$^1/_2$ ft, length 181 ft
(*Lufthansa*)

LXXIV The Airbus A300 B-2 with two General Electric engines. Wing span 145 ft, length 175 ft, range 1,118—2,360 miles

LXXV The British supersonic Concorde 002 with four Rolls-Royce/Snecma Olympus engines. Wing span 92 ft, length 223 ft *(British Aircraft Corporation)*

port with 12 million passengers. In the USA where air transport has the largest volume in the world, internal airports have had to be separated from major international ones with flights to cities all over the world. Despite a very high rate of construction American experts complain that, even before completion, each of these airports is already overloaded and out-of-date. New York's Kennedy Airport, the Tampa International Airport in Florida, and the regional Dallas/Fort Worth airport expect that in the future they will have to serve 30—40 million passengers a year. The layout of runways and taxiways allows for three simultaneous landings and take-offs. In one hour up to 200 planes can be handled.

In order to connect the individual buildings more efficiently, terminals and satellite systems are being developed based on a computer-controlled automatic suspended railway, and other novel ideas for passenger transfer. In such a system the luggage transport is computer-controlled as well. Circulating luggage carts or conveyor belts are used. The luggage is magnetically coded to make sure it goes the right way.

Automatic booking systems: The tremendous increase in air passengers necessitated the introduc-

550. A model of Frankfurt cargo airport with a fully automated operation and with an annual turnover of 1·5 million tons of goods

tion of computer-controlled systems for ticket bookings and for other services. Most of the major airlines have put their own automatic booking systems into operation. Branch offices are provided with control panels. The operators record the requirements of a passenger even for a very involved journey such as interchange of routes and takes note of other requests for services such as rent-a-car service, hotel accommodation, or tickets to shows or night-clubs and so on at his journey's end. A cable or satellite network transmits the coded requests to the central data processing department and a control unit finds the most advantageous answers, offers it to the client and after his approval, fills in the air ticket and books the seat. A booking involving even an intercontinental flight takes only a few minutes.

In order to improve the situation in freight air transport, cargo airports, with equipment for mechanical loading and unloading and with capacities from 500,000 to 2 million tons of cargo annually, are being built at an increasing rate.

The use of automation in air-control

Nearly 7,000 airliners owned by 104 companies in the IATA organisation operate about 60 million flights a year and together cover a total distance of over 6 milliard miles, so strict organisation and control of all air routes is a necessity.

The basic principle ensuring order and safety in the air where no rails or roads with warning signals can be built, is horizontal and vertical division of the air space of each respective country into zones. *Horizontally* it is divided into fixed aerial corridors outside which aircraft may not fly.

Vertically the air corridors are divided into altitude levels separated by 1,000 ft. Levels with an even number altitude figure serve aircraft flying in one direction (e.g. to the West), those with an odd number are for planes flying in the opposite direction.

Aircraft flying parallel are separated by an alti-

tude of at least 2,000 ft. Even lateral distances on the same level are strictly determined. Air corridors are internationally coded. The different types of aircraft are each allotted their own band of airspace: the fastest, for example, fly in a band with a mean altitude of 30,000 ft, the next fastest in a band with a mean altitude of 21,000 feet, the next in the 15,000 ft band.

Originally pilots used to determine their position from visible and conspicuous features on the ground indicated on charts and maps. But with the aid of radio and radio beacons it is now possible to fly in bad visibility and at night. Planes can be equipped with an autopilot which automatically maintains a predetermined direction and altitude. Navigators, moreover, have meteorological radar allowing them to identify storms and other hazards at a distance of several hundred miles. Anti-collision radar enables them to avoid collision with another plane.

Using PP1 radars with a range of 200—300 miles, regional ground control centres allocate individual flight levels or flight paths to the planes in their area. Airport control towers are equipped with radar giving a more accurate overall picture. Ground controllers follow movements of all aircraft in their

551

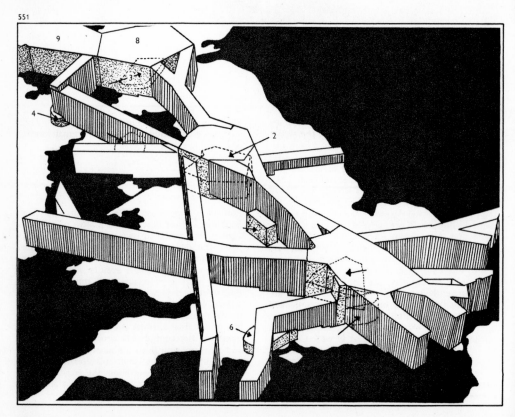

552

sector on radar screens. New types of radar facilitate control, since moving dots representing individual planes also indicate the identification number of the aircraft, its flight level, etc., all being processed through a computer.

The changing flight pattern is continuously recorded. In cases of distress, or if radio contact with the aircraft is lost, a dot in the screen representing a plane in distress is displayed, so that action can be taken.

551. The main air routes and flight corridors over Britain

552. The control tower and radar aerial at Heathrow airport (*Marconi*)

553

554

553. A view of a landing runway from an aircraft cockpit during manually-controlled landing training

554. The cockpit interior at the moment of the first automatic landing of a Boeing 727B at the Hannover airport in 1968

In some air control corridors, e.g. in the New York-Washington-Chicago triangle, traffic is sometimes so dense that aircraft movements have to be followed by 4,000 controllers. The most tricky periods are during the descent of aircraft from upper flight paths to holding areas and landing paths in the area of the airport.

In the USA this situation has led to the development of a new control system where the decision-making is once again transferred to the pilot. Aircraft will be fitted out with a system of modular navigation (MONA). The pilot's indicator screen will define the immediate position of the aircraft above specific navigation points with the aid of a magnetic tape programme. At the same time the positions and flight directions of all nearby planes

will be displayed. A board computer will determine anti-collision courses, will correct the flight path if needed, and issue instructions to the pilot in words displayed on panel screens. It is hoped that this system, to be introduced in 1980, will replace radio communication with ground control which is not foolproof due to overcrowding of air-space and unavoidable human and mechanical failures.

Take-off and landing procedures: Take-off and landing are the most critical stages of any flight, both for the crew and for the ground personnel. For that reason many attempts to automate them have been made since the end of the Second World War. The automation of the pilot's function progressed steadily until a fully-automated 'blind' landing system was established. The British have become pioneers in this field.

Weather conditions for manual and automated landing are internationally classified according to the horizontal and vertical visual range of the pilot:

Category	Min. horizontal visual range	Min. vertical visual range
1	800 m (2,625 ft)	60 m (197 ft)
2	400 m (1,312 ft)	30 m (98 ft)
3a	300 m (984 ft)	0 m
3b	50 m (164 ft)	0 m
3c	0 m	0 m

555. A chart of the Instrument Landing System: A — aerial transmitting the localizer beam; B — aerial transmitting the glide slope beam; C — glide path; 1 — at the altitude of 980 ft the pilot depresses the push-button for landing; 2 — altitude 130 ft: the autopilot continues controlling drift and controls the speed; 3 — altitude 66 ft: the autopilot flattens out the aircraft, engines are switched to idling speed; 4 — at the altitude of 10 ft the autopilot stops drift control, flattens out, and aligns the aircraft with the runway axis; 5 — after a touch-down at a speed of 93 mph the pilot takes over the landing run of the aircraft

In the use of the Instrument Landing System (ILS), a combination of three radio beams is utilized. One is the glide slope beam, which guides the pilot on his angle of descent. The second, intersecting the glide slope beam vertically, is the localizer beam. This leads the aircraft straight to the runway.

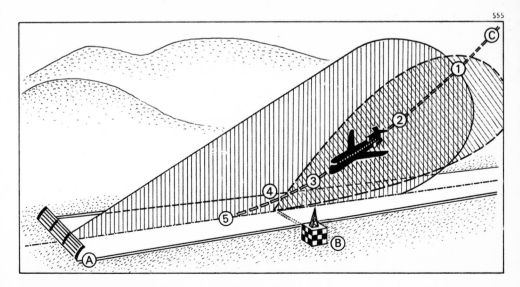

555

HOLD AT EMPIRE
IN HDG -120-

RIGHT TURN

OUT LEG TIME 1 0

OUT LEG DIST ---
DIRECT ENTRY

EXECUTE CHANGE?

556

The point of intersection of the two beams indicates the glide path. By acoustic signals the pilot is garded along the glide, at the same time compensating for lateral drift. Under category 1 and 2 visibility conditions he levels out the aircraft visually just before touch-down. The third component of ILS comprises two vertical radio marker beams, the first being located five miles out, and the second half a mile from the runway.

During automatic landing in the most frequent category, 3b, the pilot depresses a push-button at an altitude of 1,000 ft. At 65 ft above the ground the autopilot automatically throttles back the engines, so maintaining the descent along the glide path. At an altitude of 10 ft the autopilot cuts out the system countering wind drift and aligns the aircraft accurately along the runway. As soon as the undercarriage touches the ground, the automatic system immediately activates the thrust reversal, braking flaps and undercarriage brakes. When the speed drops to 100 mph the autopilot is switched off and control is taken over by the crew.

Present-day technology ensures a 1 : 10,000 reliability for such a system; experts, however, require a reliability of 1 : 10 million, which is why automatic landing systems are still duplicated.

Air transport safety: According to statistical data, the probability of a passenger being killed in an air crash — if measured in relation to the distance covered — is 210 times less than the probability of his death on the road. If he were to become a victim of an air accident, he would, statistically, have to cover more than 200 million miles by air.

Since the large-scale increase in the number of

556. The panel of the Mona modular navigation system in the cockpit of the L-1011 Tristar. On the screen the position of the aircraft and the flight path are shown. On the right and left are the computer control buttons

557. This plane crashed on 22 December 1960, in a Brooklyn street

558. On 23 March 1977, two Boeings 747s (Jumboes) crashed and exploded on the runway of Los Rodeos airport in the Canary Islands. It was the worst catastrophe in the history of aviation

jet planes during the last 25 years, about 700 air accidents have occurred worldwide, killing a total of 20,000 people.

According to Lloyd's insurance, bad weather conditions were responsible for only 5 per cent of accidents. About 20 per cent were caused by technical failure or inadequate maintenance of aircraft. But the main cause — 62 per cent of the total — were caused by pilot error and the unreliability of the human factor in general.

559

Consequently, despite advances in automation, requirements for the selection and training of pilots are ever more strict. As a useful aid, flight simulators are used on the ground which can faithfully reproduce for the trainee pilot flight situations of every kind that he would be likely to meet with in the air.

559. This simulator for pilot training has hydraulic rams to reproduce aircraft movement on the ground

Take-off development and progress

Owing to their high speed and weight, conventional aircraft require take-off and landing runways with lengths from 4,400 to 6,600 yd. Airports are having to occupy ever larger surface areas and consequently must be built much further away from big cities. As a result, the length of time it takes to travel from the airport to the city nulifies to some extent the advantages of fast communication by air. This is particularly so on short, internal flights of only a few hours, and designers are developing planes which need only short landing and take-off runways or can take off vertically like helicopters.

Conventional aircraft, designated CTOL (Conventional Take-Off and Landing) descend at an angle of 3° and take off at an angle of 5° in relation to the runway. By modifying the wing design, by the use of flaps and by installing more powerful engines, the length of the take-off runway can be reduced to some extent. Planes called RTOL (Reduced Take-Off and Landing) can take off at an angle of 8·5° which reduces the length of the take-off runway to 1,000−1,350 yd. Aircraft thus modified are used mainly to operate from comparatively small airports near provincial cities. With even greater wing modification to increase the lift at the lowest speeds, the angle of descent can be increased to 8·5 degrees and the take-off angle to 12·5 degrees. Such aircraft are called STOL (Short Take-Off and Landing). Their take-off runway length is reduced to 530−1,000 yd and they can land at even the smallest of aerodromes or reasonably flat areas.

VTOL aircraft (Vertical Short Take-Off and Landing) need an area no larger than a tennis court for their operation. The design of these planes differs aubstantially from that of all others, but between full VTOL and the traditional at least 20 transitional types can be found. These include V/STOL aircraft, descending and climbing at an angle of 20° and even more and needing a landing or take-off distance of between several hundred feet up 500 yd.

The STOL aircraft for steep take-off are already under operation in mountain regions and at small factory airfields, and plans are being put into operation for using them for connecting cities with major airports. Their structure is very light and they have powerful turboprop engines and relatively long and broad wings with complex flap systems to increase their lift way above the normal. An interesting aircraft of this type is the British Skyvan. Its clumsy-looking but practical fuselage, with a rectangular cross-section, can accommodate 19 passengers or 2 tons of cargo. A pair of turboprop engines allows it to take off and to land on 430-yd long surfaces which have not been specially prepared. A larger version is designed for 30 passengers. The French four-engine turboprop Breguet-941 with a payload of 7·5 tons needs only 155 yd for take-off, and 100 yd for landing.

The special characteristics of STOL aircraft result in a slightly lower all-round efficiency than traditional planes and they are also more demanding as far as the pilot is concerned. Recently an automatic 'Stoland' landing system has been developed in Canada specifically for this demanding type of take-off and landing.

Ideas for VTOL aircraft for true vertical take-off and landing have been tried out for at least 25 years.

560

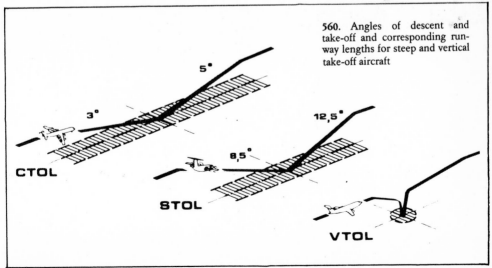

560. Angles of descent and take-off and corresponding runway lengths for steep and vertical take-off aircraft

561

562

561. The Skyvan of the Papuan Airlines is 40 ft long, wing span 62 ft. It is propelled by two turbo-prop units with 8-ft diameter airscrews

562. The American XC-142A vertical take-off aircraft with tilting wings. It has four engines with a total output of 12,000 hp and reaches a speed of 428 mph. Take-off weight 15,211 lb

563. The American VTOL Curtiss-Wright X-19

One which had a degree of success was the French Coléoptère shaped like a big barrel and using a jet engine. In 1958—59 the Coléoptère made several flights, taking off vertically, passing to level flight, reaching a speed of 500 mph and then landing with the aid of automatic stabilisers at the lower edge of the ring wing. In July 1959, however, the aircraft crashed when landing. Nowadays VTOL aircraft use both airscrew and jet propelling systems.

Airscrew VTOL aircraft carry out a vertical take-off or landing by swivelling the wing with its engines and airscrews perpendicularly to the flight path. This principle is used for example by the Vertol-76 and by the American XC-142 A. At the end of the fuselage, just behind the tail, the aircraft has a small stabilising airscrew for take-off and landing. In other VTOL systems, the engines and/or propellers can be swivelled to the vertical at the end of short wings. This principle has been applied in the Curtiss-Wright X-19, Bell-62 and Bell-XV-15, but there are several drawbacks. Enormous power and hence high fuel consumption is needed for the vertical take-off and to overcome the high drag during the flight. If the airscrews are placed in ring cowlings which also form lifting surfaces, the power utilisation efficiency is improved by 25 per cent. This type has been developed since 1950 by the American Bell Aircraft company. In this the airscrews are connected by long shafts to the four turboprop engines, which have a total output of 5,000 hp.

VTOL aircraft with jet engines can also tilt them vertically for take-off or landing and into a horizontal position for forward flight. However, experience has shown that it is better to use different engines for take-off and flight.

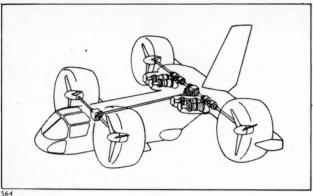

564

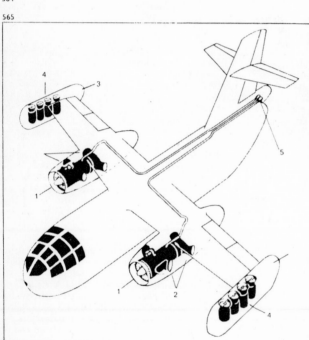

565

564. Diagrammatic view of the propeller drive layout of the American Bell VTOL aircraft

565. The propulsion system of the Dornier Do-31 VTOL jet plane
1. Pegasus engine with 13,778 lb thrust; 2. Deflectors for jet deflection during take-off and landing; 3. Wing-tip nacelles; 4. Vertical jet engines for take-off and landing; 5. Jet vane

566. The first civil jet plane for vertical take-off and landing, the Do 31

Systems deflecting the jets downwards rather than tilting the engines themselves have up to now been applied only on military planes. The most successful solution of this kind is that found in the Hawker Siddeley Harrier.

The first civil version of a VTOL jet plane was demonstrated by the German Dornier company. The high-wing Do-31 carries two Pegasus jet engines under its wings, each with a thrust of 12 tons for level flight. During take-off and landing the thrust is augmented by the deflected jets of eight engines located in nacelles at the ends of the wings.

The total thrust is 14³/₄ tons. The climb rate of the aircraft with loads of up to 5 tons is 30 ft a second, the cruising speed being 400 mph. Stabilisation and the control of the aircraft during take-off and landing is ensured by a so-called gas rudder, consisting of nozzles at the rear.

The first regular flights of VTOL aircraft for 60—120 passengers with a flight range of 500 miles are expected to take place from 1980—1985. Large-scale research is going on into safety measures in the event of failure of some of the engines, which would bring about unstability of the plane at a particularly dangerous time. The engines, moreover, must be designed so that during take-off or landing they do not eject large quantities of exhaust gases which would pollute the atmosphere around the airfield.

Helicopters

The history of helicopters: The ancient Chinese knew the principle of small propellers and possibly inspired Leonardo da Vinci in his design of small, spring-driven helicopters, and of a flying machine whose airscrew was to be driven by pedalling.

In the last century many inventors tried to construct helicopters at least in model form. Sir George Cayley designed a helico-aeroplane with both lifting and tractor airscrews. Sarti, an Italian, and a Viennese watchmaker Degen used two counter-rotating airscrews one above another. An Englishman, W. Phillips, inventor of the fire-extinguisher, built a model of a steam-powered helicopter in 1842. In this, two counter-rotating airscrews were propelled by a jet of steam from a miniature boiler. This passed up through the rotor shaft and out through holes which faced rearwards at the tips of the blades. The 6¹/₂-lb model flying machine of the Frenchman Ponton d'Amécourt, with two airscrews driven by a small steam engine, was capable of taking off and reaching the ceiling of the room in which it was tried out.

At a time, however, when Jules Verne was describing his fantastic fictional flying ship, *Albatross,* carried by 74 counter-rotating screws fixed to masts, only very few among the helicopter models which were actually built could remain in the air longer than a couple of seconds.

More serious experiments could be carried out only when designers had at their disposal a more powerful type of engine. On 24 August 1907, anchored by ropes so that it did not fly away, the French Bréguet-Richet Gyroplane No. 1 rose to a height of 2 ft and remained in the air for a minute. It was fitted out with twin-bladed rotors driven by a 48-hp Antoinette petrol engine and had a weight of 1,275 lb. Despite this promising start, for some unknown reason, the Bréguet brothers then concentrated on the development of other types of flying machines. On 13 November 1907, the helicopter of a French mechanic, Paul Cornu, took off as well, the first time in free flight. A smaller 24-hp Antoinette engine drove two rotors by means of belts. The longest flight lasted a third of a minute and the helicopter reached a height of 6 ft. His next machine with a more powerful engine had an important innovation incorporated in the rotors. The rotor blades were mounted on ball joints inside the hub of the rotor. Movement of the hub ring in relation to the rotor shaft altered the angle of incidence of the blades for hovering or for forward flight.

The concept of a single-rotor helicopter was worked out by the Russian inventor Boris Yuriev in 1912. An engine in the fuselage drove the vertical rotor shaft via a clutch; if the engine stopped functioning landing could still be made on the principle of the autogiro. The rotor blades were adjustable for incidence and the torque effect which tended to rotate the plane rather than the rotor, was overcome by a small airscrew at the rear of the fuselage.

The Spanish designer, Marquis Paul Pateras Pescara, built a number of flying helicopters in his country in the years 1918—1928. In 1924, his third machine with coaxially driven counter-rotating

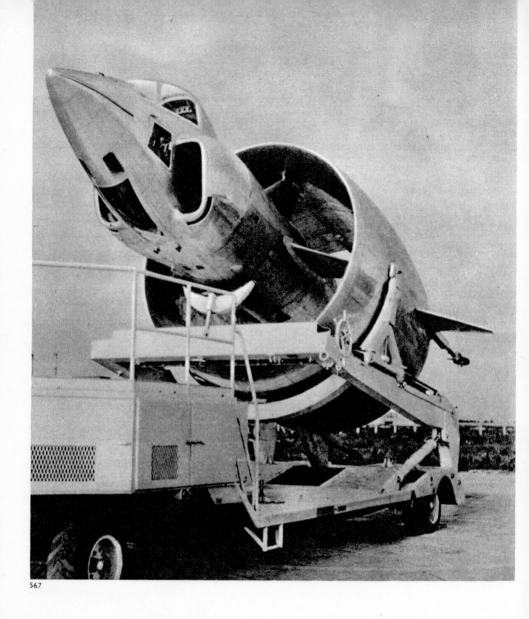

567

blades propelled by a 180-hp Hispano-Suiza engine covered a distance of almost half a mile in 4 minutes 11 seconds achieving a new world record.

At that time another Spaniard influenced the development of helicopters: Juan de la Cierva y Cordonia built an 'autogiro' with a rotor which was not driven mechanically. During flight the rotor turned like a windmill from the pressure of the air flow past it. For forward motion the machine used a tractor airscrew as in a conventional aircraft, and

567. The French Coléoptère

568. A helicopter from Leonardo's sketch-book

569. A helicopter produced by Paul Cornu in 1907 wit a 25-hp engine

434

the rotor acted as a kind of rotating, circular lifting surface as the blades turned. The very first autogiros reached speeds of up to 110 mph. When Cierva used an articulated rotor blade suspension, he solved the problem of wind forces occuring asymetrically from either side during forward flight. As was mentioned when discussing the Russian helicopter above, even if the engine failed, the rotor continued to turn and the autogiro descended safely in a gliding flight which could be controlled. The descent was similar to that of a parachute. Later on Cierva manufactured several types of autogiros in Britain, but they did not become popular because their field of application was rather limited.

Using the experience of earlier designers, the German professor Heinrich Focke designed a really practical helicopter, the FW-61. To the fuselage of a sports plane he fixed a tubular structure bearing at either end two counter-rotating rotors arranged in a V configuration to improve stability. The helicopter was driven by a radial 160-hp engine cooled by a small fan propeller. With complete reliability the machine took off and landed vertically, flew forward, backwards and sideways. In the first year of its operation it broke a number of records — it remained in the air for 1 hour 21 minutes, covered a distance of 144 miles, and climbed to an altitude of 11,000 ft. With its engine turned off it landed

568

safely, on the autogiro principle. Other Focke-Achgelis helicopters had engines with an output of 1,000 hp and were used during the Second World War to protect convoys and for mine-laying.

Modern helicopters: All over the world the most widespread type is the single-rotor helicopter. The basic design has been constantly developed and improved for 30 years by an American of Russian origin, Igor Sikorsky. In 1941, flying his own VS-300,

569

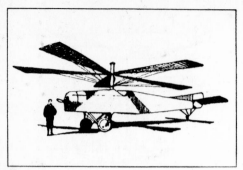

570

LXXVIII. A manual or automatic centrifugal clutch, already used in the first post-war types, enables the engine to be started uncoupled from the rotor. The angle of incidence of both rotor blades is controlled by moving a control column. A rearward movement of this and the lift and the engine power output are increased and the helicopter climbs — a forward movement and the helicopter descends. Smaller types of Bell helicopters are characterised by their glass cockpit 'bubble', offering exceptionally good visibility.

The American Kellett company started building helicopters with two rotors. More practical designs proved to be helicopters with coaxial counter-rotating rotors manufactured by Hiller in the USA just after the end of the war. At present the Soviet designer Nikolai Kamov has achieved international recognition with this type of helicopter.

he broke the record established by the Focke helicopter. Further Sikorsky helicopters with more powerful engines were produced and during the war they transported the wounded, worked in naval service, and were put to many other uses. The XR-6 of 1943, with a 270-hp engine, could fly for 5 hours and cover a distance of 375 miles. The first Sikorsky helicopters achieved cruising speeds of 115 mph.

With single-rotors, mostly with three blades, a range of helicopters with both piston and turbine engines are at present being manufactured. Among the leaders in their production is the American Bell Aircraft Company, which introduced twin-blade rotors with a gyroscopic rocker stabiliser (Plate

570. The first Cierva autogyro had a five-blade rotor without articulated blades (1924)

571. The German FW-61 helicopter of 1937. Engine output 160 hp, take-off weight 2,424 lb, maximum speed 76 mph

571

LXXVI The four-lane car tunnel leading to the main buildings of Heathrow airport, which has the greatest number of international airline passengers of any airport in the world *(British Aircraft Corporation)*

LXXVII A controller watches the Marconi radar screen

LXXVIII The Bell 222 helicopter carries 8—10 passengers at a maximum speed of 180 mph *(Bell Helicopter and Textron)*

LXXIX A Kawasaki KV-107 twin-rotor helicopter manufactured under Boeing-Vertol licence *(Kawasaki)*

LXXX Helicopters are invaluable for servicing oil rigs *(Textron's Bell Helicopter Company)*

572. The French turbine helicopter Alouette-3 in the service of the Swiss Rescue Guard

573. The French Aerospatiale SA.360 helicopter is designed for carrying up to 9 passengers and one pilot. Take-off weight 5,511 lb, maximum speed 195 mph

572

573

574

575

442

574. The Soviet Kamov Ka-26 twin-rotor multipurpose helicopter, equipped for crop spraying, can carry a load of up to 2,204 lb. Cruising speed 87 mph

575. The giant Soviet Mi-10 helicopter, with a five-blade rotor, can carry 15 tons of cargo

576. A projected Boeing Vertol heavy-duty helicopter for 20-ton container transport

After the war Frank Piasecki began building large twin-rotor helicopters with rotors in tandem. Because of the shape of their fuselages they were nicknamed 'flying bananas'. One of the first Piasecki helicopters for seven people and with a 600-hp engine, looped the loop successfully. In a passenger version, this type of helicopter has been manufactured by the Boeing company under the name of Vertol. License for its production has been granted to the Japanese Kawasaki company (Plate LXXIX).

During the 1950s these helicopters opened regular passenger services, usually connecting the centre of a big city with its airport, as is done in Los Angeles and Moscow. In 1958 a regular helicopter service was opened between Brussels, Amsterdam, Paris and London, but was cancelled after it became uneconomic.

In 1970 about 10,000 civil helicopters were operating throughout the world. Some of them were used for special purposes, e.g. for the installation of equipment in unaccessible areas, thus playing the role of aerial cranes, for spraying chemicals and extinguishing forest fires. Heavy freight turbine helicopters are used for the transport of exceptionally heavy cargoes. The Soviet Union in particular have shown initiative in their use. Turbine Mi-10 helicopters with five-blade rotors can carry loads up to 15 tons. The world's largest helicopter, the V-12, lifted a 40-ton load to an altitude of 6,500 ft. In it, four turbines with a total output of 27,000 hp drive two counter-rotating rotors. The crew consists of six men. The Americans are developing a heavy duty Vertol helicopter for transport of 20-ton containers.

Thousands of other helicopters carry out rescue services in the mountains, at sea, in deserts and other inaccessible areas of the world.

Modern helicopters mainly use light and highly

577

efficient gas turbines. Rotor blades are made of synthetic resins stiffened by carbon fibre, variable rotor geometry is electrically controlled in an automatic cycle. Sometimes the engines are carried on stub wings, which during level flight reduce the load on the rotor and make greater forward speeds possible. In 1970 the Sikorsky-Blackhawk S-67 with stub wings at the front and rear achieved a record speed of 222 mph. French and Italian designers are developing helicopters in which the rotors after take-off can be folded along the fuselage to reduce the drag, and short, telescopic wings take over. The Bell and Lockheed companies are also studying the possibility of using telescopically retractable rotors. These and other projects, e.g. rotojet, helavion, heligyro, etc. are all aimed to improve the comparatively slow and uneconomic level flight of the standard helicopter while maintaining the priceless asset of vertical take-off and landing.

577. The fastest helicopter in the world, the Sikorski S-67 Blackhawk which, with auxiliary wings, can carry 15 passengers

578. The last horse-drawn omnibus in the streets of London in 1914

7. Public Urban Transport

History of public urban transport

For centuries cities were built for pedestrians and horse-drawn carts with the occasional appearance of sedan chairs or coaches belonging to the nobility. With the onset of the industrial revolution hired coaches, fiacres and horse omnibuses began to appear in ever-increasing numbers. Iron-shod wheels rumbled over the cobbled streets, vehicles got in the way of one another, horses were frightened and accidents were numerous. The situation became even worse when streets were invaded first by steam and later on by petrol cars. In spite of the protests and even riots by cabmen, horse tramways appeared almost simultaneously in New York, Boston and London. In Britain the first horse-drawn streetcar line was built by the American G.F. Train in Birkenhead, and in 1864 one appeared in London, along Victoria Street. The upper decks of the trams were reached by a spiral staircase. In Berlin a single-track line was built from Charlottenburg to Tiergarten; in 1896 the network of Berlin horse trams covered a total of 120 miles, which was an impressive distance for that time. The tracks were laid on wood

and travelling was less noisy and more comfortable than in coaches jolting over the cobbled streets. Very soon there was not a single European city without colourful street cars—very often double-deckers—usually pulled by a team of horses. A horse could cover a distance of 12 miles per day; it had, however, to rest after one hour of work and be replaced by a fresh horse. In Berlin about 7,000 horses were in daily service. Multi-storey stables were built at terminal stops. Horse trams, however, had serious drawbacks. They could not go faster than 6 mph, caused problems with other traffic at rush hours and, moreover, the recessed rails had to be constantly cleaned out.

Cable railways grew at a very fast rate, especially in the USA. On the other hand in Europe, with the exception of Paris and Glasgow, they were never accepted. As a curiosity and attraction for visitors the city of San Francisco still maintains in operation a historic cable railway where cars are hauled by a cable and can overcome a gradient of almost 1 in 20. The cars are turned on a turntable at the bottom of the hill. Between the tracks an unending steel cable runs in a channel. A chuck collet below the floor of the car grips the cable, which then pulls the vehicle along at a speed of 6—7 mph. The service life of cables is, however, only one year at most, and the channels suffer from mud silting; cars use their

579

580

579. A double-decker horse tram in Bristol

580. This multi-storey stable for 250 horses in Berlin resembles the present-day multi-storey garage

581. One of two European cable tramways, from Kensington to Streatham in London, 1892 *(London Transport Executive)*

own momentum to keep moving at crossings, where the chuck collet is momentarily released.

Steam and petrol tramways appeared in the streets of various cities in the years 1870—1890, and were the predecessors of electric trams. The steam cars had small wheels and a narrow wheel base in order to be able to cope with the sharp curves and corners in town streets. The boiler and drive system were encased in a body so that they looked like a normal street car. However, these heavy, noisy and smoke-producing trams were incompatible with city life, and this was the main reason why electricity—in spite of its early teething troubles—took over so soon and so thoroughly.

Electric tramways were first manifested in a small electric train shown by Werner von Siemens at the Berlin Trades Exhibition in 1879. Encouraged by his success, von Siemens built in 1881 the first public electric tramway from the railway station in Lichterfelde, near Berlin, to the Cadet School. The tram was supplied by a 100-volt current from rails. But there were still horse-drawn vehicles on the streets and horses often received electric shocks when touching the live rails with their hooves, a serious drawback for the new $19\frac{1}{2}$ mile line. Electric trams developed by von Siemens for Paris and Frankfurt were supplied by current from a grooved pipe suspended on poles above the tracks. This system suffered from frequent failures, especially on damp, foggy days, when the current would short. In 1887 the American Leo Daft of New Jersey used a small four-wheeled cart moving along two conductors suspended on poles. Finally a system using electricity flowing down a spring-mounted bar with a sliding shoe or a contact roller at the end was developed. The return circuit was completed by the rails. Very often the tram hauled another behind it. Interest in the tramway transport grew enormously and double-deckers became the norm.

582

583

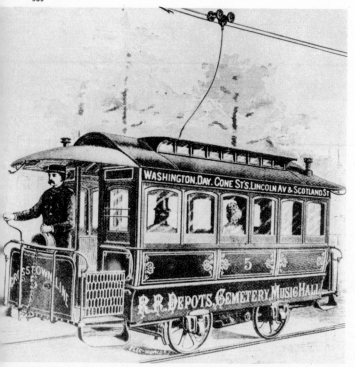

582. The first Siemens tramway in Berlin, 1881

583. A tramway using overhead current, designed by Leo Daft in 1887

584. An old Hamburg tram with trailer

585. An experimental trolleybus at West Ham, London overtaking a double-decker tram (1912)

586
587

588

586. A double-decker London bus for 24 passengers (1910). Note the old-style starting handle (*London Transport Executive*)

587. The first trolleybus in West Ham, in 1912

588. A Manhattan street in New York, USA, in 1874. On ground level are horse carriages and on the elevated section single-track trains and footways for pedestrians (*Museum of the City of New York*)

In the USA and later on in Europe, street cars were fitted with frames like the cow-catchers of early locomotives for the protection of pedestrians. Some European cities were reluctant to allow the installation of ugly overhead cables, but alternatives did not prove to be so satisfactory even though some were used.

Ever growing traffic necessitated the introduction of urban traffic control even before the era of automobiles. The world's first traffic signal was installed in 1868 near the House of Commons in London. A gas lamp shone either red or green and the switch-over was controlled by a chain pulled by a policeman until a gas explosion ended the life of this device. Traffic signals at crossings based on a safer principle were introduced in 1913 by James Hoge in Cleveland, USA, and in 1919 the first three-colour electric signals appeared in the USA. Later the Baltimore local authorities tried automatic traffic control. Drivers approaching a crossing had to blow their horns at an appointed place. Microphones recorded the noise level of the horns coming from each direction and the most noisy of the two got the green light. In Europe electric traffic signals appeared for the first time in 1926, in St. James's Street.

Buses and trolleybuses were not at first the most suitable form of transport on bad street surfaces. They became more comfortable about 1910 when the solid tyres were replaced by pneumatic ones. They had a rear entry platform and luggage platforms situated at either side of the vehicle. In good weather passengers could sit on the top deck. Efforts to eliminate engine noise and the smell of exhaust gases from petrol engines brought about

the invention of trolleybuses, which depended on a direct-current electricity supply.

Urban railways were developed in big cities in the years 1865—1875. The tracks usually led along bridges and embankments and stops were at fre-

quent intervals. Most of them provide fast electric services even today.

In the USA there were elevated railways on steel structures towering above wide and straight streets. The New York Elevated Railway (the 'El') ran the

589. The elevated steam railway in New York, in 1892. Cable tramways and electric trams run at street-level

590. The London steam Underground of 1863 ran through a system of tunnels only just below ground *(London Transport Executive)*

591. The first electric train on the London Underground, between Stockwell and King William Street *(London Transport Executive)*

length of Manhattan above Third Avenue. It was first established with steam-traction using coke-burning locomotives in 1878, and then was gradually electrified. But by the beginning of this century it became apparent that public transport in big cities would best be served by underground tunnels.

The Underground was born in London where, in 1863, four big railway stations were interconnected by several miles of tunnels. The Metropolitan Line then spread outwards into the growing suburbs. The original steam locomotives were eventually replaced by electric traction, because smoke and soot could not easily be cleared from the tunnels. While some undergrounds, e.g. that in Budapest, were built very near the surface, London started to construct the 'tube' with a circular cross-section at a very considerable depth. Underground stations communicated with the surface by means of staircases and

lifts at first, and in 1911 the first moving staircase, the so-called escalator, was installed. Passengers could enter the platforms either directly from the streets or from passages connecting various lines. Many of the first undergrounds were built without planning for future development; later on it cost a lot of effort and money to connect them with and to integrate them into the existing urban transport systems in a sensible way. Now, however, the Metro, Metropolitan, Underground, Subway, Untergrund-bahn, Sotteranea—as the undergrounds are called in different countries—are a means of fast, cheap and reliable public transport in cities.

From about the time of the first electric street cars, inventors were looking for various ways to overcome traffic jams in narrow streets and at crossings. For instance, in 1870 the American Alfred Ely Beach built a short tunnel under Broadway, where cylindrical passenger cars were driven by air pressure, just as in the pneumatic mail tubes. W. Lewis constructed for the 1900 world exhibition in Paris a 3-mile moving footway—called *passenweyor*—allowing the passengers to travel at a speed of 9 mph by stepping from one parallel moving conveyor section to another. Among the unconventional railways the only survivor is the famous suspended railway or monorail built in 1901 in Wuppertal in Germany. Its electrically-driven cars moved along a 9-mile track, situated mainly above the local river, at a speed of 15 mph. By 1960, when this railway was completely reconstructed, it had safely transported one milliard passengers. Up to the present day many daring and sometimes impractical projects to

592

build suspended, monorail, gliding, propeller driven or pneumatic railways have appeared on designers' drawing boards in an attempt to meet in various ingenious ways the ever increasing problems of overcrowded big city transport.

Development of modern urban transport

The role of cars in cities: In important centres of the USA, Europe and Japan city agglomerations are in existence with more than 10 million inhabitants. Public transport systems designed to meet their needs would work in theory, but have been prevented from doing so really efficiently by the ever-growing numbers of automobiles. Modern trams and buses capable of speeds of 50 mph crawl through the streets at a speed which can drop in city centres to an average of under 6 mph, i.e. less than the speed of the original horse tramways. Traffic congestion threatens the normal life of a city. Exhaust gases combined with the smoke from heating installations in buildings create lethal smog under certain meteorological conditions.

An individual who, when walking, occupies 1 sq yd of space, and who needs when seated in a tram or bus a total of $^1/_2$ sq yd, prefers to sit behind the wheel of a car. But the car was originally

592. The single-track suspended railway at Wuppertal, built in 1901 by O. Langen, who was one of the inventors of the combustion engine

593. A traffic jam in London

designed for free and fast roads. In today's modern cities it may have to move at a speed of a pedestrian, but occupying a surface area of 35 sq yd. The former mayor of Munich and later Minister of Construction in West Germany, Dr. H. J. Vogel, was quite justified in saying: 'The car is killing our cities.'

In perspective, the only correct and feasible solution is to replace cars in cities by a cheap and fast public transport. The struggle of cities against the automobile danger has begun.

It is now too late to build brand-new big cities where individual and public transport would be combined in a way compatible with comfortable living working and resting. *Motopia* (Fig. 594), proposed in the 1930s, was to be such a city, although present-day ideas quite certainly would not allow streams of cars to run on the roofs of houses. In cities of historical importance, any large reconstruction for the purposes of transport is strongly resisted. City authorities can only try—with little success—somehow to control and to handle stage by stage the development of that awkward triangle: city—public transport—automobile. As examples of extreme situations the big American cities of Los Angeles and New York could be cited.

Los Angeles decided to open its gates to cars without any restrictions whatever. Enormous expenditure has enabled 750 miles of multi-lane motorways to be built during the last 30 years, which occupy two-thirds of the city surface area. As soon as the cars were provided with comfortable motorways even inside the city, they started to proliferate in an unexpected manner to nearly one car per inhabitant. Even 12-lane complexes (as can be found in Chicago) became hopelessly bogged down and a solution was looked for in the building of satellite population centres. This, however, destroyed the unity and the social function of the original city. The resulting megalopolis has now a total area of 5,000 sq miles and still suffocates in smog.

New York represents the opposite extreme. In the 2-mile wide island of Manhattan between the Hudson and East Rivers cars, with the exception of taxis, are of no practical use. For lack of space residential and administrative buildings had to reach for the skies in the form of skyscrapers and streets are narrow. So, from the suburbs—the distance travelled being up to 60 miles—14 million people pour into the city, carried by the underground, buses and railways.

Zones without cars seem to be the best solution for historical city centres. Cars can approach their outer limits for a short time only. Entry permits for vehicles are issued only to those who live there, to delivery vans and various essential services. Round the circumference of the zone large underground or above-ground parking areas have to be built.

Long-distance traffic uses major highways which avoid the cities. Outside city centres cars can use large ring roads, from which minor roads radiate. The traffic signals and flow is computer controlled and police observe the situation from TV centres. New York today has 9,000 controlled crossings equipped with electronic signals which operate to the density of the traffic flow in any one direction. Approaches to car tunnels are computer controlled as well. In the struggle for capacity increase in traffic bottle-necks such as these, even a tenth of a second is important.

The confusing mass of road signs in cities is to be

594

replaced by electronic indicators guiding drivers through crossings. For this the USA are already developing an Electronic Route Guidance system.

A necessary prerequisite for the admittance of cars into city traffic will be a reduction of toxic exhaust gases. Electric cars have not yet reached such a stage of development as to be able to compete with combustion engines. Attempts in some American cities to use computer controlled small individual electric cars have not proved very successful. Although big cities continue building tunnels for automobiles, it is becoming ever more neessary to keep the car as far away as possible from the centre and to replace it by a highly efficient and clean underground or above-ground railway network. But the inhabitants of distant housing estates and visitors to cities will not be obliged totally to surrender the advantages of using their cars. At terminal stops on the railways to the suburbs, large parking lots will be built to accommodate them. The American system 'Park and Ride' is spreading even in Europe. In the USA, however, its 'Kiss and Ride' variant has become more popular—kiss your wife who brought you by car to the terminal, who then returns home with your car, while you go on, using public transport.

The era of tramways has not yet come to an end, although during the 1960s many cities gave them up as the streets could not accommodate cars, trams and buses all together. Where it is still used the tram has been updated. Its cars move on noiseless bogies and have power outputs of about 130 hp. Wheels have rubber treads. Usually, smooth starting is automatically controlled, building up to a pre-determined speed. Bogies are fitted with highly efficient

594. A projected city transport system, running on the roofs of blocks of flats. The designer is Geoffrey Jellicoe from the USA

disc and electromagnetic brakes. Ticket sales have been reorganised—passengers buy tickets in slot machines at intermediate stops and terminals. The rectangular tram bodies have automatic doors and comfortable, electrically heated seats. If a large capacity is needed, articulated units with a passage from one car to another are used. The maximum speed of these street cars, which have outstanding acceleration, is about 60 mph.

In order to prevent cars from getting in the way of trams, special lanes are reserved for tramways. Where this is not possible, some authorities have tried to run trams in city centres in underground tunnels. This idea was not a success in a number of cities, since frequent breakdowns in the tunnels caused traffic build-up. For that reason architects and designers preferred the construction of more expensive, but at the same time more reliable, underground trains.

It is surprising that the USA, the first country to desert the use of trams, has returned to them in some places. Supertrams have been put into operation in Boston and San Francisco. Their 72-ft articulated cars from the Boeing company, made of light metals, are coupled together outside the city centre to form trains with several units. The

LXXXI A three-unit set of an overhead railway in Wuppertal. It carries 48 sitting and 156 standing passengers. Maximum speed 37 mph *(Werkfoto M.A.N.)*

LXXXII The type of underground train used in Munich and Nuremberg *(Werkfoto M.A.N.)*

LXXXIII Proposed carriages for the Glasgow Underground of 1980. Trains will be automatically dispatched and computer controlled *(Greater Glasgow PTE)*

LXXXIV A simple interior, light structure, curved windows and large doors characterise the carriages designed for the Glasgow Underground *(Greater Glasgow PTE)*

LXXXV 'Cabinentaxi' car stop at the experimental circuit in Hagen, West Germany *(MBB+ Demag)*

LXXXVI The ROMAG automatic overhead railway demonstrated at the TRANSPO 72 exhibition. It is driven by a linear electric motor and has cabins for 6 passengers

LXXXVII The MONOCAB overhead railway with cars 19 ft above street level and magnetically suspended from a steel track

LXXXVIII A design for a mini underground train for smaller cities

LXXXIX A hovercraft of the future for 2,000 cars and their passengers. With engines of a total of 750,000 hp it should reach the speed of 130 knots *(Design by Schiffe und Schiffahrt von Morgen, VEB Verlag Technik Berlin)*

capacity of each line, the operation of which is very cheap, is 24,000 passengers per hour in one direction. Buses have much greater freedom of movement than trams since they do not run on rails. However, in spite of technological advances, even carefully maintained diesel engines emit exhaust gases, and as a result buses using natural gas or propane-butane in pressure bottles are being tested. In the USA and West Germany different types of electric buses are under test. The Swiss have tested a gyrobus, which is an electrobus supplied by current from its own generators which are driven by a powerful flywheel. At a route terminal the terminals of the gyrobus are connected with a charging pole, the generator is transformed into an electric motor providing the flywheel with its power.

Some progress in sorting out the traffic was made when special lanes were reserved for buses only. Sometimes independent traffic interchanges and short connecting tunnels are designed solely for buses and help to sort out bottle-necks. The time

intervals between succeeding buses on a route can be cut to 1 minute and the total travel time is reduced by a half.

'Dial-A-Ride' in the USA and Britain uses a small comfortable bus for 16—20 passengers following in the main a regular route. But the driver can temporarily leave this and call for passengers who have used the bus telephone central office to ask to be picked up. A computer processes the individual requests, combines them into rational groupings and sends instructions to the bus driver en route. The fare is in between that of a normal bus ticket and a taxi fare.

A new kind of urban travel is being developed in the USA and in Britain—as represented by the

595. Aerial view of the D. D. Eisenhower urban expressway in Chicago

596

597

'Dual-Mode-Bus' system. Small battery-electrobuses have parallel two-way lines outside the city centres. Near the centre these merge to form a single-track lane, where the bus is automatically controlled by computer. At this stage, it is driven by direct current fed from a rail—as with the underground trains—and this is also used to charge the batteries. The Dual-Mode system results in a very fast and frequent service through city centres and the buses do not produce any harmful exhaust fumes.

Modern underground railways nowadays form the backbone of big city urban transport. In the suburbs they are augmented by other means of transport such as buses and trams.

At present almost half the world's largest cities have underground systems. Dozens of others have begun construction or are at least planning it. The original methods of building them, adapted from mining techniques, have been replaced by mechanised tunneling shields with milling cutters at the face, which are followed by machines for lining the tunnels with cast iron or reinforced concrete sections. These modern developments allow 550 yd of tunnel per month to be completed.

The so-called Milanese method of surface construction of underground railways comes from Italy. Special machines dig ditches up to 65 ft in depth. They are lined with concrete and covered over with more concrete. The tunnels are rectangular in section.

Electric articulated sets of carriages, usually with 4—8 cars, for 40—60 sitting and 140—180 standing passengers, run through tunnels. On each track the traffic runs in one direction only, is electrically safeguarded and, on the latest systems, computer controlled.

599

596. The urban expressway access ramp to the Lincoln Tunnel under the Hudson River in New York, which connects Manhattan with New Jersey

597. Television used for traffic control, highlighting traffic jams and major accidents so that traffic can be diverted

598. An articulated tram for 220 passengers in Bern (Schlieren, Zürich)

599. A Tatra T-5 thyristor tram with a laminated body

The longest underground network is that of London. It has at present 252 miles of track and is still being extended. The New York underground (subway) network is only 21 miles shorter. Its history began in 1904. It has 462 stations with capacity of 5 million passengers a day. As many as four tracks converge in some tunnels. The third longest network is the Paris Métro with 14 lines and 345 stations and a total length of 150 miles. In this, older lines are being updated and the latest, No. 4, has remote control. The driver fills the role of an overseer only. He has continuous point-to-point communication with the dispatching centre. The speed of the trains is 60 mph maximum. Several lines in Paris have carriages with pneumatic bogies developed by Michelin, giving smooth and silent travel. However, they require more power to operate. The track is provided with auxiliary rails to prevent a potential accident. This type of carriage is operated on underground systems in Montreal and Mexico as well as Paris.

The fourth longest underground is the Moscow

602

Metro with its 98-mile network and richly decorated spacious stations. Lines radiating outwards are connected by a circular ring line at the circumference. The Moscow underground has the cheapest fare in the world and transports the greatest number of passengers. A complete innovation will be a 4-mile experimental pneumatic underground line. Cylindrical cars will be propelled by air pressure through a circular tunnel.

Fifth in the world is the 76-mile Washington underground (subway) network. Its special feature is

600. A Boeing Supertram for 210 passengers. Length 72 ft; maximum speed 68 mph

601. The Mercedes-Benz OG-305 experimental urban bus using natural gas fuel

602. Special traffic lanes for buses

603. A Dial-A-Ride Ford Transit bus

603

604

a 1¹/₄-mile station tunnel, the Center Station, which has three stopping places. The sixth, and in 1976 the only other city operating an underground network with more than 60 miles of lines, is Berlin. The U-Bahn was built in 1902. Just before the end of the Second World War, the tunnels were flooded by the waters of the Spree river and after the division of Berlin the underground lines were divided as well. In West Berlin the changing of trains makes use of special entry islands. The geological composition of the earth and rocks differs from place to place, so the building of any new underground system tends to produce unique problems.

The Stockholm underground is heated. The beautifully designed stations of the Hamburg underground are connected with the freeway and bus stops above ground. In Philadelphia trains have a track gauge of 62 in.

The highest rate of underground construction, about 15 miles a year, can be found in Tokyo. All those employed must have reached a certain minimum standard of education. Trains are fully automated and stop within limits of 4 in. Tunnels must be able to resist earthquakes. Passengers can enter the underground directly from ground floors of public buildings. Hong Kong is building a technologically very advanced underground under the sea.

Unconventional city transport of the future: Automated urban transport systems were first studied and tested experimentally during the last ten years. Most use comfortable and relatively fast vehicles, the size of which is somewhere between a small passenger car and a small bus. They move along independently without drivers, usually on overhead tracks, and are automatically controlled by a central computer. Whether they move on pneumatic tyres, on air cushions or are hauled by a cable, they have one common feature: they offer travel with comfort and at a speed which cannot be expected from a car in a modern city. The systems are noiseless, do not produce exhaust fumes and would avoid the necessity of building large parking areas near city centres.

Automated overhead transport would use a dense network of overhead tracks. It is projected that elevated stations in residential areas would be located at a maximum distance of 1,000 ft from every house. In the city centre stations would be at every important place, e.g. at post offices, departmental stores, railway stations, banks, theatres, etc. Supports for the tracks might become integral parts of these buildings.

The system would be computer controlled. After feeding in data about his place of destination the passenger should be able to depart for it within a minute. The car, for 1—3 people, moving at a speed of 15 mph, would automatically choose the shortest way to his destination. In the case of a blockage on the line, the cabin should automatically find a substitute route.

In Europe the CAT and H-Bahn systems are in use.

604. A dual-mode-bus
A — the passengers get in the bus at places near their homes. At this stage the bus has a driver;
B — in the centre of the city the bus is powered electrically from a side rail and is automatically controlled by a computer;
C — the now driverless bus stops in the centre of the city

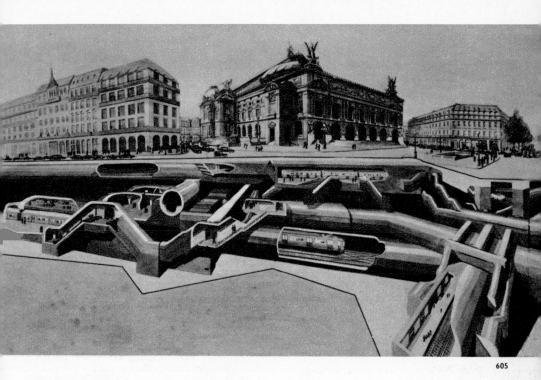

The CAT or Cabinentaxi system developed by the West German MBB and Demag Corporations was put into pilot operation in September 1974 in Hagen. In one direction the cars for three passengers ride on four pneumatic tyres along a concrete elevated road (Plate LXXXV). In the opposite direction they are suspended under the same road. Aluminium shields cover the chassis, suspension, electric motors, their collectors and the feeding trolleys. The passenger summons the car by inserting a coded ticket into a slot machine at the platform and the cabin enters the circuit. Two electric

606

605. The intricate crossing of the old and the new Paris Metro lines at the Auber station

606. The broad platforms of the new Paris Metro at the Défense station (RAPT)

607

608

607. A new London Underground train on the Victoria Line *(London Transport Executive)*

608. Interior of the latest London Underground train *(London Transport Executive)*

609. Escalators of the new Victoria Line in London *(London Transport Executive)*

610. A French Metro train running on pneumatic tyres

609

610

motors with an output of 7 hp drive it at a maximum speed of 22 mph. Sensitive automatic systems do not allow the cars to approach each other closer than 33 ft. The original plan provides for a 88-mile system with 8,000 small cars served and controlled by 25 workers. At present a CAT system with larger cars for 12 persons is being tested.

A similar system with bigger suspended cars for ten sitting and six standing passengers is being tried in West Germany by the Siemens company in co-operation with the Swiss Düwag company. It is called the *H-Bahn*. The steel wheels of the cars move along a rail and are driven by a linear electric motor. If only one passenger or several passengers with the same destination enter the cabin, it will pass through all the other stations without stopping until it reaches the one they want. In rush hours the cabins stop at each station.

Other systems, often designed for the use of larger passenger cars, run on bridges and elevated steel structures in the streets. Cars carry up to 20 passengers. Magnetic tickets are issued at the entries, and at the turnstile of the exit station an automatic machine checks that the passenger has not covered a longer distance than he paid for.

Most of the cars move on pneumatically sprung chassis driven by electric motors. The only exception to this are the American laminated Otis com-

pany cars. These move on an air cushion and are provided with a simple frame chassis. The air cushion is generated by a fan operated by an electric motor fed by current from a trolley in the wall of the concrete track.

In France smaller Aramis cars for 10—12 passengers are being tested. Equipped with pneumatic tyres they move at a maximum speed of 30 mph. In Lille large VAL system cars for 52 passengers are also being tried. The automatically controlled cars are driven by 240-hp motors and move along a concrete track at a speed of 35 mph. Both Aramis and VAL systems can couple several cars together to form a set during the rush hours. At any time the set can be uncoupled automatically.

In the USA several of these lines were put into operation to connect cities with airports or to inter-connect airport satellite buildings. At the Dallas/Fort Worth airport the Airtrans system is used which consists of cars for 13 passengers and their luggage, while the 2·5-mile South Park track in Pittsburgh uses the PAAC system where the trains consist of three cars for 100 passengers and operate at a speed of 50 mph.

Pneumatic chassis have given good results apart from minor troubles with ice on the concrete strips of the uncovered track. A little more complex and noisy but safe against the weather are the suspended

612

613

611. From the ground floor of many commercial and public buildings in Tokyo a staircase leads direct to an underground station

612. The Washington subway station

613. The most common type of subway train used in American cities

614. The CAT driving system for both large and small overhead cars *(Demag and MBB)*

615. A train movement indicator on the experimental Cabinentaxi line at Hagen *(Demag and MBB)*

616. An American Otis rail car for 6 passengers

614

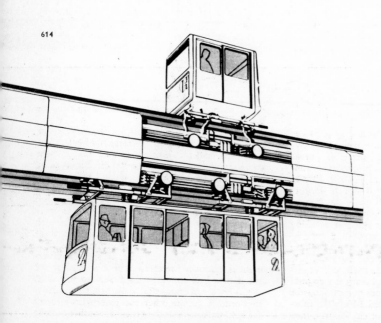

car systems. Cars are mainly made of plastic materials.

The only place where one of these systems has been in full use since 1972 is Morgantown in Virginia, USA. The 4-mile line with numerous curves and gradients has three stations. The cars move continuously along concrete strips at a speed of up to 30 mph, using 100 cabins for 8—13 passengers each. Under computer control they can run at 10-second intervals. The capacity in one direction is 3,300 persons per hour. Similar systems are being planned by a number of other towns.

Movable footways and pedestrian conveyors: Research has proved that man can cope with the speed of a belt conveyor up to 25 mph without serious inconvenience. If, however, he has to step onto a conveyor belt from a stationary position, the speed of the belt must not exceed 2·5 mph. If movable footways were to be used in city centres, they would have to have a speed of up to 12 mph for the most efficient operation.

A successful scheme for such a system has been put forward by the German Krauss and Maffei company and called *Transurban*. Two rubber belts move continuously in opposite directions along bridges with an oval cross-section and glass-covered rooves. They are driven by electric motors at a speed of 12 mph. Parallel to them are belts with laminated seats for pedestrians who wish to cover a longer distance. Every 1,000 or 1,600 ft there is an entry and exit mushroom-shaped station. In these the pedestrian steps on a circular turning table. If he walks outwards towards its edge, his speed of movement is gradually increased until it is equal to the speed of a belt running tangentially to the table. When his speed equals that of the belt, he can easily step onto it. At the other end passengers step off the belt, walk towards the centre of another turning

617

617. Passenger cars of the Airtrans system have been carrying passengers between the Dallas Fort Worth airport satellites since 1973

table and from there go upstairs or use an escalator to street level. The system has a capacity of 40,000 persons per hour in one direction and will provide economic pedestrian transport up to a distance of 6 miles.

The Dunlop company has put forward an idea for matching the speed of pedestrians to that of the main belt by means of integrators. These are parallel belts with a system of extending telescopic elements.

So-called passenger containers were developed by the American Goodyear company for their Carveyor system. Passengers enter small cars, which move off and are then transferred on to a conveyor belt running at a speed of 15 mph. At stops the containers slow down to a speed of 1·5 mph, when passengers can easily get off. The container system opens up the possibilities of people being transported not only around a city but also upwards to different floors of buildings, the containers playing the role of a lift. All this traffic would be computer controlled.

618. A central concrete rail guiding a set of three PAAC cars on the 2·5 mile South Park track at Pittsburgh

619. The interior of the Ford automatic ACT system coach for 10 passengers and their luggage

620

620. Fully-glazed passages for pedestrians are suitable for use with moving footways, not only at exhibitions and airports, but even in city centres

621. City of the future equipped with footway-conveyers of the Transurban system *(Kraus-Maffei)*

621

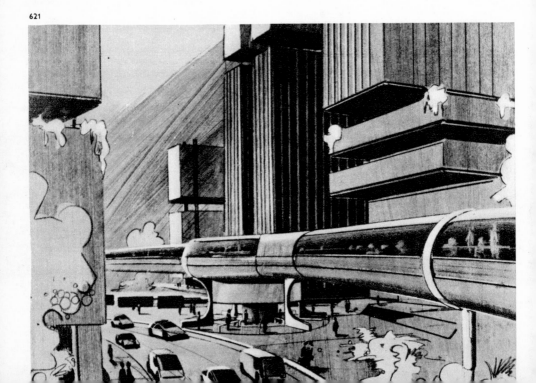

XC Transport in a city of the future *(Otis Elevator)*

XCI A futuristic design for a concrete viaduct which will carry, at an average height of 33 ft above the ground, oil and gas pipelines, telecommunication cables in its lower section. In the middle section space is provided for electric express trains, and the top section serves as a motorway *(T.Y.Lin, USA)*

622

622. A crossing of two conveyers for pedestrians,
combined with entry and exit stations

8 Transport of the future

Fifty years ago the London publisher Paul Kogan asked about a hundred outstanding scientists and authors from different fields to carry out an unusual task: they were to predict what life would be like in 50 years time, i.e. in the present day.

Bertrand Russel predicted a world government. J.B.S. Haldane believed that electric power would be a hundred times cheaper, expressing at the same time his conviction that nuclear energy—which was already a subject of discussion at that time—would never be used to generate it. John Bernal was convinced that space would be explored by rockets controlled from great distances, but without a human crew. The inventor Leslie Mitchell nearly hit the target: he predicted for 1968 the landing of a rocket on the Moon carrying a crew of five men including one Reuter reporter. But forecasts concerning world transport systems proved to be the least accurate.

J.C. Guller thought that not only railways, but roads as well would be on the decline. For cargo carrying, half-track lorries would be used which would not require roads. Another forecaster, Oliver

Stewart, believed that a combined helicopter and aeroplane would be used in cities as a major means of transport. Intercontinental transport would be provided by ships for 300 passengers provided with 10 to 20 engines, and by monster flying machines. These would reach an altitude of 4,600 ft, flying at a speed of 100 mph. Higher altitudes were declared by Stewart to be impossible, since the manufacture of a pressurized cabin was unthinkable . . .

Prospects for world transport until the year 2000: The development of world science and technology until the end of this millenium can be more surely predicted as it will be based on known scientific knowledge. Technology no longer develops in a haphazard way. Wild theories based only on an inventor's imagination no longer have a place. New ideas for means of transport no longer see the light of day in garages and small workshops but are created by teams of specialists working for state or company research institutes. Each new principle is the outcome of years of work and meticulous research by scientists and technologists. Many daring but impractical dreams of the past have had to be abandoned in consequence.

By the year 2000 wheels will still be turning as they were 150 years ago according to the claim of the chief West German railway expert Dr. Heinrich

623

623. Vehicles of the future will consist of modular sections

624. A Ford computer-controlled cabin system

625. This train, designed by Professor Odsawa of Japan, is predicted to reach a speed of 310 mph, running on an air cushion and with a linear electric motor for power

624

625

626

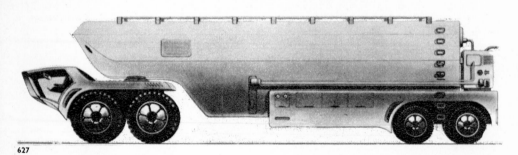

627

628

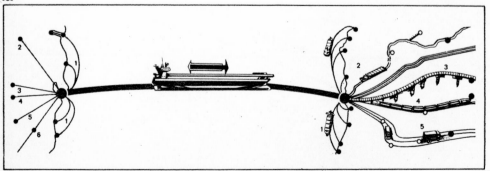

629

626. This unconventional rail vehicle developed by Japanese technicians is in the shape of a wing. It partly flies and partly runs on rails

627. This two-hundred ton tank trailer with a turbo-electric driving system is planned for the year 2000

628. A multipurpose ship shuttle service, projected for transporting goods between the USA and Europe, connects with coastal ships (1), river transport (2), pneumatic transport systems (3), railways (4), and roads (5), so that all are integrated

629. Fast overhead railways connect with a hover-craft service

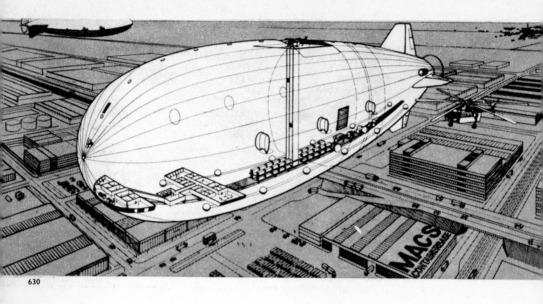

Lehmann. However, trains will be even faster and more comfortable. Magnetic principles of hovering will be used only in a limited way, provided they give good results on test circuits from about 1980 onwards. By 1985 West Germany should have built four new straight railway lines, where, theoretically, trains should reach speeds of up to 190 mph, their average commercial speed, however, being 125 mph. Japan by that time will have its national railways connected in an excellent network allowing operating speeds of 160 mph.

To ease production an ever wider international and technological co-ordination of transport methods will be realised. Very likely a standard concept of bodies for all types of vehicles will be accepted—no matter if they run on tracks or roads. These might well be made up from standardised

sections, and using universal electric motor and turbine designs. Electrically-driven computer-controlled cabin systems running on pneumatic tyres will undoubtedly be developed further and have their own special concrete tracks, mainly on elevated structures. Trains without wheels should be put into operation on long-distance lines, reaching speeds of 300—500 mph.

Electromagnetic-suspension express trains on special lines should reach speeds of up to 300 mph. A model of such a train was exhibited by Japan in 1970 at the Osaka Exhibition. The train is designed for 600 passengers and its streamlined shape helps it to achieve speeds of 500 mph. The average operating speed should be 300 mph. The driving system of this train has been tested for years by the Japanese national railway research institute.

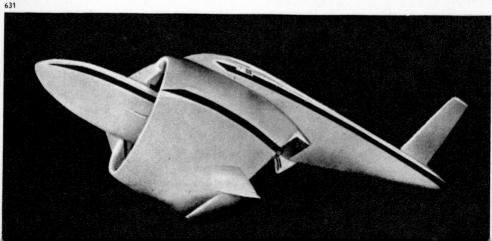

630. An atomic freight airship

631. A giant VTOL aircraft of the coleopter type

632. A model of an electrocopter powered by microwave energy transmitted by a ground aerial

632

Trains to be uncoupled and coupled while in motion, known as *rendez-vous,* have been designed by Soviet and French engineers. The basic idea is to eliminate time losses caused by stops for passengers getting in and out at stations. According to this system, the passengers wishing to get off at an approaching station will gather in the last carriage. A hydraulic system designed by a Russian technologist Pulkov will raise a wheeled suspension system from the roof; the wheels of this will link up with and start to run on a suspended rail, the carriage will be uncoupled and lifted clear of the ground, when it will run on as an independent unit to the station. Passengers wanting to join the train will board cars running along another suspended rail. These will accelerate rapidly to catch the train and computers will synchronise the speeds so that they can be coupled on, after which the suspension system would be retracted. Uncoupled carriages could, if need be, go beyond the station in question and become integrated within an urban transport system. In this way, railways might be capable of transporting passengers from house to house.

In the French system a train runs in a circular route round the circumference of a city at a speed of 28 mph. At each stop, the rear part of the train is uncoupled and departs under its own power to stations on a branch. Meanwhile, passengers wishing to join the train have been waiting in another coach, which is coupled on in place of the one which has been detached. Another idea is for the train to be approached while in motion by so-called station trains. After speed synchronisation the two trains are coupled and passengers can transfer to other carriages or get into the station train if they want to alight at the next station. For this the station train is uncoupled again.

Flying and pneumatic trains should be put into operation after the year 2000, when public transport would be expected to reach nearly supersonic speeds for intercontinental distances. The Japanese are at present testing a wing guided by rails. The American Dr. Foa, on the other hand, is a champion of pneumatic trains. A one-way tube with a diameter of 16—20 ft would contain cabins for 200 passengers. Air pressure or a magnetic system would keep the cabins aligned to the tube axis and prevent them touching the walls. The cabins, acting as pistons in the tube, would be propelled by air pressure or vacuum suction. Intercontinental trains could use tunnels at depths of several miles. Their acceleration could make use of the pull of gravity. Other designs propose airscrew-propelled units flying through a tube, in which the air pressure has been reduced. According to the Canadian, E. Bress, Europe should be connected with the USA by three tubes at a depth of nearly 400 ft. Two tubes would serve for cabin transport at a speed of 500 mph, while the third one would be held in reserve. The tubes would be provided with stabilisation stations with ship propellers maintaining them in position.

After the year 2000 means of transport are expected to be much larger. Experts believe that cargo requirements and the increased mobility of a rapidly growing population will exceed all the possibilities of present-day kinds of vehicles. Main-line railways would have a track gauge of up to 15 ft. Individual carriages hauled, maybe, by nuclear locomo-

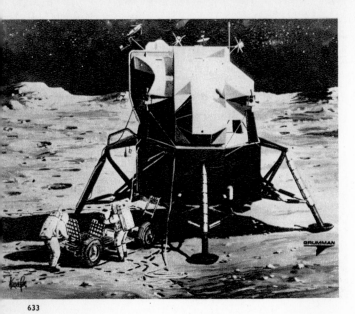

633. The Lunar Roving Vehicle, used by the US cosmonauts during the successful expedition of Apollo 15, opened a new epoch of transport

634. A transport system fed by microwave energy in the centre of a city of the future

tives, would have the same capacity as an entire present-day express train, i.e. 300 passengers. Even the wheel track of lorries should reach 15 ft, as in, for instance, a turbine tow-vehicle with 10-ft diameter wheels carrying tank or container trailers for 200 tons and more. On the sea, large specialised shuttle ships with a deck length of about 1,600 ft and a tonnage of 1 million tons are expected to be in service. Special ports for these ships trans-shipping all types of cargo will be built only at certain points in the world. They will become transport centres of key importance; the cargo of the giant ships will be trans-shipped to smaller coast or river boats, trains and road transport. Fluids and loose materials would be trans-shipped by pumping. For fast transatlantic passenger transport large capacity hovercraft will very likely be used (Plate LXXXIX). In order to improve the connection between local or urban and long-distance transport large automatically-controlled passenger cars will be used. The cars with their passengers aboard will be loaded onto larger units.

Some engineers prefer the idea of giant airships driven by airscrews powered by nuclear energy. Airships would be used mainly for the transport of gas and also as flying cranes with a lifting capacity of 200—300 tons. They could erect bridges, lay roads and rail lines in prefabricated sections, transporting them directly from the factory to the site.

Helicopters would be replaced by giant airscrew or jet aircraft of the coleopter type, i.e. with a circular wing and the ability to take-off and land vertically.

New principles for future transport: The clean-est, most simple and most efficient power system is electric. The onset of linear electric motors transforming this power without mechanical transmission or wheels into efficient traction opens new possibilities. But since it depends on cables or other such means of supply, electric drive cannot be easily extended outside the area of electric trains which run on a fixed route. A revolutionary innovation would be the transfer of electric power over long distances by wireless. With this, electric power could be fed to cars, helicopters, aircraft as well as track vehicles. First experiments were carried out in 1899 in Colorado Springs, by the Yugoslav inventor Nikola Tesla. He used models of small cars. More practically, a number of experimental cars, whose electric motors were driven by power radiating from a wire aerial erected above an experimental platform, were built in 1943—1948 by the Soviet inventor G.I. Babat. Twenty-five per cent of the irradiated electric power was transferred to the experimental vehicles.

In attempts to increase the efficiency of wireless electric power, transfer microwaves were used as well. In May 1963, at the experimental field of the American Raytheon Company, an electric helicopter took off and reached an altitude of several miles above a parabolic ground irradiating aerial. The rotor, driven by an electric motor, carried a loop aerial which transformed in a diode system a beam of microwaves, into direct current. The efficiency of a microwave transfer system should be not less than 60 per cent, even at a distance of several hundred feet.

If cars were to be fed by electric power transmit-

ted by microwaves, a cable-transmitting network would have to be installed in the road surface. Railway radiating aerials could be located on poles along the track. Aircraft would have to be automatically controlled and fly in the range of the radiated beam. Nuclear and thermonuclear energy could be used, transformed into electrical power by economical power stations.

Integrated transport in this century: Some countries have already organised transport management and planning in such a way as to ensure the highest possible benefit for national economy. But it is still usual to have independent organisation of different routes, independent management and maintenance procedures and so on. The transport of passengers, raw materials, manufactured goods etc. between big cities, industrial centres and transport centres has been concentrated in a number of arteries of various kinds. Each method of transport has occupied a certain strip of territory for its activities, has its own power and perhaps its own automated systems, its own repair and maintenance facilities. At a certain level of development such an approach becomes uneconomic and unjustified. That is why new proposals are constantly being put forward to integrate all ground transport within one perfectly organised and highly efficient system. The basic element of such a system is usually a multistorey concrete structure (Plate XCI). Express elec-tric trains run in its interior. The roadway provides motorway lanes for passenger cars and lorries. The bottom part of the bridge carries electric cables, tubing for microwave electric power transfer and oil, fuel, liquid hydrogen, natural and industrial gas and water pipelines. Even the movement of coal, metal ores and other loose materials can be carried out in such a system without the use of trucks or wagons, or liquefied hydrogen moving according to the principles of cryogenics at a temperature of $-169°$ C $(-274°$ F) can flow through a pipeline in the centre of which a superconductor runs, as part of an electric grid system.

The entire complex is computer controlled. It has its own maintenance teams. In a literal sense it would become a life artery to the human community.

The first design of such an integrated transport structure was worked up in 1972 by the Chinese T.Y. Lin for a 750-mile system connecting new Alaskan oilfields with the Canadian Valdez.

Integrated transport will be part of the architecture of future cities. Small and large electrically-driven and computer-controlled vehicles will run across viaducts, in tunnels inside them or under the ground. Speed and comfort will have the same priority as safety and economy. People, raw materials, manufactured goods and power will be transferred by the shortest possible route from house to house.

Picture Acknowledgements

AEG, BRD (193, 194, 195)
Aeroflot (522, 532, 537, 574, 575)
Aeroport de Paris (544)
Aerospatiale S. A., France (572, 573)
AFP (539)
Airbus Industrie (533, LXXIV)
Air Canada (559)
Air France (500, 501, 503, 504, 544)
Alsthom + Société MTE, France (IV)
American Machine and Foundry (189)
Ansaldi Shipyard, Italy (389, 405, 408)
Attex Corp. (298)
AUDI-NSU (269, 270, 274, 295)
Australian National Railways Comp. (179)

Balle, S., Liverpool (400)
BART, San Francisco (174, 175)
Bertone, Italy (294, XLVI)
Bitterling, K., Hamburg (444)
BL Cars (264, 266, 286, 288, 343, 376, XLIII)
Boeing Aerospace Comp. (470, 576)
Boeing Comm. Airplane Comp. (528, 531, 536, 554, 600, LXX, LXXII)
Bosch (311)
Bremer Lagerhaus Ges. (150, 414, 451)
British Aircraft Corp. (3, 499, 519, 520, LXXV, LXXVI)
British Museum, London (45)
British Railways Board, London (110, 115, 122, 156, 159)
Bürgle, K. (377)
Büssing Archiv, BRD (322)

Cable and Wireless, England (LXVI)
Canadian National Railways (137, 139, 142, 146, 152, 153, XII)
Carlevaro Carlo, Genoa (226)
Carretti e Fanfani, Milan (208)
Cessna Aircraft Comp., USA (512)
Chantiers de l'Atlantique, Saint-Nazaire (LIX, LXI)
Chrysler, USA (292)
Citroën A. (257, 272, 276, 277)
Clark, S. Essex (237)
Cockerill-Yards, Hoboken, Belgium (419, 420)
Compagnie Générale Transatlantique, Paris (398)
Compagnie Internationale des Wagons-Lits et Tourisme (124, 125, 127, 128)
Conti-Press (433)
Creusot-Loire (103, XIV)
ČTK (UPI, Pressens Bild), (22, 97, 111, 113, 187, 212, 301, 302, 309, 314, 317, 355, 359, 372, 373, 376, 382, 430, 436, 445, 465, 469, 526, 554, 557, 558, 577, 611, 618, 633)
Culver Pictures, USA (167, 454)
Cuthbert Collection, Royal Aeronautical Society, London (31)

DAF, Holland (Volvo) (342, LII)
David Burges Wise (Hamlyn), (273, 333)
DECCA (439)
Demag, BRD (614, 615)
Deutsche Bundesbahn (83, 84, 93, 160, 161, 170, 183, 184, 452)
Deutsches Museum, Munich (63, 85, 88, 243)
Dornier, BRD (535, 566)
Dunbar, Ch. (585, 593)

Ellis, H.: *The Pictorial Encyclopedia of Railways*, Hamlyn (81, 115, 122, 156)

Escher Wyss GmbH (LX)

Ferrovia della Stato, Italy (158)
Fiat (273, 367, XLI)
Finnish State Railways (72)
Flughafen Frankfurt/Main A. G. (540, 542, 543, 549, 550, LXXI)
Ford Motor Comp. (248, 249, 253, 280, 288, 290, 291, 308, 349, 350, 366, 385, 603, 619, 624, XLIV, XLV)
Four Wheel Drive Corp., USA (344)

Garret, USA (196)
General Electric Corp. (380, 525, VI, XI)
General Motors Corp. (109, 259, 289, 292, 310, 380, 381, 383, 385, L, LI)
Goldhofer GmbH, BRD (347)
Greater Glasgow P.T.E. (LXXXIII, LXXXIV)
Griebl, H., Neulengbach, BRD (74)
Grijping Nico, Nijmegen, Holland (457)

Halprin, L.: *Freeways* (356, 360, 362, 363, 594, 595, 596)
Hamburger Hochbahn Akt. (584)
Hamlyn Group Picture Library (242, 246, 247, 517)
Hawker-Siddeley, Canada (129, 130, 514, 524)
Henschel A. G., BRD (341)
Hitachi Zossen (421, 422, 427, 468, XXXI)
Hodges, D. (Hamlyn Group), (231)
Honda, Japan (227, 230)
Hovercraft B. R. Ltd., England (192, 473, 475, 476, 478, LXVIII)
Hovermarine, England (480)
Hulton Picture Library, London (387)

Indian Railways Bureau (178)
Interavia (515, 516, 518, 556, 567, 576, 634, LXXI)
Ishikawajima-Harima Ltd., Japan (423, 427, 441, LXII, LXIII, LXV, LXVII, LXXIX)

Jacobs: *Bridges, Canals and Tunnels*, USA (358, 454)
Japanese National Railways (177, 625, 626, XXXII)

Kalivoda, K., ČSSR (221)
Kangol Magnet Ltd., England (297)
Kawasaki, Japan (410, LXXIX)
Kläy-Kämpfen, Brig (172)
Klement, V.: *Z dějin automobilu*, ČSSR (43, 44, 46, 47, 48, 58, 220, 232, 233, 234, 238, 241, 304, 306, 314, 317, 319, 465)
KLM (541, 542)
Kockums, BRD (406)
Köditz, Kulmbach, BRD (180)
Köln-Düsseldorfer Deutsche Rheinschiffahrt A. G. (463, 464)
Kost, R., Luzern (20)
Král, V., ČSSR (300)
Krauss und Maffei, BRD (101, 102, 621, 622, IX, XXXIII)
Krejčí, ČSSR (XCI)
Krupp-Werkfoto (15, 140, 338, 368, 369, 379, 428, 437, 462)
Kunsthistorisches Museum, Wien (26)

Lamborghini, Italy (XLVII)
Leichbau-Zagres (XXXV, LI)
Library of Congress, USA (61, 495)
Lindemann, BRD (118)
Lohoff, H. (354)
Löchler, P.: *Die Schiffe der Völker* (20, 21)
Lockheed Corp. (518, 534)
London Transport Executive (578, 581, 586, 590, 591, 607, 608, 609)
LTV-Aerospace Corp. (617)
Luchthaven Schiphol, Holland (541, 548)
Lüden, W., Hamburg (407, 447)
Luftamt, Hamburg (440)
Lufthansa (502, 505, 506, 507, 508, 521, 523, 529, LXXIII)

Index

Italicised numbers indicate pages where
the illustrations appear